Correspondent Colorings

CORRESPONDENT COLORINGS

Melville in the Marketplace

SHEILA POST-LAURIA

University of Massachusetts Press

Amherst

Copyright © 1996 by
The University of Massachusetts Press
All rights reserved
Printed in the United States of America
ISBN 1-55849-002-7 (cloth); 003-5 (pbk.)
LC 95-37247
Designed by Steve Dyer
Set in Adobe Minion by Dix
Printed and bound by Thomson-Shore, Inc.

Library of Congress Cataloging-in-Publication Data
Post-Lauria, Sheila, 1955–
Correspondent colorings : Melville in the marketplace / Sheila
Post-Lauria.
p.   cm.
Based on the author's thesis (Ph.D.)—University of Chicago.
Includes bibliographical references (p.   ) and index.
ISBN 1-55849-002-7 (cloth : alk. paper).—ISBN 1-55849-003-5
(pbk. : alk. paper)
1. Melville, Herman, 1819–1891—Technique.
2. Authors and readers—United States—History—19th century.
3. Melville, Herman, 1819–1891—Books and reading.
4. Journalism—United States—History—19th century.
5. Popular literature—Technique.   6. Fiction—Technique.
7. Literary form.   I. Title.
PS2388.T4P67   1996
813'.3—dc20   95-37247
CIP

British Library Cataloging in Publication data are available.

This book is published with the support and cooperation of
the University of Massachusetts Boston.

This book is gratefully dedicated
to all those who helped me
make it a reality.

Contents

PART FOUR
New Audiences, New Forms

Acknowledgments

Several people have taken considerable time to read parts of this study. I am deeply grateful to Robert A. Ferguson who advised me on this project from its early stages as a dissertation at the University of Chicago (1989). I am also grateful to my Melville professors, Benjamin J. Lease, James E. Miller, John Singleton, Robert E. Streeter, and William Veeder, who helped me think about Melville and literary history in new ways. I would also like to thank particularly Charlene Avallone, Daniel A. Cohen, Wyn Kelley, Carolyn Karcher, Robert Madison, Laurie Robertson-Lorant, and Susan Belasco Smith for the time, advice, and enthusiasm they each offered in our several discussions of Melville's position within antebellum culture.

The following scholars have thoughtfully commented upon various portions of this book, and I am indebted to each: Hans Bergmann, Lauren Berlant, Walter Bezanson, Ray Browne, John Bryant, Hennig Cohen, Cathy N. Davidson, William Dillingham, Wai-chee Dimock, John Ernest, Michael T. Gilmore, Neil Harris, Susan K. Harris, Tom Inge, Christopher Looby, Kathleen McCormack, Kenneth Price, David S. Reynolds, and Eric Sundquist. Other scholars too numerous to mention here whose own works have indirectly influenced this study are acknowledged in due course in the following pages.

Parts of chapters 5 and 8 of this book have appeared in journals: "Philosophy in Whales . . . Poetry in Blubber: Mixed Form in *Moby-Dick*," in *Nineteenth-Century Literature* (December 1990); "Genre and Ideology: The French Sensational Romance and Melville's *Pierre*," in *Journal of American Culture* (Fall 1992); "Canonical Texts and Context: The Example of "Bartleby, the Scrivener: A Story of Wall Street,"

College Literature (June 1993); "Editorial Politics in Benito Cereno," *American Periodicals* (1995); "Magazine Practices and Melville's *Israel Potter*," in *American Social Texts and Periodical Contexts,* ed. Kenneth Price and Susan Belasco Smith (University of Virginia, 1995).

I would also like to thank Paul Wright, fellow Melvillean and editor at the University of Massachusetts Press for his encouragement and suggestions, as well as Pam Wilkinson, managing editor, for her superb editing. I am especially grateful to my colleagues at the University of Massachusetts, Boston, who have supported me through the completion of this project, particularly Jack Brereton, Neal Bruss, Libby Fay, Ellie Kutz, Donaldo Macedo, and Shaun O'Connell. I am most grateful to Louis Esposito who has acted as mentor, supporter, and friend. He has also understood that this research project has empowered me to empower our students at UMass Boston.

I have reserved my profound gratitude for those who have continually helped me through their support and encouragement: Melville friends Joyce Adler, John Bryant, and Carolyn Karcher, and especially my buddies Charlene Avallone, Wyn Kelley, and Laurie Robertson-Lorant; Melville students Manuel Camblor, Allan Cole, John Grosskopf, Ernesto Mendible, David Ross, Dan Scannell, Juan Marcos Salomé, Jessica Zelinski, and especially Bethany Wood, along with a host of UMass Boston students not already mentioned for their insights and interest; old University of Chicago friends Robert Chametzsky and Kevin J. Tuite, who (im)patiently saw this project through the University of Chicago years by reading drafts and encouraging me; colleague and friend, Kathleen McCormack; and most of all family supporters Ian Diego Lauria, Mary Browne Post, Shawn Post, and John Rogers (who generated enthusiasm and guidance by reading whatever work by Melville I happened to be then currently working on). I end with thanking Aldo Lauria Santiago, who patiently waited for me to close the library each night while graduate students at the University of Chicago, who solved innumerable computer problems, and who managed the household (and child) while I finished this project.

Preface

MELVILLE'S 1850 REVIEW of Nathaniel Hawthorne's *Mosses from an Old Manse* provides a starting point from which to gauge the relation between individual creativity and cultural practice. Though frequently remembered for celebrating Hawthorne's "blackness of darkness," Melville presents a bivalent formulation of genius:

> Whereas great geniuses are parts of the times,
> they themselves are the times,
> and possess a correspondent coloring.[1]

This formulation suggests a cultural indebtedness usually overlooked in studies that emphasize Melville's "classic," asocial status.

But can we assume a correspondent coloring between Melville's own progressiveness and that of his contemporaries? Certainly other "classic" writers shared Melville's views on artistry. Poe and Hawthorne too described genius as a mixture of cultural forms and personal insights: Hawthorne referred to genius as "the newspaper of a century," while Poe asserted that originality "is carefully patiently, and understandingly to combine."[2]

This book explores the relation between Herman Melville and the mid-nineteenth-century literary marketplace. American authors such as Melville who attempted both to profit from and to serve as prophets of the literary word faced the challenge of combining personal visions with the complexities of literary production at midcentury: the attempt to cater simultaneously to British and American tastes, to write for divergent readerships in America, to negotiate the critical debates over genre and style, and to "make literary" social, political, and personal views.

This project examines the nature of these mixtures, and I use the plural here for two reasons. First, I wish to underscore the heterogeneous—the compliant, developmental, experimental, sometimes discordant, but frequently simply new and different—mixtures in which Melville chose to balance the conditions of the marketplace and his own literary interests. Second, I would like to stress at the outset the necessity for recognizing the heterogeneity of cultural production that marked mid-nineteenth-century popular culture. To construe "popular culture" as a unitary concept against or within which an author wrote not only misrepresents the literary diversity that existed in the popular culture of Melville's day, but also obscures the essential multiplicity of readerships, genres, styles, and subjects that *attracted* creative artists like Melville to the marketplace.

In recovering Melville's significant—and persistent—practice of borrowing cultural forms, styles, and themes that were popular among different groups of readers in nineteenth-century culture, I attempt to demonstrate that the cultural contexts of literary production, and the diversity they entailed, were for Melville an essential basis to his literary creativity. These contexts can therefore no longer be unexamined, dismissed as irrelevant, or simply ignored.

Any study that claims to "reconstruct" Herman Melville's literary career—his compositional strategies, his creativity, and his place within antebellum culture—must resolve the contradictory assessments of these issues made by textual, contextual, and ideological critics. I participate in this debate by drawing from the insights of all three approaches, and this methodological combination produces different assessments of Melville's complex interaction with popular antebellum culture.

Through textual analyses that often rely on context, I show how Melville drew repeatedly from the popular literary trends of his times. My recovery of this dependence leads to a new understanding of this writer at work. An appropriator of forms, Melville discovered a creativity that emerged from these deliberate borrowings. The rationale for suggesting a permeability—rather than an opposition—between the works of a "classic" male writer and his culture originates in Melville's own formulation of artistry. It is Melville's fundamental indebtedness to and assimilation of antebellum cultural trends which have not yet been thoroughly explored in analyses of the author's works and career, and which I take as my subject.

Building on the methods of literary historians such as Nina Baym, Cathy N. Davidson, Buford Jones, Lawrence W. Levine, David S. Reynolds, Eric Sundquist, Jane Tompkins, and Ronald Zboray, I ground my study in the popular practices, publishing records, and critical reviews of the day, and I locate the many antebellum forms, styles, and genres on which Melville relied in his fiction.

I do not employ as a premise of this study either what I call the "transcendence" or the "subversion" models of literary analysis. While the transcendence model suggests that Melville consistently surpassed in artistic complexity the popular forms and themes he employed in his works, Hans Bergmann has recently suggested an alternative possibility: "Melville does not rise above his times so much as he helps us understand them."[3] Melville's use of and reliance on popular forms were simply not uniformly accompanied by "innovations" or "transcendence" of these forms, as is often suggested by a variety of critics. It is this complexity—that some of Melville's writings, for example, remained indistinguishable from those of his contemporaries—and the implications of this resemblance to popular forms for modern formulations of canonicity and aesthetic judgment, which I endeavor to examine here.

In this book, which is organized both thematically and chronologically, I argue that Melville planned his works and based them on existing popular narrative forms now largely forgotten; that he aimed specific works for particular readerships that included (to borrow antebellum terminology) elite, literary, cultivated, general, and mass audiences; that he enjoyed a considerable popularity among his contemporaries; and finally, that Melville considered his reliance on antebellum forms as fundamental both to his writing and to his creativity.

From the start of his writing career, Melville demonstrated through his deliberate and creative mixtures of popular forms and styles not only an interest in, but a real understanding of the subtle differences in mid-nineteenth-century literary tastes. In chapter 1, I place Melville's first work into the contexts of the trans-atlantic literary marketplace. In chapter 2, I offer an alternative perspective to reigning assumptions regarding both the "unintentional" and "limited" success of *Typee: A Peep at Polynesian Life* (1846), Melville's first novel, by comparing the narrative form, style, reviews, and sales of *Typee* to those of other best-sellers of the mid-1840s. On the basis of the different responses by cultivated and by general readers to the author's use of specific conventions in *Typee*, Melville tailored each of his next four novels to attract different segments of these audiences. Chapters 3 and 4 examine the ways Melville combined, innovated, and supported these contrasting expectations and worldviews in the novels from *Omoo* through *White-Jacket*.

Genetic scholars assume that Melville planned his "market" novels, *Redburn* and *White-Jacket,* and locate Melville's creativity in his reputedly "unplanned" works. Indeed, Melville is often praised for originality in exactly those areas where his works most conform to once popular but now forgotten forms. In chapter 5, I relate an overlooked narrative form that Melville employed in *Moby-Dick* to new contexts through which to gauge the author's creativity in this masterpiece.

This study also reconsiders the question of how successfully the author employed established practices. Chapter 6 discusses how Melville's use of specific genres in his most valued and misunderstood works aligned *Moby-Dick* and *Pierre* to particular sides of the major critical debates, which raged in the journals at midcentury, over the "proper" form of the novel.

Chapters 7 and 8 situate the author's magazine fiction within the larger tradition of the periodical marketplace in antebellum America as well as within the particular contexts of the editorial policies—and politics—of the monthlies that published his shorter fiction. The recovery of Melville's actual popularity at midcentury and his attempt to move to new and wider audiences, in addition to his creative reliance on magazine conventions, provide the background to chapter 7. Here I place the magazine fiction within its publishing environments and, on the basis of this context, I recast existing formulations regarding the author's subversive strategies by showing how Melville tailored his magazine submissions to reflect the editorial policies and practices of the individual monthlies that published his shorter works. Finally, I turn to Melville's last novel of this period. Here I reconsider the reasons why Melville turned from the novel to poetry by situating Melville's compositional methods in *The Confidence-Man* in the radically changed literary environment of the late 1850s, as well as by examining how the particular structure of this last novel signaled the direction of the author's restless move to new literary forms and audiences.

This study develops a reconstruction of Melville as a "classic" writer which challenges conventional views of an alienated, frustrated artist who felt hostile and superior to his culture. In fact, Melville's compositional practices reveal an author indebted to antebellum trends. Melville is presented in these pages as a writer who ingeniously colored his works with topical forms, themes, and styles, and through this reliance on antebellum practice created timely—and timeless—works of art.

PART ONE

Literary Culture

CHAPTER ONE

Cultural Contexts

M ELVILLE'S ACTIVE ENGAGEMENT with popular literary forms in *Typee: A Peep at Polynesian Life* (1846) placed the author's first novel at the top of the best-seller list. Indeed, Melville seemed to have arisen the morning after the publication of his book, in the words of Charles Briggs (a popular sea writer and Melville's future editor), "as Byron before him . . . to find himself famous." Chronicling the immediate success of Melville's tale of Polynesian adventures, a reviewer for The *Columbian Magazine* exclaimed that *Typee* was read "by every man, woman, and child in the Union who undertakes to keep pace at all with the current literature." By the standards of the 1840s, *Typee* was truly the most recent "successful hit in bookmaking." The *New York Sunday Times* and *Noah's Weekly Register* simply described Melville as "the greatest writer of the age in his way." [1]

This last accolade suggests that through the publication of *Typee* Melville created a niche for himself in midcentury literary culture that linked his work to the leading modes of cultural production yet reserved what he was later to call "plenty of sea room" *(Moby-Dick)* for innovation. Melville's unusual reputation among his contemporaries raises several questions. How did Melville manage to market his work at a time when George Borrow, Charles Briggs, Caroline Chesebro', James Fenimore Cooper, Fanny Forrester (Emily Chubbuck Judson), J. T. Headley, Caroline Kirkland, George Lippard, Catharine Maria Sedgwick, Anna Sophia Stephens, Harriet Beecher Stowe, and Bayard Taylor comprised the lists of leading novelists in both British and American literary circles? How did Melville's *Typee*, a first novel, with such established competition, rise to the top? What was the qualitative nature of Melville's competition? Which popular literary genres encouraged Melville to think that his sea adventures would find a market in the literary culture of the mid-1840s? The answers to these questions provide important insights into Melville's writing practices as well as into the author's stature as a popular writer in the midcentury literary marketplace. After placing *Typee* in its cultural contexts, we can then turn to the novel itself to gauge Melville's level of participation in popular practices.

The Literary Marketplace

During the years from 1842 to 1860, the number of books (both literary and nonliterary) published in the United States increased dramatically. In 1835, 64 new books were published; in 1842, the number increased only to 100. But by 1855, the number climbed to 1,092. Improved public education, diminishing illiteracy rates, increased population, and especially innovative methods of publication and mass distribution of printed materials contributed to the rise of large-scale audiences during the 1840s and 1850s.[2]

Perhaps more than any other single factor, the shift in demographics shaped new readerships at midcentury. Antebellum America witnessed what Stuart Blumin has called the "emergence" of an urban middle class.[3] Walt Whitman referred to this group as the "most valuable class"; Nathaniel Hawthorne called it the "tribe of general readers"; and it is middle-class readers whom Melville addresses as the "fireside people" in the preface to *Typee*.

Yet within this socioeconomic group, educational backgrounds and social status differed considerably. These variations account for the heterogeneity of readers within the middle class. Cultural speakers during the decade referred to the multiplicity of audiences. "General," "common," or "popular" readers referred to those middle-class audiences of both sexes who read largely for entertainment. Other individuals attempted to regulate literary production as well as the aesthetic tastes of general readers; such reviewers, literary critics, clergymen, particular authors, and other people of high social standing represented a separate audience usually referred to by their contemporaries (and themselves) as "intellectual" or "cultivated" readers. With their desire to shape literary production—and by extension, American culture—cultivated readers tended to be quite opinionated on issues of genre and ideology and to be more conservative than general readers in outlook. A third group, referred to here as "literary" readers, represented a midpoint between general and cultivated readers, two groups who differed occasionally on matters of style, tone, and subject but differed frequently on attitudes toward family, work, individuality, gender, and morality. Literary readers blended the receptiveness of general readers to progressive ideological views with the particularly formulated aesthetic standards demanded by cultivated readers.

These varied audiences within the middle class stood apart from and occasionally opposed an even larger readership commonly referred to as the "masses," or "the people." This almost exclusively working-class audience sought literature that was, among other attributes, more secular, more liberal, and even more openly defiant of middle-class values. The interests of this audience served as a mine for middle-class writers who frequently borrowed from working-class literary forms, themes, and styles when writing for middle-class readers.[4]

Cultivated American readers have historically displayed a predilection for nonfictional works, as Terrence Martin has pointed out.[5] Suspicious of fiction, the upper middle-class literary culture of the 1840s considered nonfictional works aesthetically more pleasing than novels and poetry, a bias also common among cultivated English readers of the period. Anthony Trollope recounted the conventional attitude toward fiction held by the upper classes: "The families in which an unrestricted permission was given for reading of novels were very few, and from many they were altogether banished."[6] Even as late as 1851, Susan Warner, in her successful best-seller *The Wide, Wide, World,* presents the strong bias against novel-reading through her portrayal of John Humphreys, the exemplar of cultivated middle-class attitudes. Journals ranging from the elite *North American Review* to the more popular middle-class monthlies *Graham's Magazine* and *Godey's Lady's Book* featured reviews of biographies, histories, essays, and travels in addition to poetry and stories, and antebellum readers suspicious of fictional taints included all of these various genres in their formulation of the term *literature.*

The demand for truthful, realistic narratives partially accounts for the decade's interest in particular genres, such as pseudoscientific literature. Well-attended Lyceum lectures on science, together with their wide coverage in daily papers such as the *New York Tribune,* attest to the interest of antebellum readers in scientific subjects.[7] The immense popularity, for example, of Edgar Allan Poe's purportedly authentic accounts prompted an unprecedented three hundred thousand readers to buy "The Gold Bug," though a number of reviewers for general magazines and papers located the popularity of Poe's scientific tales in the author's deliberate strategy of challenging the reader to detect the stories' essential fictiveness.

This combination of fact and fiction may explain the success of two of the most widely reviewed (and perhaps also read) genres of the decade: travel-adventure narratives and what is generically referred to as domestic or sentimental fiction. Travel writers as well as authors of domestic life greatly appealed to middle-class general and cultivated readers. Stories of individual lives and manners set within a domestic or societal framework mirrored and validated the strong emphasis middle-class individuals placed on their homes and domestic lives, as Ronald Zboray has recently shown. Indeed, the creation of materials such as wallpaper and glass objects that represented various scenes from favorite novels of the day exemplifies the strong link between the literary and the domestic.[8] Travel accounts that related interesting facts of native lives and cultures intrigued literal-minded readers and catered to the decade's demand for realistic portraiture.

Likewise, what the decade fondly called "hair-breathed 'scapes"— sensational tales of escape from native or marginal peoples—particularly fascinated general and mass readers, and the sensational mode, among other rhetorical appeals to the emotions, such as sentiment, represented styles that permeated all levels of antebellum society. Although these modes of writing vied with biographies, histories, and geographers' expeditionary accounts, the imaginative possibilities and the potential for literary embellishment inherent in the domestic and travel genres contributed to their increasing popularity as the decade progressed. By midcentury, travel narratives and domestic fiction represented the most frequently published literary genres in middle-class circles. As we shall see, the heterogeneous reading habits of antebellum middle-class audiences encouraged writers to combine forms and styles that appealed simultaneously to different readerships.

Travel Narratives

As a reviewer in *Graham's* noted in 1845, "The present rage is for voyages and travels," and indeed, the travel narrative took the decade's readers by storm.[9] With the advancement of land and sea frontiers and more expeditious travel methods, narratives about exploration, pilgrimage, escape, and migration by geographers, missionaries, immigrants, tourists, and sailors achieved widespread popularity.[10] Virtually all middle-class magazines and papers in the 1840s noticed, excerpted, and reviewed these works. For the two-year period 1845–47, *Graham's Magazine,* the popular family-circle monthly with more than forty thousand readers, published twice as many reviews of travel books as reviews of novels.[11] Detailed accounts of book publishing during the decade, including George Palmer Putnam's 1845 *American Facts* and Samuel Goodrich's account of mid-nineteenth-century literary culture *Recollections of a Lifetime,* treated travel literature—despite its fictional elements—as a separate generic category.[12]

The travel genre possesses specific attributes, the central one of which is the figurative presentation of the exotic journey itself. Resilient enough to allow for variety in tone, the form involves specific rites: leave taking, discovery, experience, homecoming, and reportage.[13] Due to this sequential pattern, travel literature inherently contains a double structure: the narrative of the reporter and the narrative of the journey itself. Melville's *Typee,* with its mixture of elements from the genre of exploration and escape, easily fits this mold. While often viewed as the result of Melville's reputed "shifting perspectives" and his "ambivalence" toward the Marquesans, the digressive form and the dual narrative of *Typee* parallel the bivalency of the travel narrative.[14] This double structure emerges from Melville's reliance on conventional expository forms and popular styles, which he creatively blended into a cohesive literary work that serves multiple purposes.

While subgenres emphasize different aspects of the recounted journey, travel accounts primarily contain informative exposition.[15] They record all facets of the journey, from topographical and climatic aspects to social and political conditions, as well as the customs, habits, and behavior of indigenous populations. The first book in the Wiley and Putnam Library of American Books series, which was the following year to include Melville's *Typee*, exemplifies this convention. In *Journal of an African Cruiser* ("edited" by Nathaniel Hawthorne), Horatio Bridge embeds his narrative in accounts of coffee production, native manners, and even the cultivation of pine and mangrove trees. Similarly, Eliot Warburton, in the popular volume *The Crescent and the Cross* (1844), a book to which some reviewers later compared *Typee*, discusses various topics, including Muslim dress, religious practices and rites, daily life of Egyptian people, and the geology, botany, and zoology of the Nile region.[16]

Paralleling this practice, Melville's *Typee* contains long passages strictly devoted to informational content.[17] In the early chapters of the novel, the narrator moves from one observation and anecdote to another. In chapter 15, for example, he suddenly interrupts his discussion of the value placed on salt by the natives and—as had other travel writers before him—he provides botanic information, in this case "a general description of the breadfruit tree, and the various modes in which the fruit is prepared" (*Typee*, 144). Such interpolated digressions provide informational content and delay the termination of the voyage. The pivotal role of pseudoanthropological information competes with plot for narrative focus in the genre of travels.

Since travels beyond familiar countries risked sounding exotic and thereby fabulous, writers employed specific strategies in an effort to appear more authentic. One common method involved validating their observations through extracting material from well-known travel narratives. This practice was so familiar to even earlier nineteenth-century readers that Frederick Marryat made it the subject of his famous burlesque "How to Write a Book of Travels."[18] In *A Visit to the South Seas, in the United States Ship Vincennes, during the Years 1829 and 1830*, Charles S. Stewart frequently mentions other travelers when he is in need of facts: "With the *Polynesian Researches* of our beloved friend [William] Ellis before you, it will be unnecessary for me to enter upon any elucidation of facts."[19] William Ellis, in turn, embeds Wouter Schouten's account of the tattooing practices on Dog Island, a remote spot in the South Pacific, in his own discussion of the practice.[20]

In particular, British and American authors of travel books published in the same series as Melville's *Typee* frequently mentioned other travel accounts. In *The Crescent and the Cross,* Warburton refers to previous descriptions of Algiers: "The reader will find some useful notices of Algiers in Wild's well-written *Narrative.* Prince Puckler Muskau, a romancer without chivalry, has nevertheless given some amusing narrative and information on this subject."[21] Likewise, in *Views A-Foot,* Bayard Taylor, a fledgling author later celebrated as the Marco Polo of travelers, links his observations to the descriptions of Germany by the popular writer Mary Howitt, in order to share in her popularity. While the practice of referencing popular authors imparted what Melville called a "life-like air to the whole," the intertextuality of these travel accounts served rhetorically as a marketing device that linked new works to established and popular practice.[22]

In a manner distinct from Harold Bloom's "anxiety of influence," travel writers seem to exhibit a proclivity for inclusion, an interest in demonstrating their willing participation in popular practice. Melville's frequent extracts from the travels of David Porter, Stewart, and Ellis, among others, parallel this convention. These quotations, once thought to be a sign of Melville's "inexperience as a writer," find a context in the genre of travels.[23]

Travel writers frequently speculate on the social, political, and moral conditions of indigenous populations. Nineteenth-century travel literature follows two distinct approaches to describing the interaction between Western and non-Western peoples, a difference that usually mirrors the socioeconomic status of the author or of the intended audience. Upper middle-class travelers or those aspiring to a higher social status (Bayard Taylor is a case in point) emphasize the superiority of their national (or more generally Western) culture over the one visited. Many other travel writers, however, especially nonformally educated sailors or those writing for general and mass audiences, openly criticize the practice of imposing Western religious and cultural practices on other countries and peoples.

In *Journal of an African Cruiser,* Horatio Bridge questions the ethnocentric attitudes and actions of American missionaries in Africa. He points out that attempts to Christianize the Liberians (a society founded by freed and/or escaped slaves from America whose philosophy was all-black rule without any help or interference from whites) undermine the ideological basis on which Liberian society was founded and that "the methodist Episcopal mission . . . possessed power almost sufficient to subvert the Colonial [Liberian] rule" (*Journal,* 72–73). While Bridge then tries to disarm readers who might oppose this view by praising general missionary acts, he concludes his analysis of African missionaries by reaffirming his original criticism: "I criticize portions of their conduct, but reverence their purity of motive; and only regret, that, while divesting themselves of so much that is worldly, they do not retain either more wisdom of this world, or less aptness to apply a disturbing influence to worldly affairs" (74).

A few daring travel writers went even further and celebrated native ways as a fortunate escape from the confines of Western civilization. A growing interest in non-Western cultures resulted in evolving formulations of the travel account. Previous approaches stressing curiosity, experiential authority, and subjective representation coalesced in the nineteenth century as inductive reasoning, natural history, and evolutionary theory shaped ethnographic and travel accounts.[24] Alfred Russell Wallace, a colleague of Charles Darwin, went so far in his account of native peoples as to suggest a devolution, the failure of the West to "train and develop more thoroughly the sympathetic feelings and moral faculties of our nature, and to allow them a larger share of influence . . . in our social organization," the kind of which he found abundant in the non-Western peoples he encountered: "There is, in fact, almost as much difference between the various races of savage and civilized peoples and we may safely affirm that the better specimens of the former are much superior to the lower examples of the latter class."[25] In literature, such a new formulation of the travel narrative found an outlet in Oriental fiction, a genre that, through its focus on non-Western cultures, contained progressive thinking which challenged the primacy of Christianity and Western traditions.[26]

Arthur W. Kinglake popularized this stance in his 1845 best-seller, *Eothen: Or Traces of Travel Brought Home from the East,* a book to which reviewers the following year linked Melville's *Typee.*

While this more radical approach to other cultures gained prestige and popularity, the more conservative, Western travel account dominated British and American markets that catered to cultivated readers. Perhaps in an attempt to maintain the objective voice of the scientific, impartial observer—coupled with an eye to the religious and cultural sensibilities of their American and British cultivated readers—travel writers, largely from the upper classes, moralized frequently on the "degenerate" condition of the peoples under scrutiny.[27] William Ellis berated the South Sea Islanders for what he considered immoral practices: polygamy and "licentious" behavior, particularly in young girls. In *The Crescent and the Cross,* Warburton adopted similar language in condemning the sexual attitudes and morals of the Muslims.

But this practice was not restricted to travel accounts of non-European regions; American travelers to Europe also judged the behavior of certain nationalities. In *Views A-Foot,* for example, Bayard Taylor harshly condemns the Irish people with rhetoric often employed in American racialist descriptions of African slaves: "The deck of the steamer was crowded with Irish, and certainly gave no favorable impression of the condition of the peasantry in Ireland. On many of their countenances there was scarcely a mark of intelligence; they were a most brutalized and degraded company of beings" (28). Criticism of unacceptable native ways reinforces the superiority of the writer's own culture to the one under observation. This stance allows the author to remain a detached observer who upholds traditional Western (particularly Anglo-Saxon) culture, and in the case of the European travel account, American society.

Several writers quickly learned the power of reader expectations and ideological demands. In first works, some travelers severely condemned missionary practices in the South Seas, as David S. Reynolds has noted. Nathaniel Ames, for example, calls Christian missionaries "the greatest scoundrels on the face of the earth." Yet authors often deliberately altered their views to attract new readerships. In his second work Ames toned down his criticism to gain acceptance among religious readers.[28] Similarly, Melville's critical comments on missionary activities in the first British and American editions of *Typee,* coupled with his willingness to neutralize and even delete them for the American Revised Edition, reveal how strongly authors considered marketplace forces.

Reader expectations did not necessarily serve as censoring devices, however; room existed for experimentation. Travel narratives that were aimed at cultivated readers occasionally reflected what might be thought of as ambivalent attitudes toward their subjects. Though establishing allegiance to Western civilization, travel writers often celebrated native customs. While condemning Muslim sexual behavior, Warburton praised the sensuality of Muslim women. Ellis, Stewart, and Porter occasionally condoned aspects of native culture, such as the hospitable and cheerful character of the people, and their low crime rate. For Ellis, the South Sea Islanders were both "criminal" and "sweetly innocent." Stewart, who found the Tahitian natives to act both "hospitably" and "unchristian-like," proclaimed of the women in their more "Christian" moments, "These beautiful women would bear comparison with any in the drawing rooms of the most polished noblesse."[29]

The multiple and occasionally contradictory views of local inhabitants are also found in many popular European pilgrimage accounts. In their travel writings, Nathaniel Hawthorne, James Fenimore Cooper, William Cullen Bryant, and Bayard Taylor both admonish and praise the English people. In *Letters of a Traveller,* Bryant remarks: "All around you are places the names of which are familiar names in history, poetry, and romance. From this magnificence of nature and art, the transition was painful to what I saw of the poorer population." Likewise, in *Views A-Foot* Taylor notes: "If London is unsurpassed in splendor, it has also its corresponding share of crime."[30] Such bivalent perspectives rhetorically curbed potentially exotic accounts by maintaining a tone of impartial objectivity and loyalty to Western (or American) ways that was demanded by elite and cultivated publishers, reviewers, and readers.

In *Typee,* Melville also presents bipartite perspectives on native life and customs. His narrator celebrates the local culture. Certain statements uttered by Tommo, such as "The horrible character imputed to these Typees appeared . . . wholly undeserved," have encouraged scholars to view *Typee* as a "defense of the Noble Savage" and as an "Earthly Paradise."[31] Melville's method, however, is more similar to the practices of a distinct group of primarily American travel writers. For example, J. Ross Browne, a popular writer, contrasts Christian with Islamic burial practices to the benefit of the latter.[32]

Yet Melville also defers to cultivated attitudes. While praising aspects of native life, the narrator of *Typee* continually looks for what James E. Miller, Jr., has called the "horror that exists not far beneath the placid surface."[33] Tommo knowingly qualifies his praise by stating: "Notwithstanding the kind treatment we received, I was too familiar with the fickle disposition of the savages not to feel anxious to withdraw from the valley, and put myself beyond the reach of that fearful death which, under all these smiling appearances, might yet menace us" (97). The author's reputed ambivalence toward the natives he describes parallels the stances of travel narrators who indirectly praise civilization over primitivism, while seeming to celebrate native customs. In this manner, travel writers maintain the allegiance to society regularly found in works read by cultivated audiences, an allegiance that Melville particularly sought in his American Revised Edition of *Typee*.

Publishers on both sides of the Atlantic published travel narratives, but John Murray in England and Wiley and Putnam in America produced the most popular books of the mid-1840s. These two houses established rigorous criteria for their travel libraries. Both insisted on objective narratives. Maintaining his publisher-father's strong opposition to fiction and poetry, John Murray specialized in truthful accounts of travels in exotic places and marketed them through his new Home and Colonial Library Series. In the prospectus written for potential subscribers, Murray described his new series of "useful and entertaining volumes" as exemplars of "good taste." By catering to the morals and tastes of "clergymen, school-teachers, and employers of labour," Murray aimed these relatively expensive books at such upper-and middle-class audiences who expected to find little morally offensive or socially disruptive content in their leisurely reading.[34]

One of the more popular books in Murray's Home and Colonial Library Series, George Borrow's *The Bible in Spain* (1843) exemplifies the inherent ambiguities of this ideological orientation. John Murray disliked fiction because he linked socially challenging accounts with fictive narration. Yet Borrow's actual travel experiences would indeed have offended Murray's targeted English upper- and middle-class readership: the author lived with a gypsy woman in Spain and then moved out to form a ménage à trois with a wealthy heiress and her daughter. None of these details found its way into the book. As one commentator on Borrow has remarked, "His are sins of omission rather than commission; his letters are always the truth, but never all the truth." [35]

Borrow served as an employee of the Bible Society—not for any philosophical identification with their goals of Protestantising the world but apparently for the rare opportunity to utilize his linguistic abilities (he spoke forty languages) and to travel to exotic places. He exploits his socially respectable position as a reputed Bible missionary to gain the support of his conservative readers. Starting his account with the statement, "I am no tourist, no writer of books of travels," Borrow distances himself from that class of writers and establishes his social superiority as a missionary. He then narrates his travels in the vein expected of him. While enticing his readers through exotic inferences such as "I have had the honor to live on familiar terms with the peasants, shepherds, and muleteers of Spain" (vii), he consistently exhibits ethnocentric views when describing the "intolerable filth" and "dishonesty" of the natives, their customs, and their "papist" religion. Through such strategies, Borrow constructed a "truthful" though ideologically hypocritical narrative which was a hit in cultivated English and American literary circles. [36]

The insistence on impartial observation by cultivated readers largely determined the publication and success of a travel book. Due to the lack of international copyright laws, American travel writers interested in protecting their royalties, before publishing in America had to publish first in England. Authors not only considered seriously the demands of English cultivated readers for truthful but culturally validating accounts but needed to combine English and American ideological perspectives to satisfy the interests of two somewhat different readerships.

THE GENRE OF TRAVEL AND *TYPEE*. Melville's engagement with the
travel genre accounts for a structure that has been described as a
"loose fictional chronicle." [37] The dual narrative design in *Typee* represented through the presence of the "innocent" and the "initiated"
narrator has not been recognized as a convention of the travel narrative. [38] Indeed, even scholars who provide the historical and "factual"
sources for *Typee* consider the novel's bivalency an example of Melville's originality rather than recognize its stature as common practice
in travel accounts. [39]

When linking *Typee* generically to established travel literature,
scholars have considered *Typee* almost exclusively in the context of
works mentioned by Melville's narrator. [40] But the expeditionary narratives and missionary accounts by Charles S. Stewart, David Porter,
and William Ellis that predate antebellum travel books were not
positively received by general readers of the travel genre and represent
conservative practice in the literature of exploration. Melville's references to these accounts legitimated his narrative for cultivated American and British readers rather than for general middle-class readers
in America, who sought entertaining instruction in popular travel
narratives of the 1840s.

In *Typee* Melville alters the method of reporting employed by his
more conservative predecessors. His emphasis, as T. Walter Herbert
observes, "rests upon the encounter, the experience of contact, rather
than on the Marquesans as a thing observed." [41] Melville moves from
observation to interaction, from detachment to involvement. This
strategy of emphasizing the narrator's response rather than his observations of primitive life diminishes the scientific tone common to the
travel narratives of Stewart, Porter, and Ellis, among others, and
augments the opportunities for sentimental and sensational rhetoric.
If *Typee* is an "alternative to the family exclusiveness of the Melvills
[*sic*] and the Gansevoorts," as Michael Paul Rogin has argued, [42] it is
also an alternative to the *literary* exclusiveness of elite travel accounts,
a detachment that distances writers from the people and cultures they
describe.

Let's consider for a moment the travel accounts usually considered
as Melville's major sources in *Typee*. Ellis's detached ethnographic

focus in *Polynesian Researches* emphasizes observation over involvement:

> Inhabitants of the islands of the Pacific—Oceanic negroes—
> Eastern Polynesians—General account of the South Sea Is-
> landers—Physical character—Expression of countenance—
> Stature, colour, &c.—Mental capacity—Ancient division and
> computation of time—Tahitian numerals—Extended calcula-
> tions—Aptness in receiving instruction—Moral character—
> Hospitality—Extensive and affecting moral degradation—Its
> enervating influence—Former longevity of the islanders.
> (4:78)

Ellis dissects his subject ("Physical character—Expression of counte-
nance—Stature, colour, &c.—Mental capacity"), a procedure that
fragments and thereby dehumanizes the people under observation.
There is no indication that the author interacted with the culture and
people he describes, and the only evaluation he offers—what he
denounced as the "moral degradation" of the native peoples—underscores his own ethnocentrism.

Now consider Melville's treatment of the same subjects in *Typee:*

> General information gathered at the festival—Personal beauty
> of the Typees—Their superiority over the Inhabitants of the
> other Islands—Diversity of complexion—A Vegetable Cos-
> metic and Ointment—Testimony of Voyagers to the uncom-
> mon Beauty of the Marquesans—Few Evidences of
> Intercourse with Civilized Beings—Dilapidated Musket—
> Primitive Simplicity of Government—Regal Dignity of Me-
> hevi. (189)

While echoing Ellis's ethnocentric bias—"Few Evidences of Intercourse with *Civilized* Beings. . . . *Primitive* Simplicity of Government"
(emphasis added)—Melville's narrator undercuts his ethnocentrism
by offering personal opinions. Placing his narrator within cultural
practices ("the festival") and thus in contact with individuals ("Regal
Dignity of Mehevi"), Melville stresses the experiential and interac-
tional nature of his narrative. Rather than dissecting and adopting a
superior stance to the culture, the narrator celebrates ("Personal

beauty ... Their superiority ... the uncommon Beauty of the Marquesans") and appears to embrace Marquesan culture.

The ethnocentric bias of Melville's reputed sources distances them from the peoples under observation. While Stewart changes the form of chapter headings used by Ellis, he certainly maintains Ellis's ideological stance. In *A Visit to the South Seas,* Stewart provides the following chapter headings for his journey to the Washington Islands:

    I. Departure from Peru
    II. Voyage to the Washington Islands
    III. Arrival at Nukuhiva
    IV. Valley of Taiohae
    V. Dance in the valley of the Hapaas
    VI. Forms of Government, and Civil and Religious Distinctions
    VII. A Day in the glen of Taioa
    VIII. Cruelty and injustice of Foreign Visitors
    IX. Removal of the Vincennes to the Territories of the Taipiis
    X. Trip to the valley of Hakahaa
    XI. Hakahaa, or the valley of the neutral ground
    XII. Departure from Nukuhiva

Although more interactive than Ellis's narrative, Stewart's account suggests only the rudiments of narrative structure: "Arrival at Nukuhiva ... Valley ... Dance ... Day in the glen." There is even less interest in stylizing the narrative.

Now consider Melville's account of the same geographic location as listed in Stewart's narrative:

> Chapter 2—Passage from the Cruising Ground to the Marquesas—Sleepy Times aboard Ship—South Sea Scenery—Land ho! The French Squadron Discovered at Anchor in the Bay of Nukuheva—Strange Pilot—Escort of Canoes—A Flotilla of Cocoa-nuts—Swimming Visitors—The Dolly boarded by them—State of affairs that ensue.

Melville intersperses his narration with sentimental images and language, such as "Land ho!" (compare with Stewart's simple "Arrival") and "A Flotilla of Cocoa-nuts," as well as with sensational imagery:

"Strange Pilot . . . Swimming Visitors. . . ." David Reynolds attributes the author's use of sensational rhetoric to the genre of sensational fiction popularized by George Lippard, among others, and he identifies one major source of Melville's bivalent discussions of missionary and native practices as the popular reform literature of the 1840s.[43] This recovery points us to some of the popular antebellum genres that Melville employed in *Typee,* but we must look further.

Melville's particular method of interpolating factual content into his experiential narrative more closely resembles the techniques employed by popular (and more liberal) travel writers, specifically Horatio Bridge, George Borrow, Eliot Warburton, and A. W. Kinglake, some of whom were published in the same British and American series of travel books that were later to add *Typee.*

The chapter headings in the works of these writers blend plot with information. For example, chapter 9 of Borrow's *The Bible in Spain* reads: "Badajoz—Antonio the Gypsy—Antonio's Proposal—The proposal accepted—Gypsy breakfast—Departure from Badajoz—The Gypsy Donkey—Merida—The Ruined Wall—The Crone—The Land of the Moor—The Black Men—Life in the Desert—The Supper" (83). Here the author moves from the scientific listing of travel places to an emphasis on plot and ends with detached anthropological observation. Likewise, in *Journal of an African Cruiser,* Bridge provides similar chapter headings that reflect the mixture of plot with observation:

> Settlement of Sinoe—Account of a Murder by the Natives—
> Arrival at Monrovia—Appearance of the Town—Temperance
> —Law-Suits and Pleadings—Expedition up the St. Paul's
> River—Remarks on the Cultivation of Sugar—Prospects of
> the Coffee-culture in Liberia—Desultory observations on
> Agriculture. (39)

Bridge shifts from the history of place—"Settlement of Sinoe" and later "Appearance of the Town"—to sensational storytelling—"Account of a Murder by the Natives" and "Law-Suits and Pleadings."

The link between *Typee* and popular travel books suggests new ways to consider the author's craft in this first work. Melville popular-

izes the conventional travel narrative by catering to the interests of
general readers as well as of cultivated readers of the British Murray
and the American Wiley and Putnam series. In *Typee*, Melville blends
sensational with sentimental rhetoric. This particular mixture links
Typee to both the current trends in the genre of travel and popular
magazine and domestic fiction and of the decade. This link to antebellum culture provides a gauge by which to measure Melville's similarities to popular practices, and this process, in turn, opens a new
door to the artistry that emerges from the author's particular mixtures in *Typee*.

The "American School" of Travels

One of Melville's great talents in *Typee* is the creative application of
the bivalency inherent in the travel genre, of different reader expectations, and of multiple ideological stances to serve complex cultural,
stylistic, and thematic ends. Yet to combine successfully different
conceptions of the travel narrative proved no easy task. Subtle distinctions existed between English and American travel books, differences that easily yielded thematic and structural discordancies.

Several American magazines characterized what was commonly
referred to as the "American school" of travels. The reviewer for
Graham's Magazine described J. T. Headley's *The Alps and the Rhine*
as a "brilliant and picturesque production, relating to men, manners,
and scenery ... full of interesting information, presented through the
medium of American ideas and feelings." An earlier reviewer, also in
Graham's, linked the particular focus and style of Headley's *Letters
from Italy* (1845) to an American audience, the general reader: "The
speculations on Italian society and politics, the anecdotes of individuals, and many of the personal incidents which occurred ... will be
found exceedingly interesting to the general reader." [44]

Yet even within the American school, differences in orientation
existed. Depending on their class status or pretensions, reviewers
endorsed specific qualities for this American school. In a notice of
Wiley and Putnam's New Library of Choice Literature and its forthcoming Library of American Books Series, Evert Duyckinck pro-

moted certain American books in the *Democratic Review* by underscoring their essentially cultivated status. Claiming that they are "of the *best class* of travels," he describes them as being "penned by men of *scholarship* and *enthusiasm,* of liberality and sentiment, fit guides for those who cannot wander, among climes and people, where history's richest landmarks are traceable, and life's bravest wonders abound" (October 1845, 317; emphasis added). Duyckinck goes on to suggest an ideological basis to these books which should "excite" the "patriotism and family pride of American readers." The *Knickerbocker,* another magazine that catered to cultivated readers, provides some insight into what Duyckinck might have meant by "patriotism and family pride." The reviewer of Headley's 1846 bestseller *The Alps and the Rhine* explains: "Being almost entirely descriptive, it has no criticisms to offend, and no peculiar views to provoke hostilities. It is a racy, vigorous, living, and life-giving book; and as such, we heartily recommend it to our readers" (*Knickerbocker,* February 1846, 164). These reviews point out two cherished aspects of the cultivated American travel book: an ideological reflector that supported upper middle-class attitudes and a lively ("racy") style. And it was the presence of both elements that Charles Wiley, the publisher of *Typee,* insisted upon for the revised edition of Melville's popular but ideologically challenging narrative.

Reviewers for the general reader, however, stressed style as the most important criterion for the American genre of travels. A review in *Godey's Lady's Book* alluded to conventional American travel writing in its notice of Headley's *Letters from Italy:* "It is a racy, lively, readable book of travels of the American school, written with all that vivacity and familiarity which is the principal charm of the books of Slidell, Stephens, Catlin and other successful American writers in this department" (December 1845, 271). As Henry Tuckerman wrote in an article called "The Philosophy of Travel" for the *Democratic Review,* traveling "is one of the few adventurous resources that remain to a prosaic epoch" (May 1844, 527). American travel writers adjusted their style to enrich their narratives for their audiences. The nation's cultivated readers demanded truthful, culturally validating yet stylistically intriguing books, while general audiences favored stylized over truthful narration. Pilgrimage narratives, written for both groups, accurately relate travels in Europe and the Orient in a light, often humorous tone, such as that found in the travels of Nathaniel Parker Willis, Bayard Taylor, and Harriet Beecher Stowe. Even the more scientifically oriented expeditionary narratives occasionally catered to the demand for stylistic flourishes and embellished their accounts: Captain David Porter romanticized his accounts of travel, while Benjamin Morrell highlighted the sensational aspects of his experiences among native peoples.[45]

Often travel writers varied their tone for rhetorical emphasis. William Ellis occasionally interrupts his factual, scientific account of South Sea flora, fauna, and manners with purely sensational rhetoric, borrowed from working-class literature, which was to become a central element of the middle-class "highly wrought" fiction of the 1840s:[46]

> Often before the new-born babe could breathe the vital air, gaze upon the light of heaven, or experience the sensations of its new existence, that existence had been extinguished by its cruel mother's hand; and the "felon sire," instead of welcoming with all a father's joy, a daughter or a son, has dug its grave upon the spot . . . and covered its mangled form with leaves.[47]

By interpolating veridical travel accounts with sensational rhetoric, writers highlighted the exoticism of the journey. This rhetoric provided an acceptable outlet where sensation could be temporarily enjoyed by all middle-class audiences. Yet this middle-class approach to sensation, unlike working-class sensational literature, did not diminish the centrality of scientific objectivity and ideological correctness, two elements essential for approval by English and American conservative readers.

For general American readers, however, it was precisely a light tone that evoked the most enthusiastic response. Reviewers of popular general magazines consistently preferred an interesting and entertaining style over instructional and informational content. The reviewer for the *New York Evening Mirror* remarked that readers unappreciative of a lighter tone "should be condemned to read Wilkes' *Narrative*," a scientific expeditionary account.[48] Discussing the same book, the reviewer for *Graham's* stated: "The striking pictures of the habits and manners of the savage inhabitants . . . will probably be sought for with greater avidity by the general reader, than the scientific facts . . . everywhere scattered over his pages."[49] *Godey's* praised the "easy and flowing style" over the factual exposition in Charles S. Stewart's *Scenes and Scenery in the Sandwich Islands, 1837–1842,* an opinion corroborated by the *Knickerbocker,* which praised the "series of sketches, illustrative of their [the natives'] present life and condition and other interesting points," because they "enliven a bare narrative of facts."[50] Instead of Bayard Taylor's "record" of Europe, *Graham's* preferred his tone, "the beautiful sweetness and healthiness of the author's mind and disposition." The *Knickerbocker* praised the style, rather than the account, of George Wilkins Kendall's *The Narrative of the Texas Sante Fe Expedition:* "It is the rich and amusing personal incidents . . . abounding with humor and wit which commends the narrative most forcibly to our attention." *Arthur's Magazine* praised Thomas Jefferson Jacob's *Scenes and Incidents in the Pacific Ocean* for its "stirring adventure" and deemed it a "very interesting book of adventures with attractions of a novel character."[51]

The reviewer for *Graham's* focused on the conflicting orientations of scientific and pilgrimage travel narratives by contrasting representative accounts of each. These disparities were further marked by national differences. The British author of the more scientific account focuses on the facts of travel, whereas the American author presents impressions:

> One loads us with detail, the other with rhetoric—one shows us countries in relation to their legislation and industrial capacities—the other in relation to himself; one is all economy, the other all poetry. There is no book of equal size which contains so much generalized information on the European mode of government and policy, and the moral and social conditions of the people, and so much criticism on both, as Mr. Laing. There are few books which give, in such small space, so many allusions to topics interesting to the lover of literature as that of Mr. Calvert. Both will find readers, but few readers will peruse both. They do not belong to the same parish.
> (*Graham's,* June 1846, 282)

Discussing the great popularity of Kinglake's *Eothen,* the reviewer for *Graham's* succinctly describes the novel's success:

> The great charm of the book consists in its *movement.* Everything is constantly in motion. The very style seems to travel. The rapid, glancing mind of the author does not dwell on a subject to weariness. Combined with the briskness of manner, there is much richness of poetic feeling, much power of picturesque description, much glow of imagination. Its highest praise is, that it is a book of travels without being disfigured with the pedantry, the simulated rapture, the mathematical exactness and pictorial falsehood, the dryness and dullness, which too often accompany works of this class. The author catches the spirit and the image of what he sees, and has sufficient skill of expression to convey both to other minds . . . and evincing a brilliant combination of the man of sentiment and the man of the world. (June 1845, 283)

Significantly, this English author who employed such American travel conventions was turned down by twenty English publishers (including John Murray), perhaps precisely because he went against British practice, and he was forced to publish his book at his own expense.[52]

These various American reviews indicate that authenticity refers not solely to mimetic representation, as John Murray and other British cultivated readers maintained, but also, at least for American general readers, to personal experience. The reviewer for *Graham's* highly praised Headley's best-selling *Letters from Italy* for its "individualities of feeling and expression" which give "freshness and colloquial grace to the style" (September 1845, 143). The reviewer for the *Democratic Review* recommended William Makepeace Thackeray's popularly constructed travel narrative *Notes of a Journey from Cornhill to Cairo* because "with less of the formality and pretension of ordinary volumes of travel, it presents a simple and often graphic picture of persons, places, and scenes, which came to the eye of the writer" (March 1846, 240). But for a travel account to be popular it must be charged. Indeed, the "simplicity" of personal reflection and a "racy, vivacious" style became, by 1846, the highest merits that a reviewer for general magazines could proclaim for a work of travels.

Popular American Styles

The major reason for the success of *Graham's* and *Godey's*, together with other general magazines of the period, was their commitment to a sentimental style, a rhetorical mode that emphasized the emotional response of the narrator over analysis. As Jane Tompkins has pointed out, sentimental fiction enjoyed great popularity during the antebellum period because, among other reasons, it reflected the beliefs of the revival movements that permeated all levels of American society, and, in effect, served as a means of cultural production.[53] Well established by innumerable contributors to the pages of *Graham's, Godey's,* and the *Columbian Lady's and Gentleman's Magazine,* sentiment replaced the "dull, dry prose" of factual travel narration. Consider the following excerpt from an account of a trip to Florence in the *Columbian Lady's and Gentleman's Magazine:* "Florence! Beautiful Florence! How many pictures in the chambers of mine imagery are filled with thy surpassing loveliness! Ah, Florence!"[54] The author, Emma C. Embury, a popular author of the 1840s, provides her emotional reaction to Florence, rather than experiential and anthropological details of the city. Highlighting her response with conventional icons (such as exclamation marks, followed by a parenthetical expression), she underscores the author's emotions and in this manner attempts to shape the reader's engagement with the narrative.

"Classic" writers of this period frequently employed sentimental rhetoric when appealing to general readers. Consider, for example, the opening passages from a story by Walt Whitman published in the *Columbian Lady's and Gentleman's Magazine:*

> Soft as the feathery leaf of the frailest flower—pure as the heart of flame—of a beauty so lustrous that the sons of Heaven themselves might not be drunken to gaze thereon—with fleecy robes that but half apparel a maddening whiteness and grace —dwells Eris among the creatures beautiful, a chosen and cherished one. (March 1845, 138)

Some of the most popular supporters of the sentiment mode were men; Nathaniel Parker Willis and later Ik Marvel (Donald Mitchell) were two of the greatest sentimentalists of the age. A *Graham's* reviewer praised Willis's writings for their sentimental style: "His works are fragrant with all the floral dam of sentiment" (April 1844, 146).

Although many of the decade's authors published both novels and shorter tales, they reserved stylistic mixtures for their magazine fiction. Periodical outlets for the general reader as diverse as the *New York Mirror, Columbian Lady's and Gentleman's Magazine, Arthur's Home Magazine, Graham's,* and the *Home Journal* published works that mixed sentimental and sensational modes.

Charles J. Peterson, former associate editor of both the *New York Evening Post* and *Graham's,* as well as a writer of sentimental and sensational sea tales, started *Peterson's Lady's Magazine,* a combination of "fashions and light literature." With Anna Sophia Stephens, a prolific contributor of stories and serialized fiction, as associate editor, *Peterson's* specialized in sensational fiction. Similarly, *Graham's* published both sentimental and sensational tales "dealing with love, American adventures, the Orient . . . along with poetry, a little travel, and entertaining book reviews." [55] The magazine praised the sensational novels of the popular French author Eugène Sue, and reviewers employed terms that indicated their support of acceptable sensational fiction. Though *Godey's* marketed sentimental literature through poems, stories, and essays that treated themes including lost love, broken hearts, mothers' sorrows, and wayward men, it too enthusiastically reviewed sensational works. The *Rover of Cuba and Other Tales,* for example, was praised as a series of "thrilling and adventurous" tales "destined to have an immense circulation among the people." [56] With the advent and acceptance of sensational fiction, *Godey's* promptly responded by including Edgar Allan Poe among its list of contributors and by publishing his story "The Oblong Box," among other sensational tales by this author. [57]

Of all the types of sensational stories, tales of the sea dominated the magazine market. With *The Narrative of Arthur Gordon Pym,* Poe bridged the gap between supernatural sea stories of the 1830s and the more realistic, though sensational, stories of the 1840s. Stories such as "Passing the Straits," "Getting to Sea," "Off Calais," and "Overboard in the Gulf" dotted the pages of *Peterson's, Graham's,* and other magazines along with other tales by Charles Peterson, Henry A. Clark, Frank Byrne, E. D. Judson, and Joseph Holt Ingraham, all sensational writers, many of whom also published in outlets aimed at working-class readers.

The later fiction by James Fenimore Cooper illustrates the use of sensation by writers interested in catering to popular tastes. Cooper's employment of this popular style has generally been overlooked, however; scholars have emphasized the increasing realism of his nautical fiction rather than the equally strong sensational elements in the fiction of the 1840s.[58] Considered a realistic novel, *Islets in the Gulf, or Rose Budd* (published in novel form as *Jack Tier*) is overtly sensational in tone. In trying to appeal to a magazine audience, Cooper sensationalized *Islets in the Gulf*, a novel written exclusively for and serialized in *Graham's*. A piratical captain attempts to abduct the innocent young Rose Budd; the rules of decorum are ignored, and women are subjected to abuse by men in reputedly high social standing, such as the captain. The best mate is cruelly left abandoned on a desolate rock to starve; the majesty of sea life is transformed into voracious sharks viciously trying to gorge themselves on human flesh. Fellow seamen deliberately cast others overboard in order to save themselves, and in a supreme act of sensation, the clutching hand of an old woman seeking to avoid drowning is abruptly slashed off at the wrist. The only element of sentiment left in this sensational novel is embodied in the character of the noble and virtuous Rose Budd. This was the story that dominated the pages of *Graham's* for two years. Such interest in sensationalism explains how Poe's stories were published in many of these magazines. Readers could freely indulge their thirst for sensational acts and yet be chastened by the middle-class values and morals that framed the tales.

The immense popularity of magazine literature, together with a growing interest in exotic travels, indicated that large audiences existed for a writer like Melville who would blend magazine and book practices. Melville applied the popular stylistic modes of sentiment and sensation (styles with which the adolescent Melville had experimented) to a new *subject;* that is, he cleverly combined these styles with the equally popular—though drier and more erudite—travel genre. The particular form of *Typee* finds an analogue in these practices.[59] With an understanding of these forms and styles, we can now shed light on some of Melville's strategies that have defied clarification in textual analyses of his first work.

CHAPTER TWO

Typee: (Re)Making the Best-Seller

Perhaps the most extraordinary aspect of the success of Melville's first book as a literary work and as a cultural artifact is how closely *Typee* reflects transatlantic literary trends and styles. The changes Melville made to *Typee,* which resulted in different editions —approximating essentially different texts—closely parallel the interests of his changing audiences. Indeed, it is somewhat misleading to refer to Melville's first work in the singular, a point recently raised by John Bryant.[1]

From the beginning of his publication negotiations, Melville indicated in several letters to John Murray, the English publisher of *Typee,* his willingness to cater to the interests of the reading public. *Typee,* he asserted, is a "bona-vide [*sic*] narrative . . . calculated for popular reading or for none at all."[2] Melville's language here implies that the author directly marketed his book to appeal to the interests of the targeted audiences, whose expectations—stylistic, formal, even ideological—appear to have shaped the various editions of *Typee.*

The *Typee* manuscript, expanded from one surviving leaf to roughly three chapters (due to the discovery in 1986 of the famous trunk, which contained family correspondence and the manuscript leafs corresponding to chapters 12 through 14 of the English edition of *Typee*), identifies the author's first intended audience. Melville referred to this group as the "fireside people" whom he directly addressed in the preface to the first English and American editions. In addition to the links between his work and the conventions of the genre of travels enjoyed by general readers, Melville displays in the *Typee* manuscript an understanding of and a debt to the conventions that marked domestic sentimental fiction. The author's direct location of his narrative within the home links *Typee* to the general readers of domestic sentimental fiction.

The earliest manuscript copy differs significantly from the first English edition. That edition of *Typee,* from which the first American edition was published (with changes), contains the author's successful attempt to blend the expectations of his bicultural readers; yet the famous Revised (expurgated) American edition amounts to what one could describe as an ideologically distinct book. Discussing *Typee* as a definitive text, then, can limit our understanding of the author at work and the multiple contexts within which the multitexts of *Typee* emerged.

Examining the manuscript against the first English edition, and in turn against the first American and the American Revised Editions, reveals an author with a sharp eye on the market and on his changing readers. It is these readerships to whom we must turn as we consider the various texts and intertexts of *Typee.*

"Here at Home": The *Typee* Manuscript and the Family Circle

Decades of Melville scholarship have confirmed that Melville consulted a myriad of literary forms, images, themes, and genres throughout his career of writing. Of all the tributes to Melville's literary appetite and to his restless reliance on various literary forms, most recently he has been celebrated for the "full range of his astonishing mobility," what Andrew Delbanco describes as "the closest thing in our literary history to an unfettered mind."[3]

Yet for several decades Melville scholarship has concentrated almost exclusively on the author's debt to classical literary heritages. Melville did align his first work within the traditional literature of travel, as William Spengeman and others have pointed out. Melville's early readings clearly demonstrate his familiarity with the travel narrative, and he adhered closely to its structure in *Typee,* as we have seen.[4] Beyond the travel narrative, scholars have looked to the libraries in the various ships on which the author served for clues to possible influences on the composition of *Typee.*[5]

But Melville's identification of his readers in the preface to *Typee* as "fireside people" indicates the author's first intended audience. The general reader of sentimental fiction, and in particular the context of the family reading circle, has been virtually ignored as an implied audience for *Typee.* Yet, as we shall see, the manuscript reflects Melville's engagement with the conventions of sentimental fiction.

When Melville returned from his four-year adventure at sea, he moved back to his mother's home in Lansingburgh, New York, a small town outside Albany. Living with his mother, a younger brother, and four unmarried sisters, Melville apparently participated —if not starred—in the evening family reading and storytelling circle. The Melville family had maintained a family reading circle that involved swapping the latest popular novels with members of the extended family, a practice that had continued since the family's move to Lansingburgh.[6] Nathaniel Parker Willis, a family friend, particularly of Melville's brother, referred to the history of *Typee* in a review of Melville's novels. The editor of the widely read *Home Journal* and a champion of sentimental fiction, Willis describes how Melville "had beguiled the long winter hours of his own home circle" with his Marquesan adventures and had published them "at their request."[7] Willis, the premier male advocate of a sentimental style, remained both a close family friend and an avid supporter of Melville's works.

Part of the family reading included the local *Democratic Press and Lansingburgh Advertiser* and the *Lansingburgh Gazette,* both of which contained literary pieces by the most famous writers of the day, including the celebrated female authors Lydia Sigourney and Anna Sophia Stephens.[8] Family members expressed at various times their interest in the sentimental mode; they also read the popular writings of the day and were particularly fond of women writers such as Catharine Sedgwick.[9] Melville's earliest writing, "Fragments from a Writing Desk," which was eventually published in the *Democratic Press,* suggests that a milieu beyond Lord Byron and Thomas Moore (the sources commonly suggested) served as a context for the overtly sentimental and sensational descriptions of the female villagers in Melville's sketches.

The surviving pages of the *Typee* manuscript relate a tale of the narrator's adventures among the Typees that is recounted in a consciously sentimentalized mode, a style in keeping with the reading interests of Melville's family circle. With descriptions of the "sweet" Fayaway, the author appears to have been aiming his tale at general American readers, much like his own siblings, mother, and extended family.

Melville's engagement with the sentimental mode is usually attributed variously to Byronic excesses, Grecian rhetoric, or to immature writing.[10] There is a reluctance to call sentimental language in *Typee* what it is: sentimental language. Consider the following evaluation of the sentimental style: "Melville's sketches also had the competition of many a lowly aspirant to Parnassus, who, by writing sentimentally of the death of a baby or of virtue triumphant, could win an audience that worshipped mawkish melancholy, piety, and a false refinement."[11] Stories by Lydia Sigourney and Anna Sophia Stephens were held up as examples of this "lowly" writing. Yet consider, for example, chapter 14, in which Tommo recounts his first encounter with the beautiful Fayaway. The manuscript records the narrator's impressions this way:

> This gentle *and amiable* being had early attracted my *notice,* not only from the extraordinary beauty *of her aspect,* but from the attractive cast of her countenance, *arrogantly* expressive of intelligence and humanity. . . . Whenever she had addressed us —especially when I lay reclining on the mats suffering from pain *in my leg that harassed me*—there was tenderness *and sympathy in the tones of her sweet voice and an expressive glance of pity in her face* which it was impossible either to misunderstand or resist.
>
> *These tokens of her kindly heart plainly assured* me that she deeply compassionated my situation as being removed from my countrymen and friends, and increasingly placed beyond *all hopes of succor or* relief. Indeed, at times I was almost lead to believe that her *gentle bosom* was swayed by impulses hardly to be anticipated from one in her condition. (Emphasis added)

The kindly heart, the gentle bosom, and the sweet voice—all unmistakable examples of the sentimental style popular in domestic novels and magazine tales of the period—were omitted from Murray's English edition, the publisher favoring objective observation over emotional responses to interactions with native peoples.

Rather than simply recount the facts of the experience (in this case, a malady), Melville stresses the narrator's emotional response to his experiences: "the malady *under which I labored*" (emphasis added). The *Typee* manuscript closely resembles this quality of sentimental writing:

> *The succor* of some proper medicines of which I stood in need
> ... his departure *oppressed me with many melancholy reflec-*
> *tions,* but *struggling against* them. . . . we were fairly puzzled,
> but in spite of these apprehensions *I could not expell from my*
> *heart* . . . *rescuing me from the dangers to which I was exposed.*
> (Emphasis added)

Indeed, the manuscript consistently stresses the narrator's *response* to his experiences, instead of underscoring the experiences themselves: "She *seemed to* overcome the scruples she might have had entertained . . . and I felt upbraided for imputing. . . . *In the first transport of my astonishment,* I accused" (emphasis added). Compare those phrases with the following changes to the English edition: "She overcame her scruples . . . I upbraided myself. . . . At first I accused"(108). While the manuscript employs words and phrases such as *heart sick, gentle bosom, sweet voice, glance of pity,* and *fall victim to,* the first English edition records these respective changes: (1) deleted, (2) "her manner," (3) "her manner," (4) deleted, (5) "be exposed to." The manuscript indicates the sentimental orientation of *Typee* and clearly projects what the author must have had initially intended for his first work be a novel of adventure in keeping with domestic and sentimental conventions.

The links between these practices and Melville's manuscript move beyond this rhetorical mode to include parallel ideological frameworks. Melville's narrator locates the source of his authorship with *Home* (a word he chooses to capitalize elsewhere in *Typee*). We have an author who locates the nexus of his narrative in the home:

> A straight, dry and partly decayed stick of the hibiscus . . . is as
> invariably to be met with in every properly furnished home in
> Typee as a box of Lucifer matches [is to be found laying] in the
> corner of [the] <a kitchen> cupboard [of our kitchens] *here at*
> *home.* (Manuscript; emphasis added)

The phrase "a kitchen cupboard here at home" locates the narrator of *Typee* in his home, writing from his home. "Home" (and "Mother") —both in the manuscript and in subsequent editions of *Typee*— serves as an ideological source as well as an ending for the narrator's values.

Melville's approach here approximates that of sentimental writers, particularly female authors, who wrote domestic fiction. Maria Jane McIntosh, whose novel *To Seem or to Be* was published when Melville was writing *Typee* and was reviewed in the local paper, also situated her authorship within the home. Nina Baym has identified this strategy as a convention of women's fiction at midcentury.[12] Dozens of domestic novels recount the story—just as the *Typee* manuscript suggests—of a character who ventures far from his or her domestic center only to ultimately return Home: to the source of an ennobling set of values.

As we have already seen in chapter 1, sentimental and sensational styles were usually blended in popular novels and magazine writing of the decade. This combination is found throughout *Typee*. Melville borrows from popular fiction and magazine writing the use of sensational rhetoric to heighten the drama of the recounted narrative. The manuscript evinces several incidents narrated in overtly sensational language:

> The sounds grew louder and nearer, and gradually the whole valley rang with wild outcries. . . . All that I could understand from him was that *something fatal had occurred in connection* with Toby. *Horrified at the thought* of some dreadful calamity, I rushed out of the house, and caught sight of a tumultuous crowd *of the savages,* who with shrieks and lamentations, *had* just *emerged* from the grove *and were approaching us* bearing in their *midst* some object, the sight of which produced all *these transports* of sorrow.
>
> In a moment the crowd opened, and disclosed *to my horror* the apparently lifeless *form* of my companion borne between two *natives,* the head hanging *over the shoulders against the breast* of the foremost, *while the lower limbs hung drooping across the arm of the other.* The whole face, neck, and bosom were *disfigured* with blood, which still trickled slowly from a

wound behind the temple. *Good God! What frightful catastrophe was this? . . . The next moment without looking backward, I became sensible from the fiendish yells behind me that the savages my enemies were in hot pursuit. Animated though I was by their fearful outcries, and heedless of the injury I had received, I instinctively shrunk to one side from a fearful whissing noise.* (Emphasis added)

The remainder of the manuscript chapter contains phrases such as "anxious though I was to be informed of the nearly fatal mishap," "the rude shock," "laid me senseless at his feet," and "a simultaneous burst of rage." Melville's reliance on sensational images and language closely parallels the language popularized in novels by George Lippard as well as by female authors who targeted general readers, such as Anna Sophia Stephens.

"A More Life-Like Air"

The literary interests of the general American reader, however, differed substantially from cultivated British readers. The changes from the manuscript version to the first English edition reveal the author's determination to appeal simultaneously to two distinct audiences. In the case of the Murray travel series, known as the Home and Colonial Library Series, an elite group of British subscribers, or financial backers, helped the publisher determine the criteria by which the forms, themes, and ideological orientation of the travel books in the series, such as Borrow's *The Bible in Spain,* Eliot Warburton's *The Crescent and the Cross,* and Melville's *Typee,* were to be produced. Though the series was intended for largely middle-class audiences whose interests might have differed from those of the cultivated subscribers, the latter group felt obliged to shape the aesthetic tastes of reviewers and readers.

Until his brother secured an English publisher, Melville was not able to tailor his book to meet a specific publisher's requirements. John Murray clearly stated his expectations to Gansevoort Melville, who, in turn, wrote a letter to his brother, Herman. Since only the author's letter to Murray regarding chapters 20, 21, and 27 is extant, I turn to these chapters, together with the English edition of the manuscript chapters 12 to 14, to examine the differences between the two versions.

In a letter to Murray sent with some additions to his manuscript, Melville described his carefully tailored material:

> The bulk of the new matter consists of three chapters, numbered respectively 20–21-& 27, which are in my humble opinion less amenable than the others to the faults you have pointed out, and from their subject matter, especially that of Chapter 27, will go far to give a more life-like air to the whole, an[d] parry the incredulity of those who may be disposed to regard the work as an ingenious fiction . . . two schedules of minor corrections & additions relating chiefly to the Taboo, the cause of Missions, and the religious belief of the Marquesans. (*Letters*, 283.)

We may infer from this letter just what was expected of authors who wished to publish in the highly regarded English travel series.

As Melville's letter indicates, chapter 27 (and the other two chapters he submitted) adds what the author called a "more life-like air to the whole." An ethnographic account of the Typees, chapter 27 consciously adopts the more detached mode of scientific reportage common to works in the Murray's series. As we have seen, travel narratives published in the Home and Colonial Library primarily recounted the *facts* of travel. Action rather than the teller's emotional response to that action is emphasized in the English edition.

Certainly Gansevoort's admitted reluctance (following his discussion with Murray about publishing expectations) to submit two of the three manuscript chapters until he had reread or "worked on" them so that they conformed more precisely to the publisher's demands suggests that the *Typee* manuscript was too sentimental, and perhaps too sensual, for British reading tastes.

Along with the more detached narrative tone in the English edition came a corresponding reduction of sensational images. Since this rhetorical mode amplifies the teller's emotional response to the narrated action, it is not surprising that the English edition contains the following significant changes from the original manuscript: The original "*horrified at the thought* of some dreadful calamity" became "*apprehensive* of some dreadful calamity"; "*something fatal* had occurred in connection with Toby" became "*some accident* had happened to Toby"; "the crowd opened, and disclosed *to my horror*" became "the crowd opened, and disclosed" (emphasis added).

If the *Typee* manuscript indicates the focus of the narrative at that stage in its composition, then Murray must have exhibited concern over the author's active engagement with and emotional response to the peoples and cultures encountered.

The manuscript emphasizes the immediacy of the narrated moment, an immediacy that was omitted from the British edition. Thus statements such as "the man now stood" (manuscript) became "the man who stood" in Murray's edition. Such attempts to distance the narrator from the cultures described reinforced the detachment and subsequent ideological superiority of travel writers in the Murray series. Melville's changes to the manuscript indicate his keen understanding of reader expectations as well as his willing acquiescence to shape his work for the marketplace.

"Fireside People"

In the preface to both the English and first American editions of *Typee,* however, Melville explicitly directs his account to the "fire-side people," an audience that rapidly comprised the majority of middle-class American readers in the 1840s.[13] The allusion places Melville's original target in the audience commonly referred to as general American readers. The author further links his work to this audience by appealing to their interest in sentimental and sensational styles, rhetorical modes not held in as high aesthetic repute with British cultivated readers. Melville hoped, in his words, to "excite the warmest sympathies" of his readers by recounting adventures "strange and romantic," two terms synonymous with sensation and sentiment to American readers of the 1840s (*Typee,* xiii-xiv).[14] This combination of popular styles connects Melville's adventures to popular literary trends of the 1840s.

While in the first English and subsequent editions of *Typee* Melville toned down his use of sentimental and sensational rhetoric in order to augment the experiences, rather than the narrator's reaction to them, the first English and American editions nevertheless reflect the author's reliance on this mode of expression. Throughout *Typee,* Melville employs sensational rhetoric, and like other writers of his day, he softens its effect by blending it with sentiment. In his delineation of the Marquesas, the author exploits hegemonic attitudes toward nativism. He counterpoints sensational and sentimental images:

> Naked houris—cannibal banquets—groves of cocoa-nut— coral reefs—tattooed chiefs—and bamboo temples; sunny valleys planted with bread-fruit-trees—carved canoes dancing on the flashing blue waters—savage woodlands guarded by horrible idols—*heathenish rites and human sacrifices.* (*Typee,* 5; emphasis added)

Through this stylistic mixing, Melville provided general readers with an exotic, sometimes erotic, attraction couched within the acceptable genre of the travel narrative.

Melville initially lures the reader with the subject of life at sea, a topic that contains its own intrinsic interest for readers: "Six months at sea! Yes, reader, as I live, six months out of sight of land; cruising after the sperm-whale beneath the scorching sun of the Line, and tossed on the billows of the wide-rolling Pacific—the sky above, the sea around, and nothing else!" (3). Though this passage has recently been described as unusual in novel writing of the day, the act of contextualizing Melville's style reveals its links to popular magazine practice.[15] The heavy use of exclamation points marking the opening passages of *Typee* recalls the sentimental tradition established in the pages of *Graham's, Godey's,* and the *Columbian Lady's and Gentleman's Magazine,* as noted in chapter 1. In a discussion of popular literature, Edgar Allan Poe described the conventional story of "life upon the ocean" as "so unfailingly omniprevalent in its power of arresting and absorbing attention that success or popularity is, with such a subject, expected as a matter of course."[16] Melville not only discussed this popular subject, but did so with a sentimental flourish that endeared him to his readers.

Interesting his readers in familiar sentiment, Melville introduces elements of sensation. The narrator of *Typee* clothes the description of his shipmate, Toby, in the romantic imagery of the sailor: "Arrayed in his blue frock and duck trousers, he was as smart a looking sailor as ever stepped upon a deck. . . ." Yet Melville immediately adds sensational elements: "He was a strange wayward being, moody, fitful, and melancholy—at times almost morose" (32). The switch from conventional, idealized description to melancholy and moroseness recalls the sensational effects in Poe's stories which catered to the demand for sensation by general and working-class readers. Whereas Poe emphasized sensation over sentiment, however, Melville reached for the balance between. With this transition from familiar icons to sensational elements, Melville does not "task or startle the intellect." Poe had maintained that this gesture "cannot fail to prove unpopular with the masses." [17] Melville's maneuver thrills the reader without shocking. Once the sensational elements have been presented, he immediately returns to the level of familiar sentiment.

In Chapter 7, "A Ravine and Waterfalls," the narrator sentimentalizes a discovery of a path by relating it to the island discovery described in *Robinson Crusoe:* "Robinson Crusoe could not have been more startled at the footprint in the sand than we were at this unwelcome discovery" (44). He then moves to a sensational description:

> Five foaming streams, rushing through as many gorges, and swelled and turbid by the recent rains, united together in one mad plunge of nearly eighty feet, and fell with wild uproar into a deep black pool scooped out of the gloomy-looking rocks that lay piled around, and thence in one collected body dashed down a narrow sloping channel which seemed to penetrate into the very bowels of the earth . . . It was now sunset, and the feeble uncertain light that found its way into these caverns and woody depths heightened their strange appearance, and reminded us that in a short time we should find ourselves in utter darkness (45).

He heightens the sensationalism by employing rhetorical questions that augment the horror: "Shall I ever forget that horrid night? . . . But the accumulated horrors of that night, the death-like coldness of the place, the appalling darkness and the dismal sense of our forlorn condition, almost unmanned me" (46). Such passages that link nature with mental states are reminiscent of Poe's method and the body of sensational literature on which Poe relied. His method involved describing inanimate objects with sensational images that symbolize mental states. Melville's "mad plunge," "wild uproar," "gloomy-looking rocks," "death-like coldness," and "appalling darkness" resemble the images in the opening passage of Poe's "The Fall of the House of Usher." Rather than continue in this manner and exploit the sensational effects through morbidity as in the case of Poe, the narrator of *Typee* abruptly switches to sentiment and ends the chapter:

> As the feverish sensation increased upon me, I tossed about, . . . I chanced to push aside a branch, and by so doing suddenly disclosed to my view a scene which even now I can recall with all the vividness of the first impression. Had a glimpse of the gardens of Paradise been revealed to me I could scarcely have been more ravished with the sight . . . Over all the landscape there reigned the most hushed repose, which I almost feared to break lest, like the enchanted gardens in the fairy tale, a single syllable might dissolve the spell. (49)

This mixture of sensation and sentiment maintained a stylistic balance that pleased general readers who desired entertaining travel books.

Melville discovered prime subject matter for catering to popular tastes in the accounts of bizarre native customs documented by some travel writers. Ellis and Stewart greatly admired tattooing practices and minutely described the procedure. Bennett, who thought his life in danger when he continued to refuse to be tattooed, calmly relates how he managed to keep his face free from the marks.[18] Melville sensationalized the horror of this practice. Though his account strongly resembles the dispassionate description of tattooing found in the volume by Georg von Langsdorff and others,[19] Melville spices his story with sensational elements:

> Horrified at the bare thought of being rendered hideous for life if the wretch were to execute his purpose upon me, I struggled to get away from him. . . . When his fore-finger swept across my features, in laying out the borders of those parallel bands which were to encircle my countenance, the flesh fairly crawled upon my bones. At last, half wild with terror. . . . (218–19).

This technique appears throughout the novel. In chapter 32, "Mysterious Feast," the author plays on sensational elements to increase the terror of the reader and the horror of the outcome:

> ... the savages were about to celebrate some hideous rite in connection with their peculiar customs, ...
>
> The sound of the drums continued, without intermission, the whole day, and falling continually upon my ear caused me a sensation of horror which I am unable to describe.
>
> ... feeling a kind of morbid curiosity to discover whether. . . .
>
> But the slight glimpse sufficed; my eyes fell upon the disordered members of a human skeleton, the bones still fresh with moisture, and with particles of flesh clinging to them here and there!
>
> ... the fearful situation in which I was placed. . . . (236–39)

Melville counterpoints these sensationally descriptive statements with an abrupt return to sentimental notions of "Home": " . . . deprived of all intercourse with civilized beings, and for ever separated from friends and home" (239). By celebrating "civilized" over native society, this strategy reinforces both the ideological views of the cultivated readers and the domestic values of general readers.

Typee as Best-Seller

Immersed in the culture of the day, mid-nineteenth-century readers easily recognized Melville's style in *Typee* as a structural device that linked sentimental and sensational modes and contributed to the bivalency of the travel narrative. Sophia Hawthorne, for example, recorded her impressions of *Typee* in a letter to her mother: "All this golden splendor and enchantment glowing before the dark refrain constantly brought as a background—the fear of being killed and eaten—the cannibalism in the olive tinted Apollos around him—the unfathomable mystery of their treatment of him."[20] Modern scholars, too, have remarked on this dual vision. Without contextualizing, as we have done, the bivalency that marks *Typee*, textual analyses have treated this doubleness in purely thematic terms. Newton Arvin described it as a conflict between the narrator's "heightened anxiety" and a "deliberate idealism," a paradigm later reformulated by James E. Miller, Jr., as a dual presence of idealism and sensation.[21] T. Walter Herbert attributes the presence of romanticism and sensation in Melville's work to the "double" narrator. Mitchell Breitweiser approaches the cultural context when he discusses the rhetorical ploy of the narrator's ambivalence toward the Marquesans, though he does not recover how this ambivalence serves as a rhetorical stance for meeting mutual demands for sentiment and sensation, one that plays off the form of the conventional travel narrative.

While thematic treatments offer useful tools for analyzing the plot structure, closer attention to the context of Melville's creativity lifts analysis from the page and into the culture. Certainly, Melville's narrator reveals both a "horror and profound admiration for the islanders," an ambivalence that becomes for Tommo the "crisis of meaning" of the novel, as Herbert has suggested.[22] Yet this theme is not separate from the narrative style.

In fact, this bivalenced view marks Melville's creativity in popularizing the travel narrative. The manner in which the author applies the double tone of sentiment and sensation to the essential bifurcation of the travel narrative—that is, how he employs sensationalism when describing the experiences while reserving a sentimental tone for "retrospective commentary"—links literary cultural forms with his own, more personal forms and themes.[23] This cultural emphasis provides greater insights into Melville's orientation in *Typee*. Thus, rather than consider how Melville tries to tell the truth through the artifices of fiction, a focus that necessarily formulates the analysis in thematic terms, I would like to suggest that it is more instructive, and more representative of Melville's own example, to consider how he tries to combine nonfictional forms (such as the travel narrative) with popular styles to present a literary text that his readers would find more engaging. This contextualization recovers the author's cultural legacies, compositional methods, and aesthetic interests, elements that reflect what Melville later called a "correspondent coloring" between individual and cultural practices.

Praise for the "sustained interest," "entertaining narrative," and "exceedingly racy and readable style" of *Typee* reverberated throughout journals and newspapers that appealed to the general reader. Entertainment was the measure of literary success for that audience. *Godey's* deemed Melville's novel "extremely entertaining," an opinion seconded by *Graham's*. The *New York Tribune* hailed it as a "very entertaining and pleasing narrative," and the *New York Morning Courier* claimed that it "abounds in anecdotes and narratives of unusual interest." The *New York Illustrated Magazine* proclaimed *Typee* "one of the most interesting, amusing, and original books of adventure we have read for many a day." Margaret Fuller of the *New York Tribune* compared Melville's characters to Shakespeare's: "Othello's hair-breathed 'scapes were nothing to those by this hero in the descent of the cataracts."[24]

American reviewers almost unanimously praised the style. "Racy and pointed," maintained George Washington Peck of *The American Review: A Whig Journal,* despite this cultivated reviewer's problem with Melville's representation of the missionary effort in the islands. The *Knickerbocker* liked the "easy, gossiping style," the *New York Gazette and Times* "the fresh, graceful, and animated style," and the *New York Mirror* "the freshness and vigor of style." Nathaniel Hawthorne's assessment in the *Salem Advertiser* agreed with the general sentiment: *Typee* was "lightly but vigorously written."[25]

Melville's calculations proved successful. American reviewers hailed *Typee* as a great achievement. Charles Fenno Hoffman in the *Literary World* remarked that "few American books awakened the lively interest excited by Mr. Melville's unique and delightful volume." Melville contributed significantly in *Typee* to the evolution of the travel genre by constructing an informative, entertaining, sensational, and sentimental narrative for the general reader. He essentially offered the public a record of adventures in an interesting form. Another reviewer described *Typee* as

> an almost unmingled *Sea Romance* of lands, waters, and people, skillfully chosen to affect the fancy of a generation highly sensuous and wonder-loving, much-rejoicing to be helped to an imaginary sojourn with barbarism and an ideal plunge into such a state of Nature as the loosest voluptuary may sigh for.[26]

As Melville's contemporary readers and reviewers continually pointed out, *Typee* illustrates an author in control of his materials and visibly sensitive to the interests of his readers.

The shift in *Typee* back from sensation to sentiment and the resulting balance account for Melville's extraordinary success among American general readers. Too much sensation leads to morbidity and the subsequent revulsion of readers, as Poe readily discovered. The public enthusiastically praised Melville's blending because it provided a spirited, tantalizing, and yet comfortable narrative.

Judging from these enthusiastic reviews, we can see that *Typee* was decidedly a hit in American middle-class reading circles. Yet we must bear in mind that this readership was small, especially according to the standards of the day. In his memoirs of his publishing career and the state of publishing in mid-nineteenth-century America, George Palmer Putnam recounts:

> The market upon which the authors and publishers depended for returns for their literature comprised the New England States, the Middle States, and two or three of the older States in the South. Even in these older states, the number of communities in which the book-buying tastes and the resources available were sufficiently important to maintain a book-shop was very restricted.[27]

As Putnam, Matthew Carey, Samuel Goodrich, and other nineteenth-century publishers continually pointed out, a best-seller during the 1840s referred to a work that sold between three and ten thousand copies. Indeed, the famous best-sellers of the 1850s—Susan Warner's *The Wide, Wide World,* Maria Cummins's *The Lamplighter,* and Fanny Fern's *Ruth Hall*—were rare exceptions to rather than the general rule of the best-seller list. It did not help that the editor of the Wiley and Putnam series, Evert Duyckinck, catered to the interests of the smaller group of cultivated, rather than to the larger audiences of general readers.

Typee competed favorably with other travel works in the series despite its more expensive price and unknown author. Melville's book was the first to sell for seventy-five cents; the cost of the first volumes had ranged from thirty-seven to fifty cents. Other authors in the series were already established names: Margaret Fuller, Edgar Allan Poe, Nathaniel Hawthorne, John Greenleaf Whittier, and George Cheever. Bridge's *Journal of an African Cruiser* had the advantage of being edited—and more important, marketed as edited—by Nathaniel Hawthorne, a popular name among middle-class readers. *Typee* sold three thousand copies in six months, while the second volume of the series, Edgar Allan Poe's *Tales,* sold fifteen hundred copies during the same period.[28] Despite the advantages that these established authors and cheaper book prices had over Melville, *Typee* did surprisingly well.

As Nina Baym pointed out in her study of antebellum women's fiction, however, it is important to establish clearly the criteria employed in determining the popularity of an antebellum work.[29] In terms of the immediate sales of the book, *Typee* sold more than two thousand copies in just half the time of the books mentioned earlier, amounting to six thousand copies in three years, from the American edition alone. Thus, according to the publishing standards of the day, established and documented through top publishers such as Putnam, Matthew Carey, and the Harpers, *Typee* was indeed a best-seller.

Melville's stylistic mixtures and subjects in *Typee* contributed substantially to establishing his reputation as a popular antebellum writer. The sentimental images of idyllic happiness that Melville created through his beautiful, "sweet" Fayaway and his Pacific island remained entrenched in the popular imagination even through the 1850s.

Melville's initial and enduring popularity with *Typee* came to serve as a mixed blessing for the author. As we shall see in our examination of his career throughout the forties and fifties, Melville discovered in his middle-class readers an audience so enchanted by his sentimental images and sensational experiences in *Typee* (and soon after in *Omoo,* though to a lesser extent) that it insisted on more of the same. But even as early as his first three novels, we discover an author who searches for new genres, different forms, and alternative audiences to his general middle-class readers.

Remaking the Best-Seller

The uproar that occurred among British readers concerning the "authenticity" of Melville's first novel indicates the seriousness of the demand for truthful narratives among cultivated audiences. The *London Athenaeum* discerned an "indication of romance," the presence of which seriously limited the "value" of *Typee,* while the *Eclectic Review* dismissed the book because it was not "authentic." [30] Moreover, Melville's reputed profession as a seaman perplexed British reviewers. Though the author purported to be a "common sailor," the *London Times* proclaimed him a "very uncommon common sailor" and considered *Typee* the work "of an educated literary man rather than of a poor outcast working seaman." They characterized Melville as a "practiced and accomplished writer rather than the inmate of the forecastle." [31]

Part of the objection to the "monstrous exaggeration" in *Typee* and the true social class of its author stems from Melville's creativity in his first work. No book of nautical adventure prior to *Typee* combined the very different voices of the formally uneducated seaman and the gentleman-sailor. The literary talents inherent in Melville's narrative induced the reviewer of the *London Critic* to proclaim the work "the joint production of an American sailor and a man of letters." [32]

Likewise, cultivated readers found *Typee* too ideologically challenging for their reading tastes. In his revisions to *Typee,* Melville learned quickly that writing for both American and British audiences required different sets of social registers. Cultivated British audiences expected a narrator to reflect—or more accurately remain within—his class status. Since Melville's narrator works as a sailor but writes as a gentleman, British readers expressed their incredulity with the notion that an uneducated sailor could write in the sophisticated and elegant manner exhibited in *Typee.* American cultivated audiences, on the other hand, more exposed to mixed-class narratives, displayed serious concern over the ideological basis of Melville's work.

As a response to such criticism, Melville shaped the American Revised Edition by toning down and sometimes altogether removing his ideological stances on culture, nativism, and missionary projects in the South Seas. In a 15 July letter to John Murray, Melville explains why he altered his book so radically:

> This new edition will be a Revised one, and I can not but think that the measure will prove a judicious one.—The revision will only extend to the exclusion of those parts not naturally connected with the narrative and some slight purification of style. . . . The book is certainly calculated for popular reading, or for none at all.—If the first, why then, all passages which are calculated to offend the tastes, or offer violence to the feelings of any large class of readers are certainly objectionable. —Proceeding on this principle then, I have rejected every thing, in revising the book, which refers to the missionaries. . . . Certain "sea-freedoms" also have been modified.[33]

Melville relates the tastes of his audience—in this case, the "class" of cultivated readers—to the nature of his revision.

Clearly, Melville's indictments of the missionary efforts had to be omitted. The "slight purification of style" applies to sexual innuendos: Melville's new edition adhered to a strict sense of Victorian propriety demanded by cultivated readers that had gone unheeded in the previous editions. Thus "naked" houris became the more innocuous "lovely" houris. A reference to the "absence" of the marriage tie became the more socially acceptable "looseness" of the marriage tie (*Typee*, 193,3).

The effect of these two changes—omission of any criticism of Western imperialism and the author's success at relativizing cultural habits—on the narrative results in radically different thematics. The first English and American editions had celebrated native culture and offered more complex formulations of the Western claim to a "civilized" ascendancy over non-Western cultures. In the American Revised Edition, Melville deleted these important thematic passages from his book, such as the following:

> How often is the term "savages" incorrectly applied! None really deserving of it were ever yet discovered by voyagers or by travellers. They have discovered heathens and barbarians, whom by horrible cruelties they have exasperated into savages. (27)

> Despite the disadvantages of his condition, the Polynesian sav-
> age, surrounded by all the luxurious provisions of nature,
> enjoyed an infinitely happier, though certainly a less intellec-
> tual existence, than the self-complacent European. (124)

> In a primitive state of society, the enjoyments of life, though
> few and simple, are spread over a great extent, and are unal-
> loyed; but Civilization, for every advantage she imparts, holds
> a hundred evils in reserve;—the heart burnings, the jealousies,
> the social rivalries, the family dissensions, and the thousand
> self-inflicted discomforts of refined life, which make up in
> units the swelling aggregate of human misery, are unknown
> among these unsophisticated people. (124–125)

Such passages openly challenged what Melville saw as the ethnocentric biases of Western cultures, and together with the celebration of
native cultures, they offered an ideological view of the world which
directly challenged that of cultivated readers, people who firmly supported manifest destiny, asserted the primacy of Christianity and
Western culture, and strictly followed Victorian social codes. By removing these ideological sections from his narrative, Melville offered
cultivated readers a travel book in the American Revised Edition that
remained clearly anchored in the mores of Western "civilization."

From this first work, a different view of Melville emerges. In *Typee,*
Melville exhibits a "design" in much more than the "rudimentary
sense" that is commonly attributed to the author's compositional
habits.[34] Far from an author who works without plan, Melville appears to have consciously strategized by shifting his orientation to
appeal to different readerships. From the start of his professional
writing career, then, Melville evinces through his deliberate reliance
on popular practices a knowledge and an understanding of—perhaps
even a commitment to—the tastes of his readers.

CHAPTER THREE

Reader Expectations and Innovation in *Omoo* and *Mardi*

I N HIS SECOND BOOK, Melville applied what he had learned about the power of readers in the marketplace and shaped *Omoo: A Narrative of Adventures in the South Seas* (1847) according to the diverse, frequently contradictory standards exacted by the various audiences of *Typee*. Seeking models that would lend a greater air of reality, a criterion that British and American cultivated readers demanded, Melville turned to the popular genre of the nautical reminiscence. To meet the expectations of both general readers for the voice of a common sailor and cultivated readers for a "gentleman's" account, Melville combined these formulations in ways that did not alienate either audience, as had occurred in *Typee*. Though his literary reputation and future success with "gentleman" readers and other advocates of cultivated narration depended on a realistic, authentic narrative, his previous success with general readers resulted primarily from the "racy" tone in which he had narrated his first book of travels. Melville discovered the approach he needed in the popular realistic sea tales of the 1840s.

Melville's reliance on this American genre of the sea narrative reveals essential differences between *Typee* and *Omoo*, differences frequently overlooked by critics who consider these first novels collectively as the "Siamese twins of the literary world."[1] The author's inclination to turn the nautical reminiscence to his literary advantage —his ability to use conventions that united different audiences as well as provided space for innovation within the genre—deserves careful study. Far from an apprentice, an "inexperienced" writer who is "unable to make the most of his materials," as was once thought, Melville displays in *Omoo* his ability to work successfully with a variety of forms and genres.[2] At this early stage in his career, he demonstrates a perceptive understanding of the marketplace and packages his new work in a form accepted by diverse readers. Yet in the face of the success of *Typee,* the author nonetheless experiments with new combinations in *Omoo.* In this light, Melville reveals himself as a writer who taps into the formulas of the successful book as well as a relentless innovator.

The Nautical Reminiscence

The nautical reminiscence evolved during the 1830s and early 1840s as a narrative form distinct from the more romantic treatment of sea adventures published the previous decade. The genre developed partially in reaction to the popularity of Cooper's romantic sea novels of the 1820s and Gothic sea tales of the 1830s, works that authors in subsequent decades considered unrealistic portraits of life at sea.

Several nautical reminiscences appearing in the American marketplace during the 1830s and 1840s achieved moderate fame among antebellum readers. The more popular of these include Nathaniel Ames, *A Mariner's Sketches* (1830) and *Nautical Reminiscences* (1832), Robert Montgomery Bird, *The Adventures of Robin Day* (1839), Richard Henry Dana, Jr., *Two Years before the Mast* (1840), Cooper, *Ned Myers: A Life before the Mast* (1843), and Charles Briggs, *Working a Passage; Or, Life in a Liner* (1844).[3]

The nautical reminiscence presents realistic accounts of life at sea from the perspective of the forecastle, the living quarters of common sailors, rather than from the foredeck, the home of Cooper's romanticized gentleman-sailors. From this perspective, writers of the genre typically relate tales of sailors' discontent, threatened mutinies, intolerable living conditions, and perilous situations.

Everything associated with the sea is presented as decidedly unromantic. In the tradition of Tobias Smollett and his nineteenth-century British imitator, the popular Frederick Marryat, American writers of the nautical reminiscence depict the ocean as a devastating force. Hostile waters replace the romantic seas of Cooper's early works such as *The Pilot*.[4] Cooper's ships, bearing the majestic names *Dolphin, Water-Witch,* and *Red-Rover,* do not fly over the waves like "sea-bird[s] on the wing" in this new genre.[5] Ships are described instead as "shabby disorderly looking crafts" named, for example, the *Viper* and the *Scattergood*. Whereas in *The Pilot* Cooper's ship appears as mountains of fortitude—"She was a gallant ship, whose large hull, lofty masts and square yards, loomed ... like a distant mountain rising from the deep"—in the nautical reminiscence ships represent everything except strength and control: "Everything was in confusion on deck; the little vessel was tearing through the water as if she had lost her wit, the sea flying over her, and the masts heaving over at a wide angle from the vertical."[6] In Briggs's *Harry Franco,* the narrator deliberately contrasts the actual appearance of a ship with romantic portrayals to underscore the realism of the genre: "She was a smaller ship, and much blacker and dirtier looking than those which had attracted my attention at first; she had neither gilding on her stern, nor a varnished waist, nor a figure-head" (1:155). Such realistic portraits discount the authenticity of their romantic predecessors.

Unlike the majestic and affable crew in the early romances of Cooper and his 1840s imitator, Charles Peterson, shipmates in the nautical reminiscence are cast as drunk, brutal, ignorant sailors:

> The hard faces of the men ... appeared like half formed beings, emerging out of chaos. They were all either drunk or in that surly and brutish state, which succeeds to a drunken revel. (Briggs, *Harry Franco,* 1:170)

> The assembling of the crew ... was a melancholy sight. The men came off, bearing about them the signs of the excesses of which they had been guilty while on shore; some listless and stupid, others still labouring under the effects of liquor, and some in that fearful condition which seamen themselves term having the "horrors." (Cooper, *Ned Myers,* 123).

> Such a stupid and greasy-looking set I never saw before.... They had brutish faces, looked like the antipodes of sailors, and apparently dealt in nothing but grease. (Dana, *Two Years before the Mast,* 176)

Captains, too, fare no better. Bird and Dana vividly depict tyrannical personalities: "Captain Brown on land, and Captain Hellcat at sea, were two very different persons; and that, however much I might have detested the one, there remained for me nothing but to fear the other" (Bird, *The Adventures of Robin Day*, 2:189); "If we get along well together, we shall have a comfortable time; if we don't, we shall have hell afloat" (Dana, *Two Years before the Mast*, 14). These captains provide scanty provisions, overwork their crew, and deny them liberty and leave.[7] Such characterizations of crew and captains augment the need for change that these narratives thematically project.

Charles Briggs was so outraged by the idealism of Cooper's early sea stories that he retaliated by writing "A Veritable Sea Story," published in the 1844 issue of the *Knickerbocker*. He attached a preface to his story, which disparaged romantic and hence unreliable sea writers:

> Those who write correctly about the sea are exceedingly few.
> Young Dana with us, and Marryat over the water,
> Are all the writers I know of, who appear to have brought a
> Discerning eye to bear on that peculiar state of existence,
> An ocean life, which looks so romantic at a distance . . .
> In naming sea-authors I omitted Cooper, Chamier, Sue, and
>   many others,
> Because they appear to have gone to sea without asking leave
>   of their mothers:
> Their descriptions are so fine, and their tars so exceedingly
>   flowery,
> They appear to have gathered their ideas from some naval
>   spectacle at the "Bowery";
> And in fact I have serious doubts whether either of them ever
>   saw blue water,
> Or ever had the felicity of saluting the "gunner's daughter."[8]

With the move toward a more truly authentic narrative in the mid-1840s, the stories of "gentleman"-sailors were subordinated to the tales of the true "tars."[9]

To maintain their stylistic simplicity, writers of the nautical reminiscence preferred the form of the sketch, an outgrowth of the picaresque novel, over deliberately fictionalized narratives.[10] American

readers approved readily of the sketch because in a period that treas-
ured "natural" writing, the sketch provided an unpretentious narrative of pure observation and sentiment. As the sketch filled the pages
of weeklies and monthlies, writers of longer works employed it as a
generic base for their travel and adventure tales. Caroline Kirkland in
Western Clearing, James Hall in *Western Scenes,* Lydia Sigourney in
Scenes in My Native Land, Anna Sophia Stephens in *Sketches of Western Life,* Fanny Forrester in *Alderbrook: A Collection of Fanny Forrester's Village Sketches, Poems, & etc.,* and Baldwin Longstreet in *Georgia
Scenes* all successfully employed the sketch in these works.

Reviewers praised works in this genre. The *Knickerbocker* commended *Harry Franco* for its "unpremeditated, natural sketch of the
different phases which the career of an American boy sometimes
assumes."[11] Until cultivated readers of the 1840s were willing to ac
cept the romance, or more fictionalized representations of life as
viable literary forms, authors relied on the sketch.

In addition, the sketch helped to validate the voice of the "ordinary
seaman." Committed to depicting the lives of working-class sailors,
writers of nautical reminiscences avoided literary pretension and employed a straight-forward and "plain" style. Many sailor-authors disapproved of the cultivated and hence literary, affected tone of
"gentleman" writers, as they were dismissively called.

Richard Henry Dana encountered this disdain for "gentleman"
sailors among some supporters of the nautical reminiscence. In the preface to his narrative of life "before the mast," the Harvard University
student-turned-sailor informs his readers of his journalistic intent:

> In the following pages I design to give an accurate and authen-
> tic narrative of a little more than two years spent as a *common
> sailor* before the mast, in the American merchant service. It is
> written from a journal which I kept at the time, and from notes
> which I made of most of the events as they happened; and in it
> I have adhered closely to fact in every particular, and endeav-
> ored to give each thing its true character. . . . My design is, and
> it is this which has induced me to publish the book, *to present
> a life of a common sailor at sea as it really is*—the light and the
> dark together.[12] (Emphasis added)

Although Dana attempted to write a plain account of his experiences as a sailor, some of his readers could not forget the elite social status of the narrator. In *Graham's,* a reviewer compared Cooper's *Ned Myers* to Dana's work:

> It will be more relished than even . . . "A Year [*sic*] before the Mast." In Mr. Dana's case, we had the commentaries (often profound and philosophical) of an educated man, upon the vicissitudes of the ordinary seaman. *Ned Myers,* on the other hand, gives us, through Mr. Cooper, the involuntary and inevitable trials of the uncultivated Jack Tar, and his reflections and comments—perhaps neither profound nor philosophical—but striking and entertaining for their freshness, naturalness, and *naivete.*[13]

The onslaught of reminiscences published by a "Fore-Top-Man," "Sailor," and so on, following in the wake of Dana's book and Cooper's realistic sea tales of the 1840s, stressed verity, authenticity, and above all simplicity.[14] Discrediting the experience of the "expert" Dana, proponents of the nautical reminiscence wrote narratives "not the result of one cruise, or of two years before the mast, but of thirteen years in various stations from the hawse-hole to the quarter-deck."[15]

Mixed Audiences in *Omoo*

This demand by certain readers for the simple tone of the uneducated sailor, popularized in the nautical Reminiscence, contributed to the public's confusion over the tone in *Typee.* To conform to the demand for unpremeditated sketches, Melville adapted in *Omoo* a structure common to the works of Briggs, Bird, and popular contemporary travel and sea writers such as Catherine Butler and J. Ross Browne, who shaped the sketch into a bivalent form in their "sea" books.

In the nautical reminiscence, action occurs both on sea and on land. For example, Browne's sailor-narrator describes life in a whaler as well as his experiences on shore in Zanzibar. Likewise, Catherine Butler describes her travels by ship to the Orient and her adventures in China. Dana's sea experiences around Cape Horn northward along the coast of South America occupy only fifty pages of his narrative; then he shifts his setting to the California coast to relate his experiences as a hide curer.

Bird and Briggs also employ this double setting in their nautical tales, though the structures of their works go beyond this duality and resemble more the rambling, picaresque novels of Smollett, Marryat, and Washington Irving. Established by writers in sixteenth-century Spain, employed by Alain Lesage in early eighteenth-century France, and popularized by Smollett in mid-eighteenth-century England, the picaresque novel was recognized by its meandering structure, its bawdy humor indicative of the lowlife of taverns, harbors, and other haunts of the working class, and its disadvantaged hero who roams from one destination to another in search of adventure within an indifferent society.[16]

Accordingly, Melville's description of *Omoo* as a more balanced record of "an eventual cruise" *and* a "comic sojourn" on the island of Tahiti illustrates a new approach for the author.[17] In *Typee,* the narrator spends only thirty pages aboard ship before moving to the land, but in *Omoo,* Melville deliberately creates both a sea and a land novel. Chapters 1 through 30 occur aboard ship, and in the manner of his predecessors, Melville then switches the scene in chapter 31 through 82 to land.

The naturalistic detail and deliberately antiromantic bias of the nautical reminiscence sheds light on Melville's radically different approach in *Omoo* as compared with *Typee.* Where the sentimental and sensational style of *Typee* generates romantic description, the conventions of the nautical reminiscence shape the author's method in *Omoo.* Melville's ship and crew closely resemble the realistic descriptions from Eliot Warburton's *The Crescent and the Cross* and Briggs's *Working a Passage:*[18]

> She was a very shabby, disorderly looking craft: her rigging all hanging in bights, points and gaskets flying from her yards, and her side and bulwarks stained with iron rust, she looked as if she had been fitted out by the parish. Her decks were in confusion, and her mates looked like anything but sailors. (*Working a Passage,* 18)

> Among the dreary wastes of swamp that surrounded us . . . the boat was towed by four wild, scraggy-looking horses, ridden by four scraggier-looking men. (*The Crescent and the Cross,* 44)

> On approaching, she turned out to be a small, slatternly look-ing craft, her hull and spars a dingy black, rigging all slack and bleached nearly white, and every thing denoting an ill state of affairs aboard. The four boats hanging from her sides pro-claimed her a whaler. Leaning carelessly over the bulwarks were the sailors, wild, haggard-looking fellows in Scotch caps and faded blue frocks; . . . (*Omoo,* 5)

Melville's description of the ship in *Omoo* not only mirrors the sen-tence structure used by Briggs, but recalls the image of Briggs's "shabby, disorderly looking craft" in his own "small, slatternly look-ing craft." Similarly, Melville's sailors, "wild, haggard-looking fel-lows," parallel Warburton's "wild . . . scraggier-looking men." Moreover, Melville presents the captain of the ship in *Omoo* just as unfit for duty as Briggs's captain:

> He was quite a young man, pale and slender, more like a sickly counting-house clerk than a bluff sea-captain. (*Omoo,* 6)

> He was a feeble little old man, dressed in a long snuff-colored surtout; his hands were encased in a pair of buckskin mittens, and he was trying to screen himself from the penetrating mist by holding a faded green cotton umbrella over his head. The ship, her master, and her crew, seemed made for each other. (*Working a Passage,* 18)

Though Melville turns his captain into a young man, the character-ization of the unfit captain made popular in Briggs's work resonates in *Omoo.*

The nautical reminiscence re-creates the daily life of the sailor by providing exhaustive accounts of sailors' duties. Long passages are devoted to the details of the ship and the language in which duties are executed:

> Again it was clew up and haul down, reef and furl, until we had got her down to close-reefed topsails, double-reefed trysail, and reefed fore-spencer. . . . Between five and six—the sun was

then nearly three hours high—the cry of "All Starbowlines ahoy!" summoned our watch; immediately all hands were called on deck. (Dana, *Two Years before the Mast*, 29–30)

True to this convention, Melville also employs sailor discourse:

> "Haul back the head-yards!" "Let go the lee fore-brace!" "Ready about! about!" were now shouted on all sides; . . . "Main-sail haul!" was now heard, as the fresh breeze streamed fore and aft the deck; and directly the afteryards were whirled round. (*Omoo*, 90)

Sea terms pervade the nautical reminiscence, and the reader learns about "watch and watch," "tricks" at the helm, and so on. Just as Dana describes the parts of the ship and the duties of the sailors, Melville relates the seaman's life on ship:

> Most persons know that a ship's forecastle embraces the forward part of the deck about the bowsprit: the same term, however, is generally bestowed upon the sailors' sleeping-quarters, which occupy a space immediately beneath, and are partitioned off by a bulkhead. (*Omoo*, 38)

Melville also devotes sections to documenting the conditions aboard ship:

> The general aspect of the forecastle was dungeon-like and dingy in the extreme. In the first place, it was not five feet from deck to deck, and even this space was encroached upon by two outlandish cross-timbers bracing the vessel, and by the sailors' chests, over which you must needs crawl in getting about. (38–39)

Recalling the "myriads of cockroaches, and regiments of rats" (39) that inhabit and occasionally dominate the living quarters of the sailors, the narrator makes no attempt to sentimentalize his experiences.

Melville borrows further from the conventions of the nautical reminiscence in fashioning his narrator's views of the native peoples encountered. The sentimental and sympathetic portraits of Tahitians celebrated by Melville's narrator in *Typee* are decidedly passed over in the nautical reminiscence in favor of greater narrative credibility and ethnocentrism. Writers of this nautical reminiscence offer disparaging views of the indigenous people they encounter. Browne describes the inhabitants of Zanzibar as "brutes" and condemns their way of life, while Dana considers the residents of California—Spaniards and Indians—as despicable, "idle thriftless people" and "the laziest of mortals."[19] Likewise, Melville presents the Tahitian natives in *Omoo* as greedy, fawning, cunning, and deceptive—a far cry from the fun-loving Fayaway and the loyal Kory-Kory of *Typee* (*Omoo*, 157–58).

Melville goes even further than the realistic presentations in travel accounts by refashioning borrowed material to fit this conventional approach to native peoples in the nautical reminiscence. In *Omoo*, he appropriates a church scene from Ellis, who praises the local people for their honesty. Melville, however, adds a description of how the natives fidgeted during a sermon on the eighth commandment and states in a deprecatory tone: "Now, there were no thieves in Martair, but then again the people of the valley were bribed to be honest" (39). Melville also argues that natives are irredeemably uncivilized and supports his view by referring to passages by other travel writers such as Beechey, Beale, Kotzebue, and the Quaker Wheeler, who all argue the same point. Of course, Melville refers to only those travel writers who agree with his opinion and at times employs their statements out of context, as Charles Anderson has demonstrated, but he does this to assert his stance as a more impartial observer than the empathetic narrator of *Typee*.[20] The ethnocentric biases scattered throughout *Omoo* reflect Melville's ruthless effort to satisfy cultivated American readers who condemned his celebration of non-Western culture in *Typee* and recall the practices of other sailor-authors who radically altered their views in second works to fit reader expectations.[21]

Yet Melville's great talent in *Omoo* almost certainly resides in his innovations of the rather dry nautical reminiscence and his clever reconciliation of the conflicting interests of his different audiences. In deference to the picaresque tradition, Melville calls his novel *Omoo*, a Tahitian term that refers to both a rover and a person who tells tales of adventure (*Omoo*, xiv). Melville creates a protagonist who engages in one adventure after another in the Tahitian islands. By thoroughly separating the educated sailor, in the form of Doctor Long Ghost from the uneducated sailor, Omoo, Melville satisfied reservations expressed by his cultivated readers of *Typee*. But the author also needed to fuse this narrative form with elements that would directly appeal to general readers. He discovered a solution through the writings of these popular sailor-writers: the realism and bawdy humor of Marryat and Briggs provided both a plausible narrative and the "racy" tone eagerly praised by general readers.[22]

Since English reviewers did not believe "that an American can be a gentleman, and have read the Waverley Novels, tho every digit may have been in the tar-bucket," Melville carefully created a working-class sailor-narrator, Omoo.[23] To overcome his own reputation as a "gentleman" sailor, he creates a sailor-narrator who participates in a mutiny aboard ship, a notable difference from the gentleman-narrator in Dana's book who avoids all altercations with authority and does not join with the other sailors in their attempts to better their situation. Melville himself did not take a leading role in the mutiny aboard the *Lucy Ann*.[24] The fact that he deliberately alters the circumstances to allow his narrator to participate fully in the incident demonstrates his interest in and his method of utilizing materials to satisfy popular demands for the novel. This alteration of facts signifies much more than a writer who "deals imaginatively" with his characters.[25] Rather, it demonstrates Melville's commitment in *Omoo* to the general reader.

Melville displays a sophisticated understanding of the literary marketplace by combining the various elements that won readerships for *Typee*. While he creates a sailor-narrator whose simplicity, unassuming airs, and plain style would assuage cultivated and elite readers, he also cleverly adds a romantic gentleman-sailor for his general readers. The veritable voice of the "common sailor" contrasts with the character of the roguish Doctor Long Ghost, who exemplifies the genteel traits attributed to the narrator of *Typee*. By personifying the characteristics of a gentleman-adventurer and rake, Doctor Long Ghost counterpoints the identity of the honest, simple sailor-narrator. Since he is introduced in the manner of adventure stories, Doctor Long Ghost is recognized as the hero of this story, and not the narrator as in *Typee*; thus the demands of disparate readers for simple narrators and romantic heroes are equally met.[26]

While the narrator supplies the naturalism expected by readers of "true" sea accounts, Doctor Long Ghost embodies the characteristics of the romantic hero:

> His early history, like that of many other heroes, was enveloped in the profoundest obscurity; though he threw out hints of a patrimonial estate, a nabob uncle, and an unfortunate affair which sent him a-roving. . . . from whatever high estate Doctor Long Ghost might have fallen, he had certainly at some time or other, spent money, drunk Burgundy, and associated with gentlemen. (*Omoo*, 12)

The Doctor, as he is familiarly called, led the romantic adventures of the conventional rogue:

> He was, moreover, a man who had seen the world. In the easiest way imaginable, he could refer to an amour he had in Palermo, his lion hunting before breakfast among the Caffres, and the quality of the coffee to be drunk in Muscat; and about these places, and a hundred others, he had more anecdotes than I can tell of. (12)

Long Ghost, rather than the narrator, is the literary character in *Omoo:* "As for his learning, he quoted Virgil, and talked of Hobbes of Malmsbury, beside repeating poetry by the canto, especially Hudibras" (12).

If the distinction between the Doctor and the narrator is not clear enough, the narrator throws a hint to his cultivated readers of the Doctor's association with the conventional literary rake Ferdinand Count Fathom. Smollett's character is an untrustworthy con artist who deceives virtuous ladies and wealthy men and is paired up with a character named Melvill. The coincidence between Smollett's characters, Fathom and Melvill, and Melville's characters, Doctor Long Ghost and the narrator, is deliberate; just as Smollett takes great pains to contrast the virtue of Melvill and the viciousness of Fathom, Melville contrasts his simple, honest sailor-narrator with the deceptive and cunning Long Ghost.[27]

By contrast, the narrator observes and records adventures, but does not initiate them. He overtly differentiates between the Doctor and himself by rebuking the rogue for his behavior:

> To tell the plain truth, things at last came to such a pass, that I told him, up and down, that I had no notion to put up with his pretensions; if he were going to play the gentleman, I was going to follow suit; and then, there would quickly be an explosion. (231)

Melville's great innovation of these conventional characters lies in his ability to relate them symbolically to the classes of readers for whom they were intended. As a true sailor, the narrator pines for life aboard ship again and takes to the sea. Unlike the narrator of *Typee* who yearns for "home" and Doctor Long Ghost who continues his rovings, the narrator of *Omoo* chooses the sea—in the conventional spirit of the sailor. The major difference between the narrator and the Doctor lies in their nationality. As an Englishman, the Doctor represents false aristocracy ("some illustrious individual, for certain reasons, going incog"; *Omoo*, 231), pretentious behavior, Hobbesian self-centeredness, and deception. The American narrator represents "plain truth" and honesty. The nationalistic captain of the whaler *Arcturian* refuses to ship the Doctor because of his nationality, though he welcomes the "true" Yankee. In order not to insult directly his English readers, Melville's narrator tricks the captain into thinking the Doctor Australian, but when told that he is English, the captain fails to distinguish the two nationalities. This scene serves a double purpose. It lightly satirizes the unsophisticated American captain who cannot even differentiate between an Englishman and an Australian, a notion that corroborated British cultivated attitudes toward "uncultivated" Americans and hence appealed to Melville's British readers. At the same time, it directly appeals to American nationalistic readers, who would certainly have appreciated the captain's patriotic favoritism.

Melville employs the humorous tone of nautical writers to his advantage. *Omoo* contains many of the mechanics of humor found in Briggs and Marryat, among others. The wit (and ethnocentrism) of Harry Franco's depiction of the Gauchos (who were part Indian) with

their "cut throat cast of eye" is echoed in the narrator's description in
Omoo of the racially mixed crew possessing an "inferior sort of rascal-
ity." Briggs is also particularly fond of puns. Harry Franco describes
his reaction to a raging storm on the Gulf: "For my own part, I
enjoyed the sublimity of the scene highly, and felt not the least fear;
indeed, the only thing which annoyed me was the water running
down my back, which rather dampened my admiration of the tempest" (189). By relating only his discomfort in a storm that frightens
the most experienced members of the crew, the narrator satirizes the
emphasis placed on experience. He, the greenhorn, merely reacts to
the sublimity, not the terror, of the scene. Melville employs both
satire and a cunning pun in a description of native singing: "The
parochial flocks may be said rather to *bleat* than *sing*" (*Omoo*, 172).
Although as flocks, they should follow the leader, the congregation
cannot even manage to sing, let alone follow the dictates of Christianity, as the narrator points out in his account of their sexual
promiscuity.

Melville also adapts humorous incidents from *Harry Franco* in his
narrative. Harry Franco deceives the crew into thinking he is seriously
injured after his fall from the topmast:

> I was scarcely for a minute insensible to all that was going on,
> but I did not choose to show any signs of life till I had been
> well rubbed, and had a glass of brandy poured down my
> throat, when I opened my eyes and made a motion with my
> hand, just in time to save myself from being bled by the doctor
> who stood by me with lancet in hand. (264)

The rascally Long Ghost in *Omoo* dons a similar garb of insensibility,
only to wake at a precipitous moment:

> By a curious co-incidence, not five minutes after making this
> observation, Doctor Long Ghost fell down into an unaccount-
> able fit. . . . The region thus denominated, exhibited the most
> unaccountable symptoms. A low, rumbling sound was heard;
> and a sort of undulation was discernible beneath the thin
> cotton frock.
>   "Colic, sir?" suggested a bystander. "Colic be hanged!"

shouted the physician; "who ever heard of any body in a trance of the colic?" During this, the patient lay upon his back, stark and straight, giving no signs of life except those above mentioned. . . . "I'll bleed him!" cried Dr. Johnson at last— "run for a calabash, one of you!"

"Life ho!" here sung out Navy Bob, as if he had just spied a sail.

"What under the sun's the matter with him!" cried the physician, starting at the appearance of the mouth, which had jerked to one side, and there remained fixed. "Hold the calabash!"—and the lancet was out in a moment.

Before the deed could be done, the face became natural;—a sigh was heaved;—the eyelids quivered, opened, closed; and Long Ghost, twitching all over, rolled on his side, and breathed audibly. By degrees he became sufficiently recovered to speak. (195)

Exaggeration, understatement, corrective wit, and puns, all abundant in the works of Melville's comic contemporaries, permeate the narrative in *Omoo*.[28] Melville uses humor to lighten the realism of the conventions he employs from the nautical reminiscence, in which storms at sea, for example, are treated with all the seriousness that the situation demands. In *Omoo*, however, Melville desensationalizes the convention by transforming the storm into a humorous episode. He first sets his story in a realistic setting:

The mild blue weather we enjoyed after leaving the Marquesas, gradually changed as we ran farther south and approached Tahiti. In these generally tranquil seas, the wind sometimes blows with great violence; though, as every sailor knows, a spicy gale in the tropic latitudes of the Pacific, is far different from a tempest in the howling North Atlantic. (58)

Here we find the interjections ("as every sailor knows") and the journalistic account of the change in weather common to the conventional narratives of storms at sea. Interspersed within his description, however, we discover figurative stylistic flourishes through the use of metaphors, similes, and personification not found in nautical reminiscences:

> For all this, the mate carried sail without stint; and as for brave
> little Jule, she stood up to it well; and though once in a while
> floored in the trough of a sea, sprang to her keel again and
> showed play. Every old timber groaned—every spar buckled—
> every chafed cord strained; and yet, spite of all, she plunged on
> her way like a racer. Jermin, sea-jockey that he was, sometimes
> stood in the fore-chains, with the spray every now and then
> dashing over him, and shouting out, "Well done, Jule—dive
> into it, sweetheart. Hurrah!" (58).

Qualifying his dry realism, Melville next moves to a broadly comic incident involving the "old black cook," Baltimore, and his desperate attempt to keep from being washed overboard in his "galesuit" and his "well-anointed sea-boots, reaching almost to his knees":

> One evening, just as he was getting supper, the Julia reared up
> on her stern, like a vicious colt, and when she settled again
> forward, fairly *dished* a tremendous sea. Nothing could with-
> stand it. One side of the rotten head-bulwarks came in with a
> crash; it smote the caboose, tore it from its moorings, and
> after boxing it about, dashed it against the windlass, where it
> stranded. The water then poured along the deck like a flood,
> rolling over and over pots, pans, and kettles, and even old
> Baltimore himself, who went breaching along like a porpoise.
> (59)

True to the nautical genre, Melville describes the living conditions of the sailors, but he adds humor into his account. Rather than select "the fore-castle described," a chapter title common in nautical reminiscences, he chooses a more humorous appellation, "A Sea-Parlour Described, with Some of Its Tenants." Though the tenants are realistic enough—the cockroaches and rats—Melville utilizes the situation for humor:

> Concerning the cockroaches, there was an extraordinary phe-
> nomenon, for which none of us could ever account.
>   Every night they had a jubilee.... Presently they all came
> forth; the larger sort racing over the chests and planks; winged
> monsters darting to and fro in the air; and the small fry buzz-
> ing in heaps almost in a state of fusion.... Nor must I forget

the rats. Tame as Trenck's mouse, they stood in their holes peering at you like old grandfathers in a doorway. (40)

Such incidents, coupled with figurative language and personification, alleviated the stark naturalism that frequently marked the overly zealous allegiance to realism found in the nautical reminiscence.

And it was the humor to which general readers responded favorably. The *New York Mirror,* the first American paper to comment on Melville's new work, proclaimed: "The author has lost nothing of the freshness and vigor of style, which, as much as the novelty of subject, gave so great a popularity to *Typee*" (1 May 1847). Most reviewers, in fact, praised the humor of *Omoo:* "Abounding in passages of wit, humor, romance, and poetry," asserted the *Boston Bee* (5 May 1847); "possessing an animated vivid style, humorous vein, and a sailor-like spirit," judged the *Southern Literary Messenger* (October 1847); containing "exuberant jollity," professed an admirer in a letter to the editor of the *New York Evening Mirror.* In a highly favorable review in the *New York Evening Mirror,* N. P. Willis described the reasons for *Omoo*'s rapid popularity:

> It is the warmth, the tropical luxuriance, the genial flow of humor and good nature, the happy enthusiasm, gushing like a stream of mellow sunshine from the author's heart—all these and a thousand nameless beauties of tone and sentiment are the captivating ingredients of *"Omoo."* (21 May 1847)

Melville raised American popular humor from the often poor burlesque found in Briggs and other writers to the art of Irving. He satisfied cultivated readers by grounding *Omoo* in the traditional reminiscence and taking their demands for the veridical narrative seriously. He catered to general readers through the bawdy humor of Bird, Briggs, and Marryat. Thus he cleverly appealed to both audiences simultaneously. Through his creation of the rakish Long Ghost, who represents gentility and yet exhibits traits common in American humor, Melville engaged proponents of the romantic as well as of the "plain style." This technique of using a form that functions on several levels is one the writer employed throughout his career in an incessant reach for wider audiences.

Melville's Popularity

By November 1847, Melville's accessible writing style had become so well known that the celebrated Grace Greenwood satirized *Typee* for a series on popular authors.[29] By the end of the year, "Typee" and "Omoo" became metaphors for idyllic happiness.[30] Indeed, Melville's family (and friends) referred to the author as "Typee."[31] A few months later, along with the "lions" of popular culture, Melville joined the celebrated Valentine's Day party hosted by the best-seller author Anne Lynch, where he met "the notables . . . the beauty and . . . genius" of New York.[32] First *Typee* and then *Omoo* clearly established the author as a popular writer.

As Horace Greeley was to point out in a retrospective of the author's works, Melville's fame stemmed from his unusual ability to write books seemingly contradictory to reader expectations, thus creating new mixtures that appealed simultaneously to different classes of readers. *Typee* and *Omoo,* Greeley marveled, have been read "with equal delight by the rough sailor, who had to spell out the words by his dim lantern, and the refined scholar who gladly turned from graver toils to these enchanting scenes—by the lawyer amid waiting clients, the seamstress at her needle, and the mechanic at his bench."[33] Melville's talent surfaced in his keen perception of marketplace conditions, which he turned to creative and literary profit by combining readership expectations.

The particular mixture in *Omoo* appealed to a new readership for Melville. While the general reader was satisfied with "stirring adventure" and the cultivated reader with the author's commitment to realistic narration, a literary group of readers, a subset of the larger cultivated readership, sought writers who could creatively utilize popular materials for literary purposes. They thought they had found their man in Melville.

Though the literary talents displayed in Melville's first two works had not impressed Evert Duyckinck, a respected New York critic and intellectual, he understood the importance of a popular writer's support in his campaign for literary nationalism.[34] The nationalistic elements of *Omoo* served as Melville's membership dues for Duyckinck's literary coterie, which consisted of writers and critics such as

Cornelius Matthews, Jedediah Auld, and William A. Jones. Melville escorted Duyckinck to the cultural events in New York where he met artists, journalists, politicians, and fellow writers. These contacts exposed the young author to the demands for a more intellectual—and national—literature.

With his marriage to Elizabeth Shaw in 1847, Melville also moved in the highest social circles, those of Judge Lemuel Shaw, the chief justice of Massachusetts. Hosting several dinner parties, Judge Shaw introduced his new son-in-law to Richard Henry Dana, E. P. Whipple (the famed reviewer of the *North American Review*), Longfellow, and other New England intellectuals.[35] The interests of this new group of writers, intellectuals, and abolitionists encouraged Melville to move beyond factual accounts of travel in his new work.

In a review in the 21 April 1847 issue of the *Literary World*, Duyckinck described the dilemma Melville faced in writing a third novel: "It is a crucial period in the life of an author, when, having received ample honors for his early productions, having on a first appearance achieved a distinguished reputation, he comes before the public again, after an interval, with a new book." It becomes a "question of the intellectual stamina" of the author who realizes that "books of Travels" and other types of popular literature "will not sustain a great literary reputation." Melville's third work, *Mardi*, needed to answer the question of whether there was "anything more in the author of *Typee* and *Omoo*."[36]

Mardi, and a Voyage Thither

In *Mardi*, Melville radically alters his relation to popular forms, yet the nature of this change is frequently misinterpreted. Scholars often cite Melville's wish in a letter to his publisher, John Murray, to "plume his pinions for a flight" from feeling "irked, cramped, and fettered" as he did during his writing of *Typee* and *Omoo*. This letter is then used to defend placing *Mardi* "in a wholly separate category" at the expense of overlooking the essential commonalities that link Melville's third work to his first two.[37]

It is not the forms that change in *Mardi*, but rather the author's relation to them. Melville innovates the conventions of the travel narrative and creates, from this genre and the popular demand for a sentimental tone, a literary travel romance. While depending on popular forms of the 1840s, in *Mardi* Melville combines, modifies, and certainly pushes them beyond their generic limits.

Early in the composition of *Mardi,* Melville referred to his new work as a "book of Polynesian adventure," a statement that indicates his reliance on the form of the travel narrative. Indeed, this work presents descriptions of sea, ship, and crew, commentary on the social, political, and religious conditions of native life, and digressions of the author's subjective impressions. Some months after starting *Mardi,* however, Melville responded to the persistent incredulity expressed by some readers toward the "authenticity" of his South Sea travel narratives. In a letter to his publisher, he stated his intention to write a travel narrative laced with fiction, a "Romance of Polynesian Adventure." [38]

While remaining loyal to the conventions of the travel narrative, Melville exploits their imaginative possibilities. He transforms the genre into a consciously *literary* travel romance.[39] In *Mardi,* he demonstrates that a "*real* romance" of his was "no *Typee* or *Omoo,* and is made of different stuff altogether."[40] Nina Baym has argued that 1840s literary culture did not distinguish between a "romance" and a "novel." These terms were employed interchangeably throughout many reviews of the period. Melville, however, distinguishes here between a "book" and a "romance." He never referred to his works as "novels." With the variability of the travel narrative, the genre contained admissible degrees of embellishment and outright fiction.

Melville referred to the structure of his "Romance of Polynesian Adventure" in the following way: "It opens like a true narrative—like Omoo for example on shipboard—and the romance & poetry of the thing thence grow continually, till it becomes a story wild enough I assure you and with a meaning too."[41] What the author relates here is not a tripartite structure as some have suggested, but one based on the traditional travel narrative, adventures described poetically and romantically with fictionalized embellishments.[42] This innovation of the travel form represented Melville's response to the challenge posed by his new literary and intellectual associates.

By demonstrating how popular materials can be utilized for aesthetic purposes, Melville could claim the allegiance of literary readers who sought writers able to transform the democratic materials of popular culture into art. This intention of Melville's has gone unrecognized by scholars who, while offering cogent analyses of the relation between form and meaning in *Mardi*, have not discussed the author's use of the travel narrative there and the rich, creative possibilities that he discovered in the genre.[43] By appealing to the "literary" world, Melville aimed to create a "new" world for the travelogue—and for himself.

Romancing the Travel Genre in Mardi

A glance at the opening passages of Melville's first three works indicates the different perspective that the author adopts in *Mardi*. *Typee* sentimentalizes the realistic setting: "Six months at sea! Yes, reader, as I live, six months out of sight of land; cruising after the sperm-whale beneath the scorching sun of the Line, and tossed on the billows of the wide-rolling Pacific—the sky above, the sea around, and nothing else!" (3). In *Omoo*, Melville consciously combines realistic detail with humor:

> On approaching, she turned out to be a small, slatternly looking craft, her hull and spars a dingy black, rigging all slack and bleached nearly white, and every thing denoting an ill state of affairs aboard. The four boats hanging from her sides proclaimed her a whaler. . . . When we came alongside, a low cry ran fore and aft the deck, and every body gazed at us with inquiring eyes. . . . A robe of the native cloth was thrown over my shoulders, my hair and beard were uncut, and I betrayed other evidences of my recent adventure. (5–6)

In *Mardi*, Melville radically alters his orientation and style:

> We are off! The courses and topsails are set: the coral-hung anchor swings from the bow: and together, the three royals are given to the breeze, that follows us out to sea like the baying of a hound. Out spreads the canvas—alow, aloft, boom-stretched, on both sides, with many a stun' sail; till like a hawk,

with pinions poised, we shadow the sea with our sails, and
reelingly cleave the brine.[44]

Rather than offer a detailed description of various parts of the ship, as
in *Omoo*, Melville moves beyond the sentimental celebration of travel
in the opening of *Typee* to stress the aesthetic in *Mardi*. This rhythmic
passage is imbued with figurative language and poetic meter. The
simile "like the baying of a hound" establishes the poetic level of the
passage. In addition, the Anglo-Saxonism "boom-stretched" and
the alliteration "alow, aloft" establish the rhythm from the trochaic
metered phrase "on both sides," through the alliterative phrases "with
pinions poised" and "we shadow the sea with our sails," to the assonance "reelingly cleave" the brine.

Reorganized into poetic format, these lines illustrate their poetic
quality:

> Out spreads the canvas—
> alow, aloft,
> boom-stretched,
> on both sides,
> with many a stun' sail;
> till like a hawk,
> with pinions poised,
> we shadow the sea with our sails,
> and reelingly cleave the brine.

Whereas Melville focuses on the narrators in *Typee* and *Omoo*, he
cleverly highlights literary language itself in *Mardi*.

From the outset, Melville emphasizes the literary rather than the
nautical interests of the narrator. Unlike the narrators in *Typee* and
Omoo who want to desert their ship, the narrator of *Mardi* does so for
literary reasons:

> Could he talk sentiment or philosophy? Not a bit. His library
> was eight inches by four: Bowditch, and Hamilton Moore. . . .
> And what to me, thus pining for some one who could page me
> a quotation from Burton on Blue Devils; what to me, indeed,
> were flat repetitions of long-drawn yarns, . . (5)

Melville underscores throughout *Mardi* his narrator's interest in the
literary, the symbolic, and the philosophical.

The manner in which Melville inscribes the perceptions and orientation of his narrators reflects the larger formal orientation of the different books. For example, consider how each narrator describes his travel companions. In *Typee*, Tommo stresses the sensational aspects of his partner's personality, as we have seen in chapter 1. The narrator of *Omoo*, however, chooses the aristocratic and effervescently comical Doctor Long Ghost for his companion, and in so doing, creates a bivalent narrative that celebrates both plain style narration and comic heroics. In *Mardi*, the narrator associates with a sailor shrouded in literary origins:

> Jarl hailed from the isle of Skye, one of the constellated Hebrides. Hence, they often called him the Skyeman. And though he was far from being piratical of soul, he was yet an old Norseman to behold. His hands were brawny as the paws of a bear; his voice hoarse as a storm roaring round the old peak of Mull; and his long yellow hair waved round his head like a sunset. My life for it, Jarl, thy ancestors were Vikings, who many a time sailed over the salt German sea and the Baltic; who wedded their Brynhildas in Jutland; and are now quaffing mead in the halls of Valhalla, and beating time with their cans to the hymns of the Scalds. Ah! how the old Sagas run through me! (12)

In noting his companion's ancestry, the narrator describes him by employing a consciously figurative language—that is, the pun on the isle of Skye, "constellated Hebrides," and the "Skyeman." Not only does Melville employ similes in his description, but he imbeds them with poetic assonance and alliteration: "brawny" and "paws"; "hoarse as a storm roaring round," "old," and "waved round." He then proceeds to create a poetic image by using literary references to Scandinavian and Germanic lore: the Scalds, Valhalla, and Brynhilda. He completes the description by donning his own literary ancestry: "Ah! how the old Sagas run through me!" The character of Jarl, in other words, compels a literary account, and the narrator's association with this embodiment of ancient saga legends links him to the literary as well.

Garbed in literary dress, the narrator transforms each of his adventures into stories. Their "literariness" distinguishes them significantly from the digressions in the conventional travel narrative—digressions that qualify some aspect of the story, usually a location of a place visited or customs of an exotic nation. In *Mardi,* digressions do qualify statements made by the narrator, but instead of presenting facts, they offer imaginative elaboration and focus on the language used to relate the story. Melville ends chapter 167 by signaling the direction of the ongoing journey: "Swan-like, our prows sailed in among these isles; and oft we landed; but in vain; and leaving them, we still pursued the setting sun" (550). He qualifies the westward direction the travelers take by presenting a figurative passage on the metaphorical meaning of "west":

> West, West! West, West! Witherward point Hope and prophet
> —fingers; witherward, at sun-set, kneel all worshipers of fire;
> witherward in mid-ocean, the great whales turn to die; witherward face all the Moslem dead in Persia; witherward lie
> Heaven and Hell!—West, West! Witherward mankind and empires—flocks, caravans, armies, navies; worlds, suns, and stars
> all wend!—West, West!—Oh boundless boundary! Eternal
> goal! Witherward rush, in thousand worlds, ten thousand
> thousand keels! Beacon, by which the universe is steered!—
> Like the north-star, attracting all needles! Unattainable forever;
> but forever leading to great things this side thyself!—Hive of
> all sunsets!—Gabriel's pinions may not overtake thee! (551)

While this passage expresses traces of the sentimental style employed in travel accounts for the general reader, which Melville made use of to great acclaim in *Typee,* the emphasis here is not on the teller's emotional response to the image or event depicted. Rather, the image evokes an aesthetic response from the narrator, a cultural and literary eulogy in richly figurative language and style that prefigures the author's later style.

The digressive stories typically employed by travel authors added sentiment, sensation, and satire to their accounts. Ellis includes some sentimental as well as sensational stories in his narrative; Benjamin Morrell was popular for his essentially sensationalized travel narrative; and Stewart rather sarcastically relates the problems inherent in what he considered amoral societies.[45] The common tendency to embed digressions within the larger travel account provided Melville with space to use stylistic modes that had brought him fame in *Typee* and *Omoo*. Satisfying the demand for another Fayaway, Melville narrates the sentimental story of Yillah, while he employs his *Parki* episode in a manner evoking Poe's *The Narrative of Arthur Gordon Pym* and a host of sensational sea tales.[46]

The *Parki* episode demonstrates the author's talent for shaping sources, forms, and images into something that becomes particularly Melvillean. While the story might have appealed to the readers of *Omoo* who appreciated realistic detail, the many allusions to literary predecessors certainly underscored the book as a literary narrative calculated to impress literary readers. At the same time, the *Parki* drama provided Melville with an arena to satisfy demands for sensational and humorous journeys. He found the germ of the story in several sources: the exploration narratives of Ellis, Bennett, and Morrell; the sensational stories in *Remarkable Shipwrecks,* a historical collection of sea deliverance narratives and supernatural occurrences; and a dramatic account related to him by Sylvester Judd, the popular author of *Margaret.*[47] In this episode, Melville continues the use of bawdy humor made popular by Smollett, Marryat, and Briggs. Yet the phantom ship also recalls English Romantic literary works, such as *The Rime of the Ancient Mariner,* while the account of the butchery aboard the *Parki* parallels the story of Dick Kirk in *Arthur Gordon Pym* as well as traditional sea deliverance narratives.

Both Melville and Poe largely relied on the same pool of nautical sources for their stories. The descriptions of the strange animals inhabiting the deep ocean, found in the works of both authors, parallel the common practice of travel writers to record observations of exotic natural phenomena. *Remarkable Shipwrecks* offered an anthology of sea deliverance narratives, and it could be argued that in addition to the popular sensational literature of the day, Melville and Poe found a style in this anthology appropriate to their own sensational accounts. Poe's and Melville's narrative recollections of past horrors recall the tone and syntax, for example, of the colonial sea deliverance narrative by Captain David Harrison included in *Remarkable Shipwrecks:*

> The weather was intolerably bad, the sea excessively heavy, and the continued peals of thunder joined to our incapacity of carrying any sail, unless for a few hours, *threw a horror over our situation, which is not to be conceived by any but those who have unhappily experienced something like our circumstances.*[48]

Richard Brodhead points out similarities between the works of Melville and Poe and argues that Melville relied on *Arthur Gordon Pym* for many details of the *Parki* episode. For example, Brodhead attributes the narrator's jumping ship to Pym's running away from home. Whether Melville actually found inspiration for this episode in Poe's work or in the author's appropriator of this material, Charles Briggs, whose works Melville most certainly read, Brodhead is certainly correct in saying that Melville's debt to Poe demonstrates the *kind* of book each tried to write. Indeed, both used "the form of the adventure narrative to conduct an exploration into other modes of reality."[49]

Furthermore, both Poe and Melville explore the realm of the linguistic. Whereas Poe seeks the limits of meaning, Melville explores the potential for the signified. Nowhere is Melville's search for literary representation more apparent than in his accounts of Yillah and the Mardian isles.

The story of Yillah allowed Melville to employ the conventions of sentiment. The voyaging boat, the maiden in distress, the winning of her heart, her mythical origins, her mysterious disappearance, and the lone, sometimes eternal search for her—all are present in Melville's story. He bases his description of the young victim on the narratives of Ellis and Bennett. His readers, however, could easily identify her story with contemporary best-sellers such as the popular *Undine.*[50]

Perhaps in an effort to appeal to his more traditional literary audience, Melville laces this story with allusions to traditional tales by romantic travelers. Readers readily noted the allusions to Shelley's *Alastor,* Keats's *Endymion,* and Robert Southey's *Thalaba,* while general readers noted its likeness to sentimental stories found in *Graham's* and especially *Godey's.*[51] Moreover, the Yillah story brims with figurative language and other literary forms, the poem in particular.

Throughout the narrator constantly highlights his literary style. In recounting the sequel before the actual story, the narrator calls attention to it as fiction. He stresses the mode of narration, claiming both that the narrative is a "credible history . . . as . . . she rehearsed it" and telling the tale in fairytale-like language: "In the verdant glen of Adair, far in the silent interior of Amma, shut in by hoar old cliffs, Yillah the maiden abode" (154). Such techniques emphasize how the story is told rather than the content of the story itself, a strategy that again underscores the literariness of the work.

In the next digression, the account of the tour through the isles of Mardi, Melville employs forms such as the burlesque and the political satire. The burlesque, which vied with the melodrama as the most popular dramatic form of the 1840s,[52] helps explain why earlier burlesques, such as Irving's *History of New York* and the *Salmagundi* papers, maintained their popularity into the 1840s.[53] James Russell Lowell's burlesque "A Fable for Critics" and Poe's rather infamous "Marginalia" were praised for their treatment of New York literati. Likewise, heated political climates, resulting in the outbreak of revolutions throughout Europe, together with a mounting storm over slavery and American political policies, spurred countless political satires. Outlets emerged specifically dedicated to satire, and magazines such as the *Knickerbocker* reserved many of its pages for this form: the popular *Pinto Papers* by Charles Briggs were printed for two years there.

Melville had experimented with these forms before writing *Mardi*. Through his satirical articles on Zachary Taylor in the *Yankee Doodle*, he had gained status as a writer of satire among politically conscious audiences and had earned the respect of Evert Duyckinck and his circle.[54] Perhaps to display his talents in creating his own "literary world," which would certainly—and did—impress Duyckinck, the aspiring author devoted several chapters to satirizing and burlesquing the political situations in various countries. Melville's use of satire proved successful; Duyckinck reprinted the author's literary burlesques of Dominora (England) and Vivenza (The United States) in an unusually long, laudatory review of *Mardi* in the *Literary World*. In an effort to highlight his satire, Melville laced the observations in

Mardi with several literary allusions to previous writers in the genre, such as references to the voyage of Pantagruel in Rabelais as well as to the third book of *Gulliver's Travels.*[55]

The philosophical discussions that dominate the story of the Mardian tour allowed Melville to display his vast reading, and allusions to philosophers like Plato and Edwards, and to metaphysicians like Browne and Burton, abound in these passages. Together, they recall the conventions of the *conte philosophique* popularized by Rousseau's *Confessions* and Samuel Johnson's *Rasselas.*[56] Like the characters in Ben Jonson's *Every Man Out of His Humor,* the travel companions in *Mardi* adhere to different philosophical positions and argue with each other throughout the narrative. Melville appears to have aimed this section at potential literary readers, such as Evert Duyckinck and his group who, easily recognizing the ideas and the literary allusions, could applaud the author's imaginative treatment of the conventional exploration theme.

Melville uses these digressions to explain his literary method in *Mardi.* He exploits the conventions of philosophical discussion to debate the various approaches to writing. Contrasting in chapter 179 the styles of Mohi and Yoomy, the narrator underscores the metafictional level of his tale:

> "And Lord Abrazza,—who is he?" asked Yoomy.
>
> "The one hundred and twentieth in lineal descent from Phipora," said Mohi; "and connected on the maternal side to the lord seigniors of Klivonia. His uttermost uncle was nephew to the niece of Queen Zmiglandi; and the one hundred and twentieth in descent from the illustrious Phipora. . . . His pedigree is endless."
>
> "But who is Lord Abrazza?". . .
>
> "Will none tell, who Abrazza is?"
>
> "Can not a man then, be described by running off the catalogue of his ancestors?" said Babbalanja. "Or must we e'en descend to himself? Then, listen, dull Yoomy! and know that Lord Abrazza is six feet two: plump thighs; blue eyes; and brown hair; likes his bread-fruit baked not roasted; sometimes carries filberts in his crown; and has a way of winking when he speaks. His teeth are good." (588–89)

Mohi, or Braid-Beard, represents the historian, or keeper of the chronicles. He argues for the veridical narrative and relates stories that furnish the listener with instruction and facts.[57] Mohi's narrative consists of an objective account of facts and incidents. As a result, it lacks personal and evaluative statements by the narrator. Mohi views his narrative as a "plain tale" and as a "simple recital of a fact to entertain the company" (280–352). Like the previous narrator of the veridical narrative, Mohi links "facts" with "truth," and disdains all narratives that vary from a "factual" account.

Yoomy, or the warbler, the minstrel or poet who endorses the sentimental mode, emphasizes the emotional implications of the narrative. His method for describing individuals differs markedly from the historian's accounts.[58] He employs a series of images in his descriptions that attempt to describe; "facts" tell Yoomy nothing. He views his narrative style as "pure conceits of my own, which have a shapeliness and a unity, however unsubstantial" (280).

Babbalanja, the mystic, upholds thematic representation and quotes from ancient authorities about universal truths. In arguing for an "inexhaustible meaning," he stresses the importance of philosophical truths over the "facts" of Mohi's histories and the sublime language of Yoomy's romances. Rather than entertain and inform, the narrative should express truths that exemplify the nature of humankind and existence.

Though Babbalanja illustrates the narrator's view of the artistic role, he acts as a mere mouthpiece for the "dark thoughts" of the past and cannot therefore "create the creative." He cannot resolve the tension between conforming to established conventions and employing imaginative language and structures. King Media, representing the "middle way," speaks for the public and thus leads the group. He urges his companions to satisfy the demands of the reader. In effect, his views on writing represent the normative position and control the approaches of the others.

In depicting these narrative styles, and in structuring his narrative to express these approaches, the narrator points to his own literary method of blending conventions to meet the varied demands of different readerships. In the last chapter, the narrator interrupts his narrative in order to identify himself as the "unreturning wanderer"

(654). Like Lombardo, the "resolute traveler" who must travel to "create the creative" (595), the narrator illustrates the creative possibilities inherent in the act of literary traveling. He reaffirms his commitment to the literariness of his narrative. He chooses a conventional literary ending, rather than the traditional ending of the travel genre. Like Lombardo, the narrator of *Mardi* does not return home to report his travels, as in the travel narrative; instead, he continues his journey west. By following the tradition of the romantic travelers and writers in Southey, Byron, and Keats, the narrator of *Mardi* continues his travels demonstrating the metaphorical implications inherent in the act of real and literary journeys.[59]

The Mixed Reception of Mardi

The critical reception of *Mardi* confirms that Melville did indeed employ forms that appealed to literary and general audiences. The reviewer of the *New York Mirror* described this heterogeneity:

> Here are points of interest for every mind. The scholar can feast upon its classical allusions, the man of erudition can add to his store, the divine food for thought and discussion, the poet luxuriate in scenes of pure fancy, the little child find entertainment, and genius salute the author as the rising sun. It remains for the future to appoint Melville his niche in the Temple of fame. (13 April 1849)

Reviewers who represented and reflected the tastes of these different readers both praised and condemned Melville's achievement in *Mardi*.

Popular literary circles readily praised Melville's work and recognized it as a travel narrative. As a travel writer himself, N. P. Willis unequivocally placed it in this genre: "The large class of readers who delights in records of travel and graphic narrative, will enjoy *Mardi* in the highest degree."[60] The *New York Atlas* linked Melville's work with the best of exploration narratives: "It is a wonder of Polynesian adventure, equalling in its characteristics the merits of Ellis and the beauties of Sir John Singleton" (22 April 1849).

With its sentimental and sensational elements, general readers easily recognized and applauded the popular conventions employed in the work. Many admired Melville's account of marine life, asserting that it represented "some of the finest nautical description that the world has ever seen . . . about the cleverest and tersest description of animated nature we ever encountered"; "No one paints a better shark than Mr. Melville."[61] They also commented favorably on Melville's use of romantic conventions.[62] With his commitment to the sentimental mode, N. P. Willis prophesied in the *New York Home Journal* that the Yillah episode would be the most popular section with readers: "We predict Yillah will turn out to be the favorite character . . . of the book—a virgin rescued from the hands of a party of priests about to lead her to sacrifice. . . . We quote this as a whet to the feast in store" (21 April 1849). Those general reviewers who did appreciate Melville's mixture in *Mardi* ranked it high. Representative of general taste, *Graham's* considered the book "decidedly the best of Mr. Melville's productions" (May 1849). Other critics classified it with traditional works of art: "The language possesses all the polish of an Irving with all the spirit of a Scott. The matter is truly poetical—philosophical as Plato, yet beautifully imaginative as Moore; the treatment thoroughly dramatic. As a whole, it is a master stroke of genius."[63]

Literary readers, too, admired Melville's work and commented favorably on the political, philosophical, and literary sections of the book. William Young, of the *New York Albion* and a sympathizer of the Young America movement, praised the structure of *Mardi:*

> Mr. Melville records a fabulous desertion in a whale-boat from a South Seaman, with all the *vraisemblance* of a log-book, interweaves, at pleasure, classical allusion and scholarly lore with such portions as suit his purpose of the mythology of the South Sea Islanders, treats his readers to some delicate satire, and some sound political hints on men and things in our own and other countries—and in short, with the Pacific Archipelago for his ground-work, has put forth a lively, pungent, instructive, and exceedingly clever bundle of his thoughts and imaginings. (21 April 1849)

By calling Melville's romance of Polynesian adventure the "romance of real life, human nature in a new setting," literary readers linked the author's achievement to their own nationalistic goal of providing American literature with a new locale.[64]

Above all, Melville's language in *Mardi* drew the highest praise. The reviewer of the *New York Atlas* noted its appeal to the higher sensibilities: "The author's romances of the real appeal mostly to the love of the sensuous and adventurous; this his ideal romance, addresses also the imagination and reasoning faculties" (22 April 1849). Even those reviewers who did not approve of an imaginative treatment of the travel narrative admired the language, "the hybrid between poetry and prose," employed in *Mardi;* Melville's poetic style remained for one reviewer the novel's "sole redeeming feature."[65] For general and literary readers alike, the poetic language transformed *Mardi* into a "new" world:

> The observations and illustrations, as the monsters of the deep are encountered, are expressed in language elegant and expressive, sometimes even beautiful to the last degree; with all its fascinations, its unique style, its genial humor, its original thoughts, its graphic descriptions, its poetic flights, its profound reasonings, its gentle religious teachings, its inimitable shows, *Mardi* stretches before us like a new world, and the mental eye can never weary of gazing upon its strangely beautiful landscape.[66]

But if there was something for everybody in *Mardi,* the mixture proved too much for the majority of cultivated reviewers. Melville's blending of a deliberate "literariness" with philosophy, satire, and travel was intolerable to cultivated audiences who demanded realistic and thereby nonfictional narration. George Ripley of the *New York Tribune* denounced the work: "It is a monstrous compound of Carlyle, Jean-Paul, and Sterne, with now and then a touch of Ossian thrown in" (10 May 1849). Likewise, British reviewers found the "improbabilities" overwhelming. Henry Forthergill Chorley wrote in the *London Athenaeum* that "as we proceed the improbability deepens: the author trifles with his tale for some purpose too deep for our plummet to fathom—becomes more and more outrageous in the fashion of his incidents and in the forms of his language" (24 March 1849), and a *London Examiner* critic stated: "From first to last it is an outrageous fiction; a transcendental *Gulliver,* or *Robinson Crusoe* run mad" (31 March 1849).

The mere presence of forms popular with a specific class of readers was not enough. For cultivated readers, a conscious use of literary language and philosophy destroyed the veridicality:

> The truth is, that we have been deceived, inveigled, entrapped into reading a *work* where we had been led to expect only a *book.* We were flattered with the promise of an account of travel, amusing, though fictitious; and we have been compelled to pore over an undigested mass of rambling metaphysics.[67]

Melville committed the most serious crime for cultivated readers. By choosing literary pretension over naturalness, he exerted "a continual strain after effect, an effort constantly at fine writing, a sacrifice of natural ease to artificial witticism."[68] The "new world" that Melville had created in *Mardi* violated too strongly the dictates of the old.

From the reception of *Mardi* Melville learned that certain mixtures were unacceptable to particular groups of readers. In *Redburn* and *White-Jacket,* he coordinated style with theme in an attempt to get along with the existing literary world.

CHAPTER FOUR

Writer and Community in
Redburn and *White-Jacket*

THE RELIANCE OF the "classic" writers Poe, Hawthorne, and Melville on popular antebellum practice has often been seen as an act of aesthetic degradation and self-limitation. Scholars have usually presented these writers as ideologically superior to their culture.[1] The marketplace, so the argument goes, forced these "alienated" artists to preserve prevailing ideologies in their fiction against their personal wishes. Where financial necessity failed to control literary impulse, the shackling influence of the Puritan, Revolutionary, and genealogical fathers did.[2]

Considering the works of Poe, Hawthorne, and Melville as responses to economic necessity and societal pressures risks obscuring the personal artistic impetus that distinguishes their works as well as any creative reliance on popular materials these authors might have maintained. Certainly, as authors dependent on their writings for financial support, they shared a common economic necessity. The presence and preservation of what Emory Elliot has termed an "American ideological consensus" of popular ideas and conventions, however, does not necessarily mean a common denominator. Poe's criticism of morality and ethics in the fiction of the period represents a stance ideologically antithetical to Melvillean aesthetics, which include ethics and social morality as integral components. Then again, Hawthorne's view of his cultural inheritance as potentially dangerous and inimical to artistic creativity is considered by Melville the very key to artistic survival.[3]

Critics usually treat *Redburn* and *White-Jacket* as works consciously shaped for the marketplace.[4] On the basis of Melville's own references to these novels as "two *jobs,* which I have done for money," such interpretations seem justified. Yet the author's language deserves closer inspection. In directing these comments to the two men most artistically and economically important to him (Evert Duyckinck and Judge Lemuel Shaw), Melville needed to maintain a balance between sustaining their necessary support of his literary endeavors and his desire to treat them as confidantes. The author's criticism of his works also came months after they were written, when his readings and thoughts indicated a shift in his attitude toward the relation between the artist and his culture. As William Gilman, Hershel Parker, and James Justus have suggested, Melville began writing *Redburn* with literary as well as monetary aspirations.[5]

Rather than accept statements that served a specific rhetorical purpose as definitive authorial assessments of *Redburn* and *White-Jacket,* we should reconsider Melville's disparaging comments in light of his artistic development. *Redburn* and *White-Jacket,* novels reputedly written for the marketplace, were not the only works Melville disparaged. In a letter to Evert Duyckinck, he also criticized *Mardi,* a narrative written for literary rewards: "I am glad that you like that affair of mine. But it seems so long now since I wrote it and my mood has so changed that I dread to look at it, and have purposely abstained from doing so since I thanked God it was off my hands." Melville could also speak of his own necessity in *Redburn* and *White-Jacket.* In a letter to his father-in-law, Melville wrote, "I have not repressed myself much—so far as they are concerned, but have spoken pretty much as I feel." Indicating as he had in his letter to Duyckinck that his "mood had so changed" from the conscious stylistic isolation in *Mardi* to a sociable compliance with popular conventions, he registers a change in ideological perspective in *Redburn* and *White-Jacket.*[6]

Melville's earlier works presented both the lure of creating an identity free from societal conventions and the problems that inevitably results in isolating oneself from society. *Typee* celebrates the charms of a "world elsewhere" and records its debilitating effects (in this extreme case, physical deterioration and death).[7] *Omoo* depicts the lure of the life of the rover but stresses the relief in reestablishing one's place within the social hierarchy. Clothed in popular conventions and in the metaphor of the travel narrative, *Mardi* records the search for an alternate, personal ideology and the void that results from deliberate isolation. In *Redburn* and *White-Jacket*, Melville returns to a reliance on themes popularized in the works of his contemporaries. Mirroring the themes found in popular domestic novels largely written by women authors, *Redburn* and *White-Jacket* recount the process of socialization. Recording the growth of the individual consciousness, they dramatize their protagonists' increased awareness of the structure and strictures of society. In *Redburn*, Melville ultimately integrates the alienated narrator into a recognized social community, while the narrator of *White-Jacket* negotiates a place for himself within the social hierarchy. These stories parallel the plot structure of dozens of tales written about female characters in similar situations.

Melville indicates a willingness to endorse cultural aesthetic values and norms. In their forms, styles, and themes, *Redburn* and *White-Jacket* reflect the cultural-historical consensus of Melville's culture, a set of beliefs promulgating a sense of social responsibility and civic duty.[8] The presence of these beliefs, however, reveals more than the employment of formulas necessary for economic recompense. His support of the cultural ideology and rhetoric—the "middle way," the "jeremiad," middle-class norms, and morality—indicates his understanding and desire for community and sociability much more than it does those feelings of hostility commonly ascribed to him.[9] Melville's use of popular materials and attitudes in *Redburn* and *White-Jacket* marks a development in his artistic perspective, a change from the defiant vow of artistic individuality and isolation asserted in *Mardi* to a reconciliation with his historical-cultural legacies and literary norms provided by popular culture.

Contemporary arguments hold that Melville's talent in *Redburn* and *White-Jacket* appears despite the conventions employed there. These popular materials, however, supplied the author with a style that required linguistic discipline and encouraged stylistic refinement. They also offered a theme in which he could legitimately depict cultural and personal beliefs. Together, style and theme provided an aesthetic through which artistic development could occur. One may go further. The popular materials that Melville utilized in these works illustrate his recognition of their artistic potential.

Many writers have employed cultural norms creatively in their works. Benjamin Franklin, for example, secularized his Puritan theological inheritance into an economic-philosophical ideology.[10] In his exploration of the individual's relation to his culture, Hawthorne reformulated his Puritan legacy as a psychological doctrine.[11] Myra Jehlen locates in the hegemonic structure of middle-class America the belief that self-realization away from society is impossible, a philosophy found in such works as *The Scarlet Letter* and *Moby-Dick*.[12] Melville seems to share this belief. Fully comprehending that preservation as an author depended on loyalty to established practice rather than a deliberate literary isolation, he individualized his historical legacy and cultural norms by formulating them into a literary aesthetic that guided his subjects, style, and themes. In *Redburn* and *White-Jacket,* Melville consciously explores the possibilities for developing an artistic style by coordinating his personal visions with cultural norms.

Innovations of the Nautical Reminiscence

In *Redburn* and *White-Jacket,* Melville turned again to the nautical reminiscence, a genre that, as we have seen, he had successfully employed in *Omoo*. Presenting true accounts of life from the quarters of the simple or "common sailor" (*Redburn,* iii), this genre chronicles the inexperienced narrator's exposure to and ultimate mastery of the sailor's duties.[13] Detailed accounts of the daily life and "the general tenor of life aboard ship" (*Redburn,* iii)—the living conditions, daily routines, meals, duties, watches, and "the purpose behind every procedure"—dominate the narratives of the nautical reminiscence.[14] Occupying large segments of *Redburn* and *White-Jacket,* such details parallel established practice; they are certainly more than the "filling" for a "sketchy" narrative that some have intimated.[15]

The power of Melville's depiction of sea life lies in his exploration of the artistic potential of the nautical genre. Previous writers emphasized and valued technique and performance, concentrating on the duties and work aboard ship. They translated the narrative of the sailor's experiences into a story of initiation, the sailor's transition into manhood, a movement defined by performance and mastery of action.[16] Melville unearthed deeper symbolic implications in this convention. In addition to recording physical achievements, he stressed cognitive development. In *Redburn,* Melville chronicled the growth of his protagonist's social consciousness, while in *White-Jacket* he portrayed his hero's understanding of the social structure and its effect on individuality. Through these orientations, *Redburn* and *White-Jacket* suggest the necessity for integration within society.

To depict this growth in social consciousness, Melville chose narrators who emphasized either their adolescence, as in *Redburn,* or their simplicity, as in *White-Jacket.* Such characters were popular with readers who distrusted artistic, pretentious, and deliberately self-conscious narrators.[17] A favorite persona of the period, the "common sailor," like the "b'hoy," offered honesty, integrity, and above all, simplicity. With the emphasis on facts, this voice lent a plainness to the narrative that the refined voice of a cultivated "gentleman" narrator, or, for that matter, the philosophizing narrator of *Mardi* could not.

Through its patent simplicity, the boy/adolescent narrator gained popularity with general readers. Marryat popularized this persona in several works, namely *Mr. Midshipman Easy, Peter Simple,* and *Frank Mildmay.* Probably using these examples as models, Charles Briggs employed a boy narrator in *The Adventures of Harry Franco* (1839) and *Working a Passage* (1844).[18] Dickens used the character in some of his novels (including the serialized *David Copperfield* in 1849). Melville's adoption of this practice suggests an openness to popular forms.

An alleged "discrepancy" in the narrative voices of *Redburn* and *White-Jacket* has led some scholars to question Melville's sophistication in handling this technique. *Redburn* is criticized for its inconsistent voice, its "abrupt change" from an adolescent to an "adult" narrator. By placing Melville's narrator into its literary cultural context, I would like to suggest that far from "a ruinous defect" of *Redburn,* the complex narrative voice marks a major development in Melville's handling of this technique as well as in the practice of the convention.[19] The boy narrators in the works of Briggs and Marryat remain static; their growth from exposure to mastery of a sailor's trade does not stimulate a "cognitive" development. Paralleling the development of the female characters in the period's domestic or sentimental novels, Melville's narrator grows psychologically. He matures as he develops in his trade. Interpreted by some as a satirical treatment of Redburn, the practice of focusing on the young narrator's naïveté in this work develops as a thematic representation of the young narrator's awareness—the growth of cognitive, moral, social, political, and ethical consciousness followed by the subsequent recognition of the importance of integration with and awareness of society, just as female protagonists do in works written by women authors. Through the dual narrative voice, the author connects style and theme. This balance reflects the coordination of inner and outer worlds that Redburn must maintain.

Redburn, His First Voyage

Redburn begins by establishing the voluntary segregation of the narrator from his community. He recounts his overwhelming sense of alienation: "Cold, bitter cold as December, and bleak as its blasts, seemed the world then to me" (10). Melville shifts the conventional leave-taking scene in sea fiction from its traditional use as a sentimental device of grieving mother and sisters, found in the works of Marryat and Briggs, to an emphasis on the narrator's isolation: "Yes, I will go to sea; cut my kind uncles and aunts, and sympathizing patrons, and leave no heavy hearts but those in my own home, and take none along with me but the one which aches in my own bosom" (10).[20] Everywhere he goes, Redburn feels the same sense of isolation from the "stony-eyed and heartless" people around him: "I sat apart, though among them" (12).

The practice of exploiting the naïveté of the adolescent narrator, the focal point in the stories by Marryat and Briggs, is employed by Melville to stress one of his major themes—the growth of the narrator's insight into the importance of home and family, a theme likewise central to domestic novels by women authors. The source of Redburn's naïveté lies in his youthful imagination, a cognitive faculty not triggered by any experience in the world. He desires to ship to

Bremen because he imagines the romance of a ship comprised of "foreigners . . . men of dark complexions and jet-black whiskers, who talked French" (4). His imagination mars his vision of reality and prevents him from integrating himself within the community around him. Redburn's isolation is cognitive, self-imposed.

Melville adopts a narrative mode conducive to the narrator's youth and innocence. Appropriating a stylistic device common to conventional tales of humor, he employs puns that reflect the narrator's nascent observation of the world. The common fare of Marryat's and Briggs's narratives, puns highlight the inexperience of the narrator; in Melville's tale, they serve an additional purpose by exhibiting the narrator's understanding of the symbolic correspondence between physical and mental states. The hooked-nosed pawnbroker is rather astutely regarded, in Redburn's eyes, to be "ready to hook anything that came along . . . and would gladly hook my gun" (21). Similarly, the impoverished man reduced to stealing for a living expressed his degeneration in his "seedy red cravat" and "pimply face, that looked as if it were going to seed likewise" (21). These harsh puns indicate Redburn's early powers of observation of what he sees as a harsh world. A source of humor in Briggs and Marryat, conventional puns in *Redburn* point to the possibility of a more mature understanding of life.

Melville also employs puns to depict metaphorically Redburn's own state. As the ship leaves the harbor, Redburn recounts his feeling as it enters the open sea: "About sunset we got fairly 'outside,' and well may it so be called; for I felt thrust out of the world" (36). Redburn notices that the physical world reflects inner thoughts and feelings. Thus Max the Dutchman's "hair, whiskers, and cheeks . . . of fiery red" did not "belie him; for his temper was very inflammable" (79).

Through such correspondences, Redburn begins to develop a psychological understanding of the ways of humankind. In the works of Marryat and Briggs, adolescent narrators receive incessant abuse from the sailors for their ignorance and inexperience. Employed to depict the sordidness of sailors, this convention in Melville's works is instead a means to describe Redburn's developing awareness. After a severe grilling from the sailors for his cowardice and fear when a drunken sailor jumped overboard, Redburn observes that their abuse of him results not so much from his cowardice as from theirs: "And they did not say I was cowardly, because they perceived it in me, but because they merely supposed I must be, judging, no doubt, from their own secret thoughts about themselves" (65).

As Redburn observes the reflection of mental states in the realm of the physical, he begins to see the ways of humanity in the ways of the sailor. The sailor shares with his fellow human beings a common ontology of experience. He interprets the narrow escape of the ship as a comment on human nature:

> And even, as suddenly as the bravest and fleetest ships, while careering in pride of canvas over the sea, have been struck, as by lightning, and quenched out of sight; even so, do some lordly men, with all their plans and prospects gallantly trimmed to the fair, rushing breeze of life, and with no thought of death and disaster, suddenly encounter a shock unforeseen, and go down, foundering, into death. (94)

As in the opening sketch in Irving's *Sketch Book* on which this passage is modeled, *Redburn* shifts from individual incident to universal significance, a movement anticipating much of the best passages in *Moby-Dick*.

Paralleling established practice, the narrator recounts his mastery of the seaman's duties, a process that dominates the narrative of the conventional nautical reminiscence. Redburn's account, however, occupies less than one chapter. His narrative stresses the development of cognitive as well as physical performance. Rather than remain a simple celebration of Redburn's initiation into the world of the sailor, his mastery of sailor's duties introduces a new level of cognitive insight. Though Redburn has earned the title of "sailor-man" for his seamanship, he discovers the existence of a social hierarchy. He also learns to accept his assignment of place within the social hierarchy and to endure his situation "like a young philosopher . . . in the spirit of Seneca and the Stoics" (122).

Redburn's awareness of the hierarchical levels in society colors his English experiences. Though complying with the established conventions of the travel narrative, *Redburn* describes not the architecture of historical, religious, and cultural sights, but rather the architecture of society—the distribution of people to different socioeconomic strata. Throughout his Liverpool account, Redburn observes the different classes of people who comprise that society. He constantly focuses on the social stratification and the impossibility of social progress for the underclass within such a system:

> There are classes of men in the world, who bear the same relation to society at large, that the wheels do to a coach: and are just as indispensable. But however easy and delectable the springs upon which the insiders pleasantly vibrate: however sumptuous the hammer-cloth, and glossy the door-panels; yet, for all this, the wheels must still revolve in dusty, or muddy revolutions. No contrivance, no sagacity, can lift *them* out of the mire; for upon something the coach must be bottomed; on something the insiders must roll. (139)

His argument is based not on the theological concept of allotment, but on conventional notions of Western capitalistic society.

Exploring the streets of Liverpool with his father's travel guide, Redburn learns perhaps the most painful lesson in his study of society: the uselessness of "fine old family associations" in determining his place within the social hierarchy. The society with whom Redburn's merchant father associated—the world of theaters, libraries, restaurants, and hotels—is unavailable to the sailor-son. The "port wine and cigars" of his father are transposed into "swipes and chaws" for the son; the father's aristocratic castle is the son's tavern; Birkenhead Abbey, home of the earls of Derby, is a jail for the criminal and impoverished. As only a "common-carrier across the Atlantic" (160), the sailor-boy and his reminiscences of travel remain a meager recollection of a "chain of tap-rooms surrounding the Globe," because, unlike the more aristocratic travelers, sailors only "go *round* the world, without going *into* it" (133). This strategy, adopted by sailors who recognize the limits their social status imposes on them, becomes for Redburn, and later for White-Jacket, the key to survival and coordination with society. This observation is also a testimony to the nature of narrative in *Redburn*. There is perhaps no better indication of Melville's awareness that *his* story is more than a nautical reminiscence.

Historical legacies—"family relics"—are no more fit to serve as guides "amid avenues of modern erections" than "the map of Pompeii[?]": "Yes, the thing that had guided the father, could not guide the son" (157). Redburn's journey in the Old World revealed to him ("a new light broke in upon me") the inapplicability of historical legacies in the contemporary "march of improvement" (157). Rather than a society of stasis, "this world . . . is a moving world; its Riddough's Hotels are forever being pulled down; it never stands still; and its sands are forever shifting" (157). The key to survival in society lies not in personal historical legacies denoting the "highest style of art," but in individual senses. "Hereafter," Redburn admonishes himself, "follow your nose throughout Liverpool; it will stick to you through thick and thin" (159).

Survival always lies in the present, in accepting contemporary cultural values. Redburn's Liverpool travels focus on strategies of survival in the city's unyielding, stratified society. Land sharks and enterprising beggars cross elite gentlemen, peasants, and rag pickers. The city's forlorn occupy Redburn's observations as he tries to understand their strategies for surviving the "cold charities of the world" (213). The now "sadder" but "wiser" Redburn reaches out to the community to compare his awareness of the ways of the marble-hearted world to other stances toward society and survival. In considering other views and reactions to the necessity for adaptability and assimilation, he depicts both the destructiveness of isolation and the importance of integration into society.

Through his interactions with Harry Bolton and Carlo, the Italian immigrant, the narrator tests his theory of survival. The story of Harry Bolton confirms the truth of the narrator's insight into existence; as such, it is more than an "afterthought" for expanding a "sketchy" narrative. Perhaps a model of what Redburn "might have become," as Christopher Sten has suggested, Harry flouts the wisdom gained by the narrator and reinforces Redburn's belief that survival is an individual act.[21] The tragedy of this "incontrovertible son of a gentleman" (216) lies in his unwillingness to assimilate into a new society where the social stratification of the Old World is blurred—gentlemen can be sailors, and sailors gentlemen. Rather than participate in the initiatory rites of nautical manhood and join the community of sailors, Harry refuses "in a pet and a pique" (255) to obey any further orders by the mate to go aloft—"but go aloft again he *could* not, and *would* not" (257). A part of the physical prowess and initiation scene common to sailing stories, this episode serves a radically different purpose in Melville's narrative.

Harry and Carlo represent individuals with the aesthetic sensibilities of the narrator.[22] Both feminine in build, Harry and Carlo must survive on attributes other than sailorlike physical performance and strength, but they present alternate strategies for survival. The narrator contrasts the two man's behavior: as "one who had certainly seen much of life," Harry could "evince such an incredible ignorance"; Carlo exuded "experiences so sad and various . . . humility, deep-seated thoughtfulness, yet a careless endurance of all the ills of life" (253, 247). While Harry taunts his mates with his aristocratic heritage and refuses to serve them in their desire for his songs, Carlo adapts the opposite strategy and cajoles people through his music. Where Harry had failed in England, Carlo had succeeded: "Ah! I succeeded very well!—for I have tunes for the young and the old, the gay and the sad" (248), a statement that may indeed have served as a model for Melville. With his aesthetic sensibility, Carlo readily assimilates to marketplace society. Interpreting the various faces he encounters, he plays "what airs will best please them" (248).

Although Harry and Carlo share similar age, talents, and physical stature, Harry's reluctance to carry out the sailor's duties links him more to the misanthropic Jackson, whereas Carlo's immigrant belief in future prosperity links him to the immigrants residing in the steerage. Jackson's malevolent, cynical view of humankind alienates him from the beneficence of social bonds, causing his destruction.

The narrative of Redburn's growth develops into a narrative of survivors and failures. Through his observations of people's strategies for survival or destruction, Redburn discovers the philosophical implications of his American heritage and culture. He recovers the meaning of his cultural ideologies, a set of values that fosters not social stratification but the formation of "one federated whole"—

values that promise a future for the "estranged children of Adam" by restoring them to the "old hearth-stone in Eden" (169).

Redburn chooses America, its ideologies, and its values. In the end, he chooses to make America "home," because "being an American and returning home" guarantees survival (279). Certainly, Redburn chooses home over his friendship with Harry. Harry's estrangement from society like the malevolent influence of Jackson, alienates those in contact with him. Redburn has embarked on a journey away from home only to discover that survival lies in supporting and being supported by the community: "Oh! he who has never been afar, let him once go from home, to know what home is" (300), a motif that both recalls the narrator of *Typee* and parallels many female characters in domestic morals of the day. To choose one's community, culture, and home over individual bonds that threaten social survival indicates maturity, not the "retrogression" many critics have imputed to Redburn's final stance toward Harry Bolton.[23] In returning home and opting for social bonds over the isolating individuality of Harry, Redburn helps himself despite having to renounce a friendship. This renunciation of a friendship that directly conflicts with a sense of community is necessary for Redburn's survival. Self-preservation, however, is a mixed blessing. *Redburn* depicts the painful compromises necessary, the relinquishment of cherished historical legacies and friends, bonds inimical to survival within society. Far from an "unresolved maturation," Redburn reveals a mature, if sober, understanding of society.[24]

White-Jacket, or, The World in a Man-of-War

In the opening pages of *White-Jacket*, Melville presents a narrator fully primed with the lessons that Redburn learned on his voyage of social consciousness and survival. White-Jacket affirms the importance of home, community, and society. Unlike Redburn, who alienated himself from his community by leaving home, White-Jacket celebrates his return:

> Homeward bound!—harmonious sound! Were you ever home-ward bound?—No?—Quick! take the wings of the

> morning, or the sails of a ship, and fly to the uttermost parts of
> the earth. There, tarry a year or two; and then, let the gruffest
> of Boatswains, his lungs all goose-skin, shout forth those magi-
> cal words, and you'll swear "the harp of Orpheus were not
> more enchanting." (6)

White-Jacket's ready use of nautical language and commands indicates his integration within the community of sailors. Proud of his
mastery of the sailor's duties, he flies to answer difficult commands
issued in nautical terminology at which the young Redburn could
only balk. Unlike the friendless Redburn, White-Jacket claims a
brotherhood with his fellow shipmates: "We main-top-men were
brothers, one and all; and we loaned ourselves to each other with all
the freedom in the world" (15).

While Redburn experiences the gradual development of his social
consciousness, White-Jacket exhibits a true understanding of society.
His narrative focuses on the divisions "into which a man-of-war's
crew is divided" (8) and minutely describes the various levels of
command from the quarter-deck officers to the fore, main and

> Boatswain's mates, . . . Coxswains, Quarter-masters, Quarter-
> gunners, Captains of the Forecastle, Captains of the . . .
> Maintop, . . . Coopers, Painters, Tinkers, Commodore's stew-
> ard . . . Mess-cooks, hammock-boys, messenger boys, cotboys,
> loblolly-boys, and numberless others, whose functions are
> fixed and peculiar. (11)

This focus on each sailor who make up the "world in a man-of-war"
distinguishes the narrative from *Redburn*. *White-Jacket* portrays how
these various individuals, while retaining their personal sense of
uniqueness, integrate themselves within the hierarchical man-of-war
society.

In the preface the narrator reveals the nature of representation in
his story by asking the reader to "conceive" the characters he describes. Individuals serve as "portraits" in the work, and they focus
the reader on the act of creating. White-Jacket's individual portraits
are not static; in his narrative, portraiture is reified into literary art.
The iconographic representation of Jack Chase—"tall and well-knit,
with a clear open eye, a fine broad brow, and an abounding nut-

brown beard" (13)—is followed by literary representation: "Here, I must frankly tell a story about Jack" (17).

Within this context the symbol of the narrator's white jacket acquires significance beyond the alienation that it allegedly engenders for the narrator. As a sailor, he creates through his jacket a mark of individuality within the man-of-war society. As a writer, however, by "manufacturing an outlandish garment of my own devising" (3), he distinguishes his work from the conventional nautical reminiscence. The jacket marks the narrator more as a sailor-narrator than as an alienated individual—one who has a defined place within the hierarchy.

This garment is transformed into a literary artifact, a chapter, which in turn clothes the narrative. By referring to his white jacket as a "novel" (3), and by calling his story after it, the narrator signals the metaphoric significance of his man-of-war tale as a *literary* narrative about the white jacket, or the narrator. *White-Jacket* assumes the shape of a narrative about a writer as well as about a sailor and his world. The isolation of an idiosyncratic style and its potential threat to literary survival within popular culture is reflected in the narrator's unique jacket, which could indeed inhibit integration into the community of sailors. White-Jacket, however, "pads" his jacket with old materials. The idea of quilting and painting is based on incidents found in popular sea tales, as Howard P. Vincent has pointed out.[25] Far from making the jacket "impervious" to environmental influences, the padding transforms it into a "universal absorber" (4–5). The narrator's creativity in mixing old materials with his unique design transforms the jacket into a trope for the writer at work. The point is, however, that Melville combines old materials with new purposes. He does not suggest here that his story relates the struggle of "the artist seeking his own organic form of expression," as Vincent contends.[26]

Rather, *White-Jacket* tells a double story. Melville interweaves the narrative of the role of the individual in man-of-war society with the story of personalizing literary conventions. *White-Jacket* relates the narrative of individuals like the sailor-writer who wish to coordinate their individuality with their sense of integration into the prevailing social hierarchy aboard the ship, to the story of a writer's necessary integration and role in society. Instead of relating how he must isolate himself for "art," the sailor-writer describes how he, as well as everyone else aboard ship, must join in the community of sailors, the brotherhood of humanity.

Melville's focus on social structure echoes a general concern of the nautical reminiscence. In *Thirty Years from Home*, Samuel Leech cogently depicts the social hierarchy of the man-of-war:

> A vessel of war contains a little community of human beings, isolated, for the time being, from the rest of mankind. This community is governed by laws peculiar to itself; it is arranged and divided in a manner suitable to its circumstances. Hence, when its members first come together, each one is assigned his respective station and duty.

Leech exemplifies this hierarchy by describing the absolute authority of the captain: "A Ship contains a set of *human* machinery, in which every man is a wheel, a band, or a crank, all moving with wonderful regularity and precision to the *will* of its machinist—the all-powerful captain." Likewise, Cooper's Ned Myers attributes the hardships which the sailors endured to the inequalities inherent in the social hierarchy aboard the man-of-war. Charles Briggs faulted this system in *Working a Passage* by severely criticizing naval tyranny attributing it to "the inevitable effect of a system ... which has reared in the midst of our boasted democracy, an absurd aristocracy." [27]

Melville shares with fellow sailor-writers an abhorrence of the abject tyranny inherent in the social hierarchy of the ships to which sailors were subjected in addition to the conditions under which they lived and worked. Combining images from both Leech and Briggs, he describes the parameters of the captain's authority:

> For a ship is a bit of terra firma cut off from the main; it is a state in itself; and the captain is its king. It is no limited monarch. . . . The captain's word is law; he never speaks but in the imperative mood. When he stands on his Quarter-deck at sea, he absolutely commands as far as the eye can reach. Only the moon and stars are beyond his jurisdiction. He is lord and master of the sun. (23)

By depicting how officers exploit their levels of command, Melville records the social inequality and moral degradation inherent in the social structure itself.

Writers of the nautical reminiscence transformed the pervasive secular interest in morality and the subsequent reform bias of popular novels into a plea for social reform in the life of the sailor.[28] Briggs, J. Ross Browne, Frederick Law Olmsted, and Samuel Leech, among others, argued persuasively for reform on the sea. Narrative after narrative plainly recounted the horrors of sea life, inhumane living conditions, and psychological and physical maltreatment. Pleas for reform similar to Melville's reverberate through the narratives of Dana, Briggs, Browne, Cooper, and Leech.

Despite the similarities in subject matter, moral tone, and narrative form, Melville's narrative differs markedly from the reminiscences of Leech, Cooper, and Codman. *White-Jacket* focuses almost entirely on the social structure and the individuals who comprise "the world in the man-of-war." The conventional nautical reminiscence stresses action, adventure, and daring exploits of ship and crew. Melville's delineation in *White-Jacket* of man-of-war society, rather than man-of-war glory, indicates a very different perspective. The narrator records the individual's relation to his society: "Conceive him now in a man-of-war; with his letters of mart, well armed, victualed, and appointed, and see how he acquits himself" (1).

White-Jacket depicts the effects of social position on the individual. He observes the metamorphosis of a top-mate man promoted to the station of quarter-gunner, attributing it to "the wondrous influence of habitual sights and sounds upon the human temper" (46). He warns that "all people should be very careful in selecting their calling and vocations": "Many an angelic disposition has had its even edge turned, and hacked like a saw; and many a sweet draught of piety has soured on the heart, from people's choosing ill-natured employments, and omitting to gather round them good-natured landscapes" (45).

Throughout his narrative, White-Jacket observes the strategies that various individuals adopt in enduring both the beauty and the brutality of society aboard the man-of-war. He depicts the "wicked, unhappy, inefficient," the "skulkers and idlers," together with the "poets" and the "gallant fore, main, and mizen top-men aloft." Despite society's ill will, they adhere to their duty: "We . . . still trim our craft to the blast" (399). This society represents society at large; the world of the sailor reflects the universe itself: "We expatriate ourselves to nationalize with the universe" (76). Likewise, the sailor's experiences at sea reflect the experiences of human beings in the world: "But sailor, or landsmen, there is some sort of a Cape Horn for all" (109).

Though condemning atrocities such as flogging, abuse of authority, inadequate living conditions, and sparse provisions, White-Jacket endorses individual compliance with social ideologies and norms. In what some critics have termed "undemocratic language," White-Jacket stresses "the necessity for precision and discipline" (8).[29] Without "regulations," the large number of men aboard the man-of-war would be quickly reduced to an ungovernable "mob" (9). Thus when "an order is given to loose the main-royal, White-Jacket flies to obey it; and no one but him" (6). He recognizes the balances on which society is sustained. White-Jacket esteems his shipmate Jack Chase above all others aboard ship for his sociability, his creativity, and his sense of social duty: "No one with greater alacrity sprang to his duty" (13). The narrator acknowledges his understanding of—and pride in—his own defined place within this social order: "White-Jacket was where he belonged" (8). He thus exhibits an understanding of what Sacvan Bercovitch has called the "ritual of consensus," which represented a significant element in antebellum middle-class ideology.[30]

Despite the injustices of society, White-Jacket condemns mutiny, viewing it as an act of inevitable self-destruction. He knows that his own rebellious but justified instinct to revenge an unmerited accusation of negligence and the subsequent infliction of a punishment through flogging would only transform the innocent White-Jacket into a "murderer and suicide" (281). A sense of divine retribution for immoral and unethical acts, expressing the cultural ideology of the period, colors White-Jacket's narrative. Because of the ultimate alienation that results from individual rebellion—at least open, violent rebellion—against social norms, the narrator pleads for a reconciliation with society:

Let us not mutiny with bloody pikes in our hands. Our Lord
High Admiral will yet interpose; and though long ages should
elapse, and leave our wrongs unredressed, yet, shipmates and
world-mates! let us never forget, that, Whoever afflict us,
whatever surround, Life is a voyage that's homeward-bound!
(400)

In praising the importance of vocation and duty, in acquiescing to
the structure and strictures of society, in locating one's own groups
within society, and in working within the confines of duty, place, and
society, White-Jacket delineates the strategy necessary to survive in
the world of social inequity, violence, and immorality. By asserting
that "from the last ills no being can save another; therein each man
must be his own saviour" (399–400), the narrator reaffirms beliefs in
community and sociability that were central to mid-nineteenth-
century cultural hegemony.

White-Jacket concludes his narrative by circling back to its title,
"the world in a man-of-war," and points out the double vision of the
work: "As a man-of-war that sails through the sea, so this earth
sails through the air. We mortals are all on board a fast-sailing,
never-sinking world-frigate, of which God was the shipwright; and
she is but one craft in a Milky-Way fleet of which God is the Lord
High Admiral" (398).

This doubleness signals the literary level of the book. Melville's
characters act as artistic representations who comprise what one of
the book's contemporary reviewers called the "great portrait-gallery"
of White-Jacket's man-of-war.[31] They enhance Melville's larger "portrait" of the man-of-war world. In this respect, they function rhetorically as "characters" in a fictional world. In addition, the narrative
continually enlarges the narrator's own self-portrait. Observations
and opinions, scattered throughout the story, further depict his personality. For example, White-Jacket discusses conventional moral issues, highlighting his "rhetorical" rather than his "logical" abilities.[32]
This focus encourages the reader to view the narrative as constructed
art rather than recorded reality.

White-Jacket's unrestricted literary references throughout his narrative point both to his identity as a man of letters and to the literariness of his text. He clearly depicts himself as a literary person who

associates solely with the "literary" group of sailors aboard. Together they create, discuss, and refer to literature. In White-Jacket's narrative, references adopt a metaphorical significance. The literary display of the Cape Horn episode, the metaphoric parallels of the sailor's experience around the Cape to the experiences of "Orpheus, Ulysses, or Dante," coupled with references to the representations of Cape Horn in Byron, Coleridge, and Dana, indicate the literariness of White-Jacket's narrative—as Denis Berthold, in pointing out the factual errors and fictional aims of this episode, has suggested.[33] In Melville's hands, the experience of Cape Horn becomes a conscious act of literary representation beyond mere storytelling.

Literary references metonymically represent characters in White-Jacket's narrative: "He was a Thalaba the Destroyer at the helm." This metonymy of references in his narrative metaphorically transforms the man-of-war reminiscence into a man-of-war fiction. By extension, the relation of the man-of-war ship to the world at large reflects the relation of the writer to his society at large.

By exploring the creative potential of popular conventions and ideologies, Melville discovered metaphorical implications embedded within those conventions. The story of the author's initiation and fellowship in the literary community follows the same types and levels of experience as the sailor's integration into the sailor community. The narration of White-Jacket's experiences and understanding of man-of-war society expresses the individual artist's awareness of the parameters of his or her environment and the necessary balance between personal interests and sociability.

Reviewers praised Melville's "union of culture and experience . . . the sharp breeze of the forecastle alternating with the mellow stillness of the library."[34] They argued that White-Jacket stood out among other nautical reminiscences of the day due to its metaphoric doubleness: "It is not often that the stains of the tar bucket and the ink stand are seen on the same fingers."[35] This move to subsume thematic and existential concerns within literary conventions—this coordination of an artistic style with cultural attitudes—provided the impetus for artistic balance between "philosophy and whales" and "poetry and blubber" in Moby-Dick.[36]

Critical Debates

CHAPTER FIVE

Originality: The Case of *Moby-Dick*

WHILE MOST TEXTUAL CRITICS assert that Melville planned his "market" novels, *Redburn* and *White-Jacket,* by deliberately employing popular forms of the day, they locate Melville's "creativity" and "originality" instead in his "unplanned" works. In these critics' view, creativity and originality bear little relation to compositional planning and indeed seem antithetical to it. For these reasons, genetic theorists have continued to endorse the idea that Melville did not plan what is considered his most original and creative work, *Moby-Dick.* Yet we have already seen how Melville deliberately—and creatively—employed popular forms in *Typee, Omoo, Mardi, Redburn,* and *White-Jacket.* We have also discovered how innovative Melville was in these "market" novels—a term that applies equally to all of these early works. Such exceptions to standard formulations of Melville's compositional methods should encourage modern readers unfamiliar with the literary trends of antebellum culture to adopt Ishmael's suggestion and "look at this matter in every light."

Beyond a linear realism, the author's compositional method is commonly associated with the improvisational habits of realist writers. With meaning derived from minute observations of experience, these writers reputedly discovered the thematic significance and content of their stories not through a priori schemes, but rather through the act of writing. As Edwin Eigner has painstakingly recovered in his examination of Victorian attitudes toward literary writing, many realist writers upheld the romantic theory of literary inspiration: Scott maintained that he "could never lay down a plan," Trollope never thought about a novel until he "was doing it," and Thackeray wrote from "brilliantly resourceful improvisation." [1]

In this light, Melville's practice of "energetically creating parts," in the words of Richard Brodhead, stems from a "preference from writing without plan." [2] The narrative form of *Moby-Dick*, Harrison Hayford has suggested, results from unplanned changes—"shifting, expanding, and not altogether seamlessly blending conceptions of the work." [3] In short, Melville's great masterpiece is largely considered an unplanned coincidence.

Scholars unfamiliar with or disinterested in the literary trends of Melville's day provide instead psychobiographical explanations for the author's compositional practices. Rather than link such practices to mid-nineteenth-century conventions, critics such as Howard P. Vincent, Richard Brodhead, James Barbour, and most recently John Samson treat Melville's act of mixing fact with fiction either as the author's personal innovations of the factual materials of whaling or as "defiant anomalies of genre," [4] Viewed from these perspectives, the multiple genres, plots, characters, and modes of literary narration in *Moby-Dick,* for example, seem "unnecessary duplicates," as Hayford has suggested, elements that indicate "shifting intentions" for the work. In fact, the author's creativity is thought to stem from his "revisions" to stories "already well-developed." [5]

Grounded in textual and biographical explanations, such theories seem to dismiss the contextual basis of narrative form in *Moby-Dick* and unnecessarily segregate personal and cultural influences, as Eigner argued almost two decades ago. Despite Eigner's recovery of a narrative form that the peculiar structure of *Moby-Dick* parallels, many scholars persist in separating Melville's work from its obvious narrative paradigm. [6] In a recent discussion of Melville's compositional methods, Brodhead projects an isolated view of the writer: "When the author of *Moby-Dick* thinks of literature . . . he associates it scarcely at all with the literary forms most active in his own time." [7] Many critics continue to seek explanations and sources *beyond* Melville's literary culture. The author's reading of Shakespeare, according to Charles Olson and Larzer Ziff, provided lessons of craft and "dark intensity." Yet a cultural penchant for "darkness," as David S. Reynolds has demonstrated, pervaded sensational rhetoric in antebellum literary culture, and Lawrence W. Levine has shown that rather than lying beyond, the plays of Shakespeare were fully integrated within popular antebellum culture.[8]

Genetic accounts of compositional and revisionary practices, as Hershel Parker has persuasively argued, do not need to dismiss or ignore contextual information.[9] Yet many formulations of Melville's compositional strategies overlook the actual genres and styles that the author employed in his earlier works. Melville's reliance on popular practice was too consistent, thorough, and deliberate for scholars to present him persuasively as one who wrote without plan. Instead, we gain greater insight into the nature of the author's writing habits by contextualizing his novels within the prevailing genres and styles of his day.

The heterogeneity of *Moby-Dick*—often attributed to the author's "soared ambition," "fluid consciousness," "shifting . . . conceptions," and even "lessons of craft from Shakespeare"—actually reflects a narrative license of the times.[10] The metaphysical discussions, genre shifts, use of Shakespearean conventions, and the mixture of facts and romance, typically considered Melville's improvisations, also appear in "mixed form" narratives, a genre (in)famous at midcentury but now largely overlooked. Through this heterogenous form, Melville links his work to a popular yet subversive trend in both English and American antebellum literary cultures. Indeed, Melville's debt to "mixed form"—which Eigner calls a subgenre of the romance—is central to understanding the narrative form and Melville's intentions and method in *Moby-Dick*.[11] Recovering this complex narrative form represents the first necessary step to reconsidering Melville's actual creativity, as well as resolving the disparate readings by contextualist and genetic scholars of *Moby-Dick*.

Mixed Form

The genre of the mixed form novel emerged in transatlantic literary circles as a response to early nineteenth-century critical strictures on literary realism. Praise for a literary work by reviewers supportive of realistic fiction almost always included the positive comparison of the author's representational approach with seventeenth-century Dutch realist painting. With this genre as the model of portraiture in mid-nineteenth-century culture, realist writers depicted their fictional worlds with the minute detail of a Rembrandt, Vermeer, or Steen. They observed a strict fidelity with almost daguerreotype accuracy.

Edward Bulwer-Lytton (1803–173), one of the first serious literary theoreticians and practitioners of mixed form in England, credited the publication of *Wilhelm Meister* by Wolfgang von Goethe in Germany as the first example of what he called the "metaphysical" novel. Bulwer-Lytton defined this new genre as "neither wholly allegory, nor wholly matter-of-fact, but both at times." Radically multiple, the mixed form novels simultaneously present different perceptions of experience through mimetic and philosophical modes. As a result, Bulwer-Lytton called them "metaphysical" narratives, since they depict the "truth of causes" and deliberately mix levels of approach.[12]

David Masson, a leading Victorian literary critic, differentiated in his revisionary account of the period's fiction, realistic "novels of English life and manners" that represent experience through a "portraiture of outward society" from "art and culture novels" that present "the nature of experience itself."[13] The latter, also called mixed form or metaphysical narratives, sought to accomplish something other than mainstream realistic portraiture. The very nature of their mixture suggests an alternate view—a subversion even—of the world of facts.

Masson discusses the use of mixed form narratives as a literary strategy. Typically, they combine a Lockean positivistic worldview—the belief that there is a "definite complement of truths related to human procedure which may be ascertained by reason, experience, and a scientific study of the natural laws"—with a reflective, mystical, often visionary, Kantian point of view. As such, these novels stress the necessity of "a deeper faith, a faith metaphysical, in which these very truths must be rooted out ere they can function so powerfully as they might."[14] The need for metaphysical truth within the world of facts informs the structure of mixed form narratives and helps to explain this "mixture."

Masson describes the conventional structure of the genre. In his words, the metaphysical novel chronicles the individual's "progress through the very blackness of darkness, with only natural reason, or the revelation that can come through reason, as his guide":

> There is the mind preying on its own metaphysical roots; there is the parting, piece by piece, of the old hereditary faith, and yet all the remaining torture of the ceaseless interrogation which that faith satisfied . . . there is the burden of sin and the alternate sullenness and madness of despair. . . . Sometimes the mind under probation is made to ascertain for itself that its perpetual metaphysical self-torture, its perpetual labour on questions which cannot be answered, is a misuse of its faculties, and so take rest in the philosophic conclusion that "man was not born to solve the problem of the universe, but to find out where the problem begins, and then to restrain himself within the limits of the comprehensible. (287–88)

Compensating for the deficiencies of the experiental, empirical perspective in realist writing, which—according to metaphysical writers—lacked thematic, philosophical, and symbolic truth, metaphysical narratives portrayed the general ambience of a scene or individual through impressionistic portraiture. Metaphysical writers employed representational techniques that revealed inner impressions, since the depiction of insights, visions, and perceptions about existential matters guided both their compositional method and their thematic articulations.

In travel, historical, and nautical narratives, facts supported the veridical orientation of the genres. In metaphysical narratives, facts were used to subvert the materialist world that facts represent. While presenting the world bound by regular laws, the metaphysical writer then contradicted that world and its facts from an idealist point of view. While the linear plot depicted the empirical approach to experience, the retarding digressions, multiple genres, and interpolations elucidated the preferred ideal view.

Uniting formal elements with thematic concerns, metaphysical writers wrote from an a priori scheme. The formal complexity and multiplicity of their narratives originated from preconceived ideas. Emily Brontë, one of the most famous metaphysical writers, revealed in her notebooks copious plans and outlines for novels considered the work of a "wild, unregulated improvisor" by realist critics.[15] Charles Dickens, another writer of mixed form narratives and a reputed improviser, worked from concrete preconceived plans; his letters refer to his outlined ideas for various works.[16] Bulwer-Lytton indicated the preconceived nature of the mixed form narrative by locating the source of the metaphysical writer's pleasure in his or her completed work, less in "proportion as it is good, than in proportion as it fulfills the idea with which he commenced it."[17] Visionary insights—the metaphysical writer's impetus for writing—come before, not through, the act of writing.

Like other metaphysical writers, Melville planned his works; a prevailing idea, or vision, guided his writing. In a 1 May 1850 letter to Richard Henry Dana, Melville described the narrative form of his forthcoming novel:

> It will be a strange sort of book, tho', I fear; blubber is blubber you know; tho' you may get oil out of it, the poetry runs as hard as sap from a frozen maple tree;—& to cook the thing up, one must needs throw in a little fancy, which from the nature of the thing, must be ungainly as the gambols of the whales themselves. Yet I mean to give the truth of the thing, spite of this.[18]

While frequently cited as evidence for Melville's changing conception of what was to become *Moby-Dick, or The Whale,* this letter reflects the author's intention to construct a mixed form novel. In a 17 November 1851 letter to Hawthorne regarding *Moby-Dick,* Melville alluded to this notion of a central idea that informed his writing: "You did not care a penny for the work. But, now and then as you read, you understood the pervading thought that impelled the book —and that you praised."[19]

Melville's creation of a mixed narrative form that blends science and fiction, philosophy and poetry, urges the modern reader to consider this matter of mixed form, as Ishmael repeatedly counsels his readers, "in every light." Certainly Melville's masterpiece shares a consensus of aesthetics with such English "mixed form" novels as *Bleak House, David Copperfield,* and *Wuthering Heights,* as well as with popular American works like Richard Burleigh Kimball's *St.*

Leger; or, The Threads of Life (1850), William Starbuck Mayo's *Kaloo-lah* (1849), and Sylvester Judd's *Margaret: A Tale of the Real and Ideal, Blight and Bloom* (1845).[20] This consensus is crucial to understanding Melville's relation and contribution to the tradition of the mixed form novel. To appreciate the author's creativity in *Moby-Dick*, however, we need first to understand the complexities of compositional method during the period.

Mixed Form Narratives

Combination of the veridical and the visionary pervaded the mixed form novel. Readers of metaphysical narratives *expected* a blend of fact and philosophical fiction. The conflation enabled writers to represent both the materialist world, through the familiar form of a veritable record, and the idealist or visionary view, through more figurative language. In this context, Melville's act of mixing the facts of "commodity" with "cosmological knowing," or improvising on the necessary "narrative of facts"—often seen as the author's personal interpretation of narrative form—begins in a consensus of mixed form.[21]

Antebellum Practices

A glance at a few of Melville's contemporaries depicts some of these commonalities. The most striking characteristic that distinguished mixed form novels from other narratives of the day lay in their particular bivalent structure. While the nature of this mixture of realism and philosophy differed according to the interests of individual authors, mixed form narratives juxtaposed empiricism with idealism.

Bulwer-Lytton—with Goethe as his model—first experimented with this narrative mixture. To augment the verisimilitude of a genre considered an "ideal fable," Bulwer-Lytton "heavily documented" his historical novels through copious footnotes and endnotes. In this manner, he added a perspective and authenticity to the historical novel that Scott and his followers had not, an authenticity that met the genre's responsibility to faithful depiction. By providing historical accuracy, the author could then focus on themes that emerged from its historicity.

In *St. Leger*, Richard Burleigh Kimball cleverly juxtaposes his chronicle of the cognitive and philosophic journey of his hero and an essentially historical narrative. By providing extensive genealogical facts, Kimball represents the traditional position of realist writers. These facts offer an epistemology and perspective different from the protagonist's search for intuitive knowledge. Kimball ultimately challenges the thematic value of realistic narration through his philosophical, intuitive account of metaphysical discoveries of his protagonist. The understanding gained in the realistic narrative through studying family tradition is spurned by the narrator for the visionary insights gained through philosophic inquiry.

Other authors represented a multiplicity of views in their narratives. In *Margaret*, Sylvester Judd thematized the cultural and ideological bases to individual perspectives by presenting alternative cultural views, including classic Greek, Native American, Arabic, and Anglo-Saxon. Sometimes writers subverted reader expectations. In *Nile Notes of an Howadji*, George William Curtis transposed the two levels by creating an instructional travel narrative from the conventional light and amusing "sketch" of travel. His "notes" stressed the informational content of his story and added a level of reflection not found in the conventional European travel narrative.[22]

Other writers mixed science with fiction. In the historical romance *Kaloolah*, William Starbuck Mayo provided ethological accounts of ocean birds, fish, and dolphins.[23] Even in his more realistic *The Berber*, Mayo conflated geographical information and romance, a combination described by a *Harper's* reviewer:

> The scene is laid in Morocco, affording the writer an occasion for the use of a great deal of geographical and historical lore, which is introduced to decided advantage as a substantial background to the story, which, in itself, possesses a sustained and powerful interest. (December 1850)

The reviewer then located that powerful interest specifically in the narrative's mixed form: "These sudden and decided transitions form a striking feature of the volume. . . . They constantly pique the attention of the reader, keeping curiosity alive, and presenting the combined charm of surprise and alternation." Mayo's descriptions grounded his romances in the world of science—a contrast that satisfied readers who required realistic depictions. With such factual safety belts, the reader could embark on the romantic journey without fear of colliding with opposing stylistic views.

Some writers mixed scientific and literary genres as a way of presenting different epistemological schemes. Judd's *Margaret*, whose title alone blends the scientific ("blight and bloom") with the philosophical ("real and ideal") juxtaposes polytheistic, Native American forest lives and a Christian, Anglo-Saxon village. Village life dramatizes the philosophical, whereas forest life portrays the natural world of geology, botany, and biology. Here the "real," natural world offers an epistemology represented variably through Native American and other non-Christian worldviews which, in turn, serve as an alternative to the "ideal." Through a lesson in geology (anticipating the anatomy lessons of *Moby-Dick*), Judd compares the geological formation known as a geode to the human head:

> Man like this stone is geodic. . . . expressing all men collectively viewed in their better light. . . . Much depends upon this light, phase, or aspect . . . an Indian head in one position. . . . If I could crack any man as I do this stone, I should lay open beautiful crystals. (240)

Again anticipating Ishmael, who contrasts different philosophical views in the Whale's head chapters (74–75), Judd underscores here the relativism inherent in philosophical perspective.

In this light, the "cetological center" of *Moby-Dick* reflects both the mid-nineteenth-century interest in natural science and the necessary empirical realism of the mixed form novel.[24] *Moby-Dick* correspondingly abounds in statistical, historical, economic, and anatomical facts interspersed through the philosophical chronicle of Ishmael's developing metaphysical insights. As a codified form within this tradition, the "mass of cetological and whaling data" is not the "extra material" inserted into a "story already well-developed," as Vincent contends, but an integral element of narrative form in *Moby-Dick*.[25] In terms resembling the *Harper's* review of *The Berber*, the *New Haven Daily*

Palladium praised the mixture of forms in *Moby-Dick:* "The work possesses all the interest of the most exciting fiction, while, at the same time, it conveys much valuable information in regard to things pertaining to natural history, commerce, life on shipboard, and etc." (17 November 1851). This conscious alternation of facts with fiction signals a deliberate approach to narrative form by metaphysical writers.

To portray the alternate worldviews signaled by either a narrative of facts or one of inspiration, philosophy, or vision, metaphysical writers employed various stylistic devices. Different literary genres depict alternating perspectives of reality. Dickens, for example, incorporated poetry into his narrative in the *Pickwick Papers,* a fairy tale in *Little Dorrit,* and drama in *Nicholas Nickelby* and *Great Expectations.* Judd relied on poetry and Native American oral traditions, while Kimball interpolated poetry and soliloquies into his narrative. Though resembling Melville's Ahab, the following soliloquy comes not from Ahab, but rather from the narrator of Kimball's *St. Leger:*

> Be still, rebellious temper. Dare not disturb the calm current of my thoughts. Down, ye mocking suggestions. Away, ye dark, thick, brooding fancies—hence, all! all! At any rate, your time is not *yet.* The mysterious union of body and spirit still is, though faintly indeed does Vitality in me perform her office; but the wheel is not yet broken: I am at the helm still! therefore, Doubt, thou supple, coward slave of evil, avaunt!
> I *WILL* that I believe.
> I *DO* believe! (232)

This work, like *Moby-Dick* after it, also contains the different genres of poetry and drama. Shakespearean conventions "share textual space" with decidedly less classical materials in Kimball's book, just as they do in *Moby-Dick.*[26]

In Melville's era Shakespeare was truly a popular playwright with all audiences and not the icon of "highbrow" culture, a status assigned to him only in the late nineteenth-century.[27] Melville shares with others of his day "many lessons of craft from Shakespeare," including the use of the soliloquy to dramatize "psychological states," lessons that scholars too often assign to Melville's uniqueness. Ge-

neric mixtures, frequently associated with Melville's greatness of vision—or attributed to "Hawthorne's example" and "classicist
readings"—reflect a common strategy of mid-nineteenth-century
metaphysical writers.[28]

Melville's reputed "defiant anomalies of genre" cohere in the conventions of mixed form.[29] Working within this tradition, Melville
does not need to "accept that part of the traditional compact" that
necessitates "while writing one kind of work, one must give up the
will to be writing another"—a compromise that Richard Brodhead
recently asserted as a necessity for Melville.[30] Rather, the author ac-
cepts the *metaphysical* compact that stipulates the use of multiple
genres in one narrative. Indeed, the author's use of mixed form offers
an alternate perspective on alleged stylistic inconsistencies. When
viewed textually, the multiple genres, plots, characters, and modes
of literary narration in *Moby-Dick* have seemed to be "unnecessary
duplicates," elements that indicate "shifting intentions" for the
work.[31] Considered contextually, however, these inconsistencies represent a deliberate attempt to create an orchestrated whole that contains segmental, alternating perceptions of reality—a structure
favored by metaphysical writers.

Originality in *Moby-Dick*

Because most modern readers have not identified Melville's attempt
to "illustrate a knowledge different" from cetological facts as common practice in the mixed form novel, they must look for originality
in exactly those areas where Melville conforms to once-accepted but
now forgotten standards. Howard P. Vincent considers Melville's
strategy in *Moby-Dick* as the author's great "innovation" of facts.
James McIntosh attributes to the example of Hawthorne—rather
than to the larger tradition of mixed form narratives to which Hawthorne himself was indebted—Melville's use of multiple explanations, something that purportedly sets the works of both novelists
above their culture. McIntosh also signals Melville's "multiple quest"
as "a new invention in romanticism . . . virtually unique," a view that
he is forced to assert since he considers only classic quest romances
and not the mixed form quests popular in Melville's day.[32]

Melville's use of mixed form (a form that the author clearly knew was not accepted by all) did not restrict the author's creativity, contrary to critics who have ascribed a "marketplace" necessity to antebellum writers.[33] Indeed, relating Melville's narrative form in *Moby-Dick* to the larger tradition of mixed form does not need to diminish or even negate the possibility for creativity. We need to understand the role that Melville's use of mixed form plays in the creative process.

When Ishmael narrates *Moby-Dick,* he repeatedly urges his readers to "look at this matter in every light."[34] This suggestion links narrative form to theme, a balance that represents Melville's innovations of popular practice. For Melville, originality lay in a combination of established forms, as he attested in his statement on genius made in his review of Hawthorne's *Mosses from an Old Manse.*[35]

Mixed Form in Moby-Dick

Melville innovates the genre of mixed form in his great American epic by reshaping it to suit his thematic purposes. Unlike other metaphysical writers—particularly, Kimball, Judd, and Mayo, who thematized the superiority of the ideal to the real—Melville combines in *Moby-Dick* both realistic and impressionistic methods of depicting reality to convey their complementariness. He vivifies his narrator's perception, for example, by qualifying his description with a metaphor or simile. In "The Line," Ishmael contrasts the different materials from which whale lines are constructed: "Of late years the Manilla rope has . . . superseded hemp as a material for whale-lines; for though not so durable as hemp, it is stronger, and far more soft and elastic" (278). He then offers a metaphor that vividly distinguishes the two:

> Hemp is a dusky, dark fellow, a sort of Indian;
> but Manilla is as a golden-haired Circassian to behold. (278)

The descriptive elaboration serves a twofold purpose. It clarifies by offering more realistic detail and yet simultaneously renders the narrator's intuitive impression of the significance of the ropes.

Melville does not present alternative worldviews for the purpose of endorsing one over the other; rather, he advocates a necessary

multiplicity of views. This combination suggests an orientation different from other metaphysical narratives. Kimball's narrator asserts the
noncompatibility of opposing views:

> If a man serves his passions, he must exclude the higher enjoy-
> ments of the moral and intellectual. Or if he seeks the intellec-
> tual, he must exclude those baser things which enervate and
> enslave the mind. If he determine upon moral and religious
> culture, he must exclude the influences of time and sense.
> (*St. Leger,* 193)

Likewise, Kimball argues for an epistemology that is fundamentally
sequential in nature: "For no person can at the same time walk in a
given direction and in a direction exactly the opposite. Attempt first
one and then the other, and no progress is made" (194). At times,
Melville seems to endorse this view: "Out of the trunk, the branches
grow; out of them, the twigs. So, in productive subjects, grow the
chapters" (289). Yet he challenges and radically reconstructs such
views by reaching beyond physical reality to include the literary world
of narrative. Thus, by mixing these different ontological levels, Melville offers a new metaphysical—and metafictional—level that successfully accomplishes what Kimball had deemed impossible:

> In the tumultuous business of cutting-in and attending to a
> whale, there is much running backwards and forwards among
> the crew. Now hands are wanted here, and then again hands
> are wanted there. There is no staying in any one place; for at
> one and the same time everything has to be done everywhere.
> It is much the same with him who endeavors the description of
> the scene. We must now retrace our way a little. (319)

Stressing the nonsequentiality of experience, Melville ingeniously
moves both forward and backward simultaneously: through retracing
plot, the narrator advances the narrative. Through such mixtures, the
author innovates established use of mixed form.

Melville simply creates a new (metaphysical) world for the mixed
form narrative. The philosophy of "try[ing] all things" (345) is central
to Ishmael's "multiple quest."[36] In this novel, comprehension and
insight occur through considering existence "in every light," seeking

truth through empirical, metaphysical, theological, and economic approaches. In Melville's view, since different circumstances and conditions influence perception, no one truth or ontological position dominates.

Through the story of Ishmael's developing understanding of the link between surface and signification, Melville instructs his readers how to view the particular form that his narrative assumes. Ishmael recounts his discovery early in the narrative that "nothing exists in itself" (53). Phenomena gain meaning through their potential for opposing referential signification: "There is no quality in this world that is not what it is merely by contrast: Truly to enjoy bodily warmth, some small part of you must be cold" (53).

Melville improvises on metaphysical practice by positing in *Moby-Dick* the notion that comprehension of physical manifestations provides an understanding of the inner nature of objects and people. "Admonitions and warnings" act as physical correlates to inner states: "But rather are ye predictions than warnings, ye shadows! Yet not so much predictions from without, as verifications of the foregoing things within" (165). In "The Pulpit," Ishmael observes the famous sailor-minister, Father Mapple, isolate himself within his pulpit by drawing up the rope ladder. "Without fully comprehending the reason for this," Ishmael hypothesizes that the physical act of isolation "must symbolize something unseen": "Can it be, then, that by that act of physical isolation, he signifies his spiritual withdrawal for the time, from all outward worldly ties and connexions?" (39). This ability to discover spiritual and psychological meaning in physical elements informs Ishmael's increased understanding of Father Mapple:

> While he was speaking these words, the howling of the shrieking, slanting storm without seemed to add new power to the preacher, who, when describing Jonah's sea-storm, seemed tossed by a storm himself. His deep chest heaved as with a ground-swell; his tossed arms seemed the warring elements at work. (47)

By considering opposing perceptions, Ishmael discovers insights that resolve these disparate elements into an organic whole. At first,

Father Mapple's double occupation of sailor-minister seemed an unlikely mixture. By considering these ostensibly insoluble elements,
however, Ishmael perceives a higher, visionary significance: "What
could be more full of meaning?—for the pulpit is ever this earth's
foremost part; and all the rest comes in its rear; the pulpit leads the
world. . . . Yes, the world's a ship on its passage out, and not a voyage
complete; and the pulpit is its prow" (40).

Melville's portraits mark the essential difference in perspective between the typical metaphysical narrative and *Moby-Dick*. In "Ahab"
Ishmael recounts his first view of the captain of the *Pequod:*

> I was struck with the singular posture he maintained. Upon
> each side of the Pequod's quarter deck, and pretty close to the
> mizzen shrouds, there was an auger hole, bored about half an
> inch or so, into the plank. His bone leg steadied in that hole;
> one arm elevated, and holding by a shroud; Captain Ahab
> stood erect, looking straight out beyond the ship's ever-
> pitching prow. There was an infinity of firmest fortitude, a
> determinate, unsurrenderable wilfulness, in the fixed and fear-
> less, forward dedication of that glance. (124)

Ishmael begins with the detail of a realistic portrait, and though he
uses exact measures and technical terminology, he supplements his
depiction with impressionism. This representational mode does not
serve here to counterpoise the realism. Unlike other metaphysical
narratives, *Moby-Dick* illustrates the intrinsic semantic relation between these perspectives. By observing the physical staunchness—
"Ahab stood erect, looking straight out"—Ishmael can observe
Ahab's mental "willfulness" in his "fixed" expression. Qualifying his
realistic mode of description with an impressionistic representation,
Ishmael points out the significance of the scene described. He demonstrates that "some certain significance lurks in all things, else all
things are little worth, and the round world itself but an empty
cipher" (430–31). Facts, in themselves, are meaningless without a
referential signification. In this passage Melville directly relates form
and theme.

In "The Carpenter" Ishmael applies the same kind of understanding to his description of the carpenter aboard ship. Paralleling Judd's treatment of the same topic, Melville's narrator considers humankind from opposing perspectives:

> Seat thyself sultanically among the moons of Saturn, and take high abstracted man alone; and he seems a wonder, a grandeur, and a woe. But from the same point, take mankind in mass, and for the most part, they seem a mob of unnecessary duplicates, both contemporary and hereditary. (466)

However, by considering these disparate views, Ishmael comes to understand that the carpenter is something more than the mixture itself: "But most humble though he was, and far from furnishing an example of the high, humane abstraction; the Pequod's carpenter was no duplicate" (466). The point here is that after contemplating these opposing viewpoints individually, Ishmael goes beyond them to realize that meaning stems not from contrast but rather from the mixture.

Blending contrasting modes of representation, Melville offers some unusual mixtures. In addition to mixing descriptive modes, he combines seemingly unrelated subjects. Nineteenth-century reviewers praised this intermingling of topics. The reviewer for *John Bull*, a British journal, admired Melville's method and referred readers to "The Blanket," which represents "the manner in which the author extracts lessons of life from the carcass of a dead whale."[37] Recounting the process of skinning the whale, Ishmael mentions that sailors call the strips of skin "blanket-pieces" (307). He then compares the skin of the sperm whale to an actual blanket:

> For the whale is indeed wrapt up in his blubber as in a real blanket or counterpane; or, still better, an Indian poncho slipt over his head, and skirting his extremity. It is by reason of this cozy blanketing of his body, that the whale is enabled to keep himself comfortable in all weathers, in all seas, times, and tides. . . . Oh, man! admire and model thyself after the whale! Do, thou, too, remain warm among ice. Do, thou, too, live in this world without being of it. Be cool at the equator; keep thy blood fluid at the Pole. Like the great dome of St. Peter's, and like the great whale, retain, O man! in all seasons a temperature of thine own. (307)

Ishmael finds a lesson for humanity in the "rare virtue of a strong individual vitality, and the rare virtue of thick walls, and the rare virtue of interior spaciousness" of the whale (307). This method involves employing the facts of the whale and, through the meaning that the facts supply, detecting a larger perspective where the facts and their signification are metaphors for the human condition. This process of relating facts and their meaning as the signifier of a larger perspective on the human condition and experience remains one of Melville's great creative uses of the mixed form.

Melville also applies the facts of whaling to the narrative process itself, as we have already seen. In "The Monkey-Rope" Ishmael equates "the tumultuous business of cutting-in and attending to a whale" (319) with his compositional method of description, two seemingly unrelated tasks; the process of whaling thus becomes a metaphor for the narrative process. This perception provides the reader with a wider perspective on the particular form this narrative assumes. Changes in narrative form exemplify the philosophy of a necessary multiplicity of perspective. Ishmael demonstrates how his understanding of the whale acts as a metaphor for the reader's understanding of the narrative at hand. His methodological approach to representing the whale complements his own narrative method. Both Ishmael, regarding the whale, and the reader, regarding the narrative, need to "look at this matter in every light" to gain a "thorough, sweeping comprehension" of things (448). It is a necessary multiplicity of approaches that yields meaning.

In depicting this multiple approach, Melville illustrates the link between the image under scrutiny and the method of representation: the mutability of the signified and the signifier. Ishmael reinforces the relative nature of portraiture by prefacing many of his descriptions with references to mental perception. Before describing an action of Stubb, Ishmael urges the reader to "look now at Stubb, a man" and "look at him, he stands." In this manner, Ishmael demonstrates how individual methods of perception frame the nature of the portrait.

Ishmael's observations of other crew members also furnish clear insights into the nature of perception. In "The Doubloon" Ishmael watches Ahab's movements on the deck:

> When he halted before the binnacle, with his glance fastened
> on the pointed needle in the compass, that glance shot like a
> javelin with the pointed intensity of his purpose; and when
> resuming his walk he again paused before the mainmast, then,
> as the same riveted glance fastened upon the riveted gold coin
> there, he still wore the same aspect of nailed firmness, only
> dashed with a certain wild longing, if not hopefulness. (430)

The nailed doubloon, which denotes the firm intent behind the whale hunt, conveys its physical and inner states of firmness to the observer. Ahab's "riveted" glance mirrors the "nailed firmness" of his intent. The language in which Ishmael's observation is portrayed is likewise "riveted" in unity of its depiction; Melville repeats the stasis and fixedness of the first two verbs, *halted* and *fastened,* in the adjectives and nouns employed in the description: *javelin, pointed, intensity, riveted, nailed,* and *firmness.* A common approach to narrative mode and portraiture in *Moby-Dick,* this multiple and yet harmonious method marks Melville's originality within the genre of the metaphysical novel.

Melville moves to the existential. In "The Mat-Maker," Ishmael recounts an epiphanic moment that occurred one afternoon when he helped Queequeg weave mats. By considering both the feeling that "an incantation of revery lurked in the air" (214) and the physical actions involved in constructing the mats, Ishmael perceives a view of things more complete than the sum of the parts:

> it seemed as if this were the Loom of Time, and I myself were a
> shuttle mechanically weaving and weaving away at the Fates.
> There lay the fixed threads of the warp subject to but one
> single, ever returning, unchanging vibration, and that vibra-
> tion merely enough to admit of the crosswise inter blending of
> other threads with its own. This warp seemed necessity; and
> here, thought I, with my own hand I ply my own shuttle and
> weave my own destiny into these unalterable threads . . . this
> savage's sword, thought I, which thus finally shapes and fash-
> ions both warp and woof; this easy, indifferent sword must be
> chance—aye, chance, free will, and necessity—no wise incom-
> patible—all interweavingly working together. (214–15)

Ishmael concludes his examination of the whale through "compre-hensiveness of sweep" (456). In trying to describe the center of the whale through the skeleton, he finds that it is necessarily tied to the other parts of the whale's anatomy—a lesson not learned earlier in the narrative, where Ishmael presented the various parts of the whale separately. In "The Fossil Whale" Ishmael describes the essential unity of the whale. He discovers that his account must include "the whole circle of the sciences, and all generations of whales, and men, past, present, and to come, with all the panoramas of empire on earth, and throughout the universe, not excluding the suburbs" (456).

As the narrative moves toward the final chase, Ishmael consolidates his own multiple quests for a viable ontology. "The Symphony" represents his personal conclusion to his ontological search by blending together the elements of life into a symphonic composition, so to speak. He presents the essential organic harmony between disparate elements through his view of the sea and air:

> It was a clear steel-blue day. The firmaments of air and sea were hardly separable in that all-pervading azure; only, the pensive air was transparently pure and soft, with a woman's look, and the robust and man-like sea heaved with long, strong, lingering swells, as Samson's chest in his sleep. (542)

The chapter becomes a "symphony" of different perspectives on life. Ishmael contrasts his understanding of the sea and air with Ahab's perspective: while Ishmael observes and relishes the femininity of the air, Ahab remains unresponsive to its graces. Ishmael describes how the "stepmother world" of the "winsome sky . . . now threw affectionate arms round [Ahab's] stubborn neck, and did seem to joyously sob over him, as if over one, that however wilful and erring, she could yet find it in her heart to save and bless" (543).

In contrast to Ishmael, Ahab will not allow his "splintered helmet of brow" to unite with "the fair girl's forehead of a heaven." Instead, he turns to gaze at his sinking shadow in the "mannish" water. Like Ishmael, who thought of "wife, the heart, the bed" when he established physical contact with the crew, Ahab sees his wife and child when he gazes into the "human eye" of Starbuck (544). Rather than uniting with the image he finds in Starbuck's eyes, he averts his glance, only to stare into the "two reflected, fixed eyes" of Fedallah, the symbol of the evil, darker aspects of individuality. Where Ishmael celebrates the necessary unity of life, Ahab turns away, to chaos, to destruction.

Ishmael's perspective allows him to see unities where he once saw unrelated entities. Sylvester Judd had anticipated Melville's own thematic treatment of what his character Margaret had called "diversities":

> That we have diversities is certain, but what shall we do with them? Wink them out of sight; agree to disagree, bear with one another in silent consuming pain? No. Let them be thrown in the common crucible of our affection, and fused together onto some *tertium quid*, some new homogeneous form. (*Margaret*, 440)

Paralleling Margaret's solutions, Ishmael subsumes in "The Chase— The Second Day" multiple quests into an organic vision:

> They were one man, not thirty. For as the one ship that held them all; though it was put together of all contrasting things— oak, and maple, and pine wood; iron, and pitch, and hemp— yet all these ran into each other in the one concrete hull, which shot on its way, both balanced and directed by the long central keel; even so, all the individualities of the crew, this man's valor, that man's fear; guilt and guiltlessness, all varieties were welded into oneness. (557)

Melville's text, like the ship with its diverse yet unified crew, represents an organic approach to narrative composition. For the reader, these perspectives build into an organic whole. Whaling encompasses a multiply motivated search—for money, revenge, and ontological meaning. It allows for a variety of approaches—empirical, metaphysical, theological, and economic—as do Melville's subjects, whaling and existential questing. The ability to blend realistic and impressionistic representational modes with a multiplicity of philosophical approaches to his subject, and to create organic unities from these combinations, represents Melville's view of narrative form. He instructs the reader how to look at this narrative form "in every light." This suggestion regarding his intention in *Moby-Dick* aids the reader in understanding the point behind an apparent fragmentation. These segments, while meaningful in themselves, build together into a more profound understanding of Melville's conception of narrative form.

Reconsidering Melville's Method in *Moby-Dick*

Recognizing the forms of the conventional metaphysical narrative of *Moby-Dick*, we may now "consider this matter" of narrative form in a larger perspective. Melville's demonstration of the multiplicity of literature encourages a reconsideration of existing genetic theories of his work. The "two" and "three *Moby-Dicks*" theories should be revised to include an understanding of Melville's commitment to the metaphysical narrative.[38] The hypothesis, posited by the editors of the Northwestern-Newberry edition, that "it seems likely that Melville started to write *Moby-Dick* on the pattern of his five earlier books, as a sailor-voyager's firsthand account of his experience and observation" seems unlikely, given the foregoing insights into Melville's growing allegiance to the metaphysical narrative.[39] Mixed form assumes as a basic premise that the "unnecessary duplicates" Hayford has conjectured regarding Melville's compositional method are actually necessary. They stress the varying perspectives that are essential to reading and comprehending the narrative form of *Moby-Dick*. Rather than "unintentional," "flawed," or "blurred," Melville's concept of narrative form in *Moby-Dick*, based on mixed form, helps us understand its intentionality and distinction in depicting the disparate segments of experience—or as Ishmael proclaims in *Moby-Dick*, the "separate citation of items" (203).[40] The suggestion by the Northwestern-Newberry editors that Melville built "better than he knew" (to borrow Emerson's phrase) should be reformulated to suggest that Melville built better than *we* knew.[41]

In our "national tale of questing," Melville explores the nature of whaling, whales, humankind, imagination, comprehension, existence, and the creative act of writing itself.[42] As in "The Doubloon," where it is not "commodity or materialism with which we conclude, but the very act of perception itself," as Bryan Wolf has remarked, *Moby-Dick* explores the act of perceiving the nature of the quest.[43]

This emphasis on perception induces modern readers to reconsider their own perception of *Moby-Dick*. Melville's orchestration of many forms liberates the novel from restrictive categories. Mixed form is an aesthetic foundation that stimulated the remarkable artistic creativity portrayed in *Moby-Dick*. The author's masterpiece simply reflects, and yet transcends, genre. In the hands of the author, the mixed form of *Moby-Dick* is a catalyst to this timely—and timeless—mixture.

CHAPTER SIX

(Un)Popularity: *Moby-Dick* and *Pierre*

Two MID-NINETEENTH-CENTURY critical debates that raged in British and American journals provide a central context for gauging the popularity of Melville's novels. During the antebellum period and particularly at midcentury, reviewers argued vehemently over the "proper" form of the novel. This critical debate, gone largely unnoticed by later scholars, is central to recovering the popularity in Melville's day of *Moby-Dick* and *Pierre, or, The Ambiguities.* As we have already discovered in assessing the reception of the earlier novels, especially *Typee* and *Omoo,* different readerships reacted strongly to the presence of certain forms and perspectives, and this is particularly true in the cases of *Moby-Dick* and *Pierre.* Like the responses to *Typee, Omoo,* and *Mardi,* which were decidedly mixed depending on whether readers perceived Melville to be following or challenging cherished conventions and themes, the reception of *Moby-Dick* and *Pierre* is more complex than previously thought. The author's use of specific narrative forms aligns him with particular sides of the debate and provides insight into the types of audiences that he intended for his two works. Our recovery of the heterogeneity of midcentury critical appraisals is contingent on placing the reviews of these individual works into their cultural and ideological contexts.

Mixed Form Novels and the Reception of *Moby-Dick*

Failure to recognize the split in critical appreciation between reviewers supportive, on the one hand, of realistic novels or, on the other, of metaphysical novels has distorted our understanding of the narrative form and the popularity of Melville's work in mid-nineteenth-century culture. Praise for the mixed form of the metaphysical novel depended mostly on the reviewer's literary allegiance. Those critics who approved of mixed form commended Melville's adherence to these conventions, as well as his contributions to narrative form. Yet the popularity of mixed form narratives depended substantially on critical approval. While reviewers readily acknowledged Melville's work as mixed form, they did not all approve. Those loyal to the realist tradition treated metaphysical narratives with disdain, despite the author's popularity. They condemned novels that did not utilize conventions of dramatic unity, a paradigm that informed the genre of realism. It was this aspect of a novel on which reviewers of realist fiction based their evaluations.

This overall critical split helps to explain the negative response that some literary masterpieces received. John Forster, a reviewer for the *London Examiner,* denounced *Wuthering Heights,* proclaiming it "a strange book . . . as a whole, it is wild, confused, disjointed, and improbable." He later found the "autobiographical form" of *David Copperfield* similarly disconcerting: "It admits of deeper insight into secret mental workings with less apparent violation of probability, but is apt to mislead into vague psychological wanderings, overstrained metaphysical niceties, and mawkish effusions of sentiment."[1] Attributes such as "disjointed" and "wandering," anathema to proponents of the realist school, were frequently used to describe and condemn metaphysical form.

Forster had no trouble aligning *Moby-Dick* with the class of mixed form novels, and in his review of Melville's work he stressed his contempt for the narrative method of metaphysical writers. In *Moby-Dick,* he asserted, "all the regular rules of narrative or story are spurned and set at defiance." In this context, Forster's criticisms reveal neither more nor less hostility toward Melville's work than the reviews displayed toward other novels that failed to conform to realist demands for a dramatic unity.[2]

The critical debate appeared in American literary circles, and some American reviews reflected Forster's opinions. In June 1849 the reviewer for *Holden's Dollar Magazine* denounced Cooper's *The Sea Lions* for the mixture of various genres "interwoven into" his tale of

the sea. E. P. Whipple in the *North American Review* faulted the
"heterogeneousness" of Bulwer-Lytton's *Harold, The Last of the Saxon Kings:*

> Fact and fiction are either placed side by side, or huddled
> together, instead of being fused into one consistent narrative.
> Harold, the Saxon King of history, and Harold, the hero of
> Bulwer Lytton's romance, so modify each other, that the result
> somewhat resembles Mrs. Malaprop's Cerberus,—he is "two
> gentlemen at once."[3]

Authors once praised were now being held up to different standards
of aesthetic accountability.

The debate on aesthetic form caused some reviewers to change
their critical allegiance toward authors whom they had previously
admired. This shift largely accounts for the mixed reception of *Moby-
Dick* in America. Evert Duyckinck, founder of the *Literary World* and
the man who had marketed the author to the cultivated New York
literati, once tolerated formal "experimentation." Though originally
noting "the *extreme* free style" of William Starbuck Mayo's *Kaloolah*,
he praised the work in a 23 June 1849 review. By 1850, however,
his reviews shifted toward a more conservative perspective in their
advocacy of a dramatic unity of form. In support of Mayo's *The
Berber*, he retracted his favorable opinion of the literary powers of
Kaloolah; instead he favored the more "traditional" realistic work,
The Berber:

> The present book is a much severer test of his powers than
> *Kaloolah*; there he had the field to himself, and was able to
> violate the unities *ad libitum*; but now that he has put him-
> self into the traces as a novelist of the orthodox and estab-
> lished school, he must, perforce, submit to all the rules and
> ordinances.[4]

Duyckinck's 1850 reviews of other metaphysical narratives indicate
this abrupt change. He found the mixed form of Kimball's *St. Leger*
perplexing: "It is not an essay, a metaphysical discussion, a love
story." With dramatic unity as his critical guide, he criticized the
novel: "As an entire work, it seems wanting in unity of design. Differ-

ent spirits animate various portions."[5] Moreover, he urged his favorite writers to alter their literary styles. In a private conversation with the author of the popular *Nile Notes of an Howadji*, Duyckinck warned Curtis that experimenting with formal unity was "dangerous," a term Duyckinck reiterated in his review of *Moby-Dick*.[6]

In the context of this growing disapproval of metaphysical novels, Duyckinck's discomfort with the mixed form of *Moby-Dick* becomes more meaningful: "A difficulty in the estimate of this, in common with one or two other of Mr. Melville's books, occurs from the double character under which they present themselves. In one light they are romantic fictions, in another statements of absolute fact."[7] A supporter of Melville's early works, especially *Redburn* and *White-Jacket*, Duyckinck treated the writer's metaphysical narrative with the same suspicion that he viewed other works within this genre.

Many prominent American journals and papers, however, avidly supported the metaphysical school of writing. The mixed form of the novel intrigued a reviewer in *Harper's*, who praised Hawthorne's *House of the Seven Gables* for its "skilful blending of the tragic and the comic . . . and deep vein of reflection."[8] The reviewer for the 15 November 1851 *Hartford Daily Courant* acknowledged that in *Moby-Dick* "there is the same want of unity of subject—of a regular beginning and end—of the form and shape of a well-built novel," a sufficient cause for condemnation by supporters of realistic writing. However, this "happy carelessness of style" distinguished it as "the most interesting and best told" of all Melville's works.

Moby-Dick received considerable acclaim for its interesting mixture; the mixed form absorbed reviewers, many of whom attempted to describe it to their readers. A London reviewer wrote:

> High philosophy, liberal feeling, abstruse metaphysics popularly phrased, soaring speculation, a style as many-colored as the theme, yet always good, and often admirable; fertile fancy, ingenious construction, playful learning, and an unusual power of enchaining the interest, and rising to the verge of the sublime, without overpassing the narrow boundary which plunges the ambitious penman into the ridiculous: all these . . . are exemplified in these volumes.[9]

Reviewers intrigued by the metaphysical narrative distinguished *Moby-Dick* as a unique mixture within that genre. The 14 November 1851 *Morning Courier and New York Enquirer* located the book's "bewitching" interest in the mixed form: "It is ostensibly taken up with whales and whalers, but a vast variety of characters and subjects figure in it; all set off with an artistic effect that irresistibly captivates the attention." "Who would have looked for philosophy in whales, or for poetry in blubber?" mused the reviewer in *John Bull,* 25 October 1851, noting a combination that placed the novel "far beyond the level of an ordinary work of fiction. . . . The author has succeeded in investing objects apparently the most unattractive with the most absorbing fascination." The 14 November 1851 *London Morning Post* reviewer described the "wild and wonderful fascination in the story against which no man may hope to secure himself," proclaiming *Moby-Dick* a "book of extraordinary merit . . . one of the cleverest, wittiest, and most amusing of modern books." Thus, reviewer allegiance to a particular belief in narrative form shaped not only their critical response to a given work but also helped to determine its reception by readers.

The French Sensational Romance and *Pierre; or, The Ambiguities*

Underestimating the role that the critical debates played in the popularity of a novel in mid-nineteenth-century America has distorted our ability to consider the question of Melville's popularity accurately. This is particularly true in the case of Melville's next work, *Pierre; or, The Ambiguities.* The case of *Pierre* is further complicated by the fact that Melville's ostensibly sentimental yet highly enigmatic work has suffered from misperceptions of the author's purpose by twentieth-century readers. Considered a "flawed grandeur," the novel is commonly viewed as Melville's failed attempt to attract female readers of the sentimental mode.[10] Contemporary reviews of the period, however, suggest that Melville targeted a much wider audience. These reviews indicate that Melville traded in the market for the general reader when he shaped *Pierre* in the form of the popular romance. Yet *Pierre* is no *sentimental* romance, or even a "permutated" Gothic romance, as some critics have posited.[11] The narrative form of this most misunderstood of Melville's novels, like *Moby-Dick* before it, mirrors a once highly controversial—and popular—genre in mid-nineteenth-century culture.[12]

The form of *Pierre* prompted Evert Duyckinck, among other reviewers, for the first time in Melville's literary career, to consider the author's work in the tradition established and popularized by the best-selling writers E.D.E.N. Southworth, Alice Cary, and Caroline Chesebro'—women authors whose fiction offered radical alternatives to socially prescribed gender roles.[13] Melville's contemporary reviewers argued that in *Pierre* (rather than in *Moby-Dick* as twentieth-century scholars have asserted), Melville "combined . . . the peculiarities of Hawthorne and Poe," a combination associated with the French sensational romance (*Graham's*, October 1852).

Melville's *Pierre* closely resembles French sensational fiction. This genre stood in stark contrast to literary forms demanded by cultivated readers which validated, rather than directly challenged, hegemonic perspectives. Writers such as Eugène Sue, Victor Hugo, and George Sand popularized the genre in France. Capitalizing on the French models, authors such as George Lippard, George Thompson, Joseph Holt Ingraham, Anna Sophia Stephens, Alice Cary, Caroline Chesebro', Osgood Bradbury, F. A. Durivage, and E. Z. C. Judson (also known as Ned Buntline), magazines such as *Holden's* and *Graham's*, and publishers such as Fredrick Gleason, Robert Bonner, Peterson and Graham, and Dewitt and Davenport popularized the sensational romance among a large variety of working-class and middle-class readers, audiences that Melville referred to as the "general tribe of readers."[14] This group of readers, as David S. Reynolds has demonstrated in *Beneath the American Renaissance*, rejected the conservative and self-congratulatory fiction favored by cultivated audiences. In fact, general readers preferred sensational fiction, which portrayed the elite, to borrow Melville's phrase, in "less exalted lights" and emphasized instead the humanity of the lower classes.[15]

These ideological complexities have been lost on twentieth-century readers when we view antebellum culture in hierarchical terms. In order to unravel the various ideological allegiances that much of antebellum fiction dramatizes, the modern reader requires a "clearer sense," as Hershel Parker and Brian Higgins have suggested, of the actual generic context from which complex novels like *Pierre* evolved.[16] Recovering the conventions of this lost but once popular form is essential to understanding Melville's intentions in this most popularly clothed and ideologically challenging of works.

The French Sensational Romance

Reviewers of the 1840s and 1850s praised, blasted, and defended the sensational romance. Cultivated reviewers strongly condemned the works of French sensational authors, notably Balzac, Hugo, Sue, de Kock, Sand, and Stendhal. Evert Duyckinck, a champion of "cultivated" literature, attributed the popularity of sensational romances to the genre's "morbid anatomy of the passions":

> The hidden workings of the impassioned heart, stung and tortured by ill-directed passions, long suppressed but never thoroughly subdued, and bursting forth at last only the more fiercely because of that long restraint, are laid bare with a terrible fidelity and force, which fixes and fascinates our unwilling interest. (*American Review,* March 1846)

Cultivated reviewers commonly referred to a stylistic "morbidity" when they criticized the sensational fiction of Poe, Hawthorne, Cary, Southworth, and Chesebro'. In his review of *The Scarlet Letter,* the respected literary critic Edwin P. Whipple complained of the "almost morbid intensity with which the characters are realized, and the consequent lack of sufficient geniality in the delineation" in Hawthorne's romance (*Graham's,* May 1850). George Ripley found that in *The Scarlet Letter,* Hawthorne "derives the same terrible excitement from these legendary horrors, as was drawn by Edgar Poe from the depths of his own dark and perilous imagination":

> He brings before us pictures of death-like, but strangely fascinating agony, which are described in the same minuteness of finish—the same slow and fatal accumulation of details—the same exquisite coolness of coloring, while everything creeps forward with irresistible certainty to a soul-harrowing climax —which made the last-named writer such a consummate mas-

ter of the horrible and infernal in fictitious composition. (*New York Tribune Supplement*, 1 April 1850)

This trait served as the literary trademark for a "school" of fictional style. In the *Literary World*, Duyckinck faulted Alice Cary's popular *Hagar: A Romance of Today* for its allegiance to the dark school of romantic fiction: "The story belongs to the sombre and somewhat morbid school of fiction, now apparently striving to become the literary fashion of the day" (18 September 1852, 185).

English reviewers detected in the works of American sensational romance writers a national fascination with darkness. Blaming French models, the reviewer for the *London Atlas* lamented:

> It is a melancholy sign for the prospects of a rising American literature that some of its most hopeful professors should have, in recent works of fiction, been evidently laying themselves out for that species of subtle psychological romance, first introduced to the reading public by such authors as Balzac and Sand. (December 1852)

American writers readily borrowed from the "French school." The sensational romance in the United States contained sentiment, sensation, horror, psychological aberrations, and the erotic:

> Mr. Nathaniel Hawthorne and some others of his country-men have adopted the style of a bastard French school, and set themselves to the analysis and dissection of diseased mind and unhealthy and distorted sentiment . . . and then proceed with the dryest minuteness to describe the pathology of the morbid structure, to trace and dissect the anatomy of the monstrous moral and intellectual abortion . . . to let us into the secret turnings and windings of unhealthy and abnormal power and promptings. (*London Atlas*, December 1852)

With the plethora of published romances in the United States, the notion of a distinctly American romance emerged after 1850, a phenomenon described by a leading British reviewer:

> There is such a genuine outcoming of the American intellect as can safely be called national . . . a wild and mystic love of the supersensual, peculiarly their own. To move a horror skillfully,

with something of the earnest faith in the Unseen, and with weird imagery to shape these phantasms so vividly that the most incredulous mind is hushed, absorbed ... to do this American literature is without a rival. What *romance* writer can be named with Hawthorne? Who knows the horrors of the sea like Melville? (*London Leader,* 8 November 1851)

While this notion of an American romance contradicts Nina Baym's suggestion regarding the blurred divisions between formulations of the romance and the novel, it demonstrates the importance for considering the different interests among the various readerships during the period.[17] In transforming their European sources, American romances clearly borrowed from the eroticism and sensationalism that characterized popular French fiction.

French sensational fiction patently appealed to the American general reader, an audience characterized as that "class of readers, those who have theories of seduction and adultery modeled after the French school of novelists" (*Literary World,* 30 March 1850, 323). This genre attracted such a wide readership in America that it made its way into even purportedly middle-class sentimental and "family circle" magazines, a phenomenon that demonstrates the importance for differentiating, as antebellum reviewers did, between different *classes* of readers during the period. With sections of these monthlies dedicated to French fashions, the latest French novels, and gossip of famous French personalities, the general reader received constant exposure to French popular culture in the pages of *Godey's Lady's Book, Peterson's, Graham's,* and *Holden's Dollar Magazine,* as well as in the myriad of working-class penny papers which some middle-class readers also purchased.[18]

Melville located *Pierre* within this pervasive fascination with French fiction and culture. He referred to the form of *Pierre* in a letter to his publisher as "a regular romance, with a mysterious plot to it, and stirring passions at work."[19] The term *romance* represented a large genre of novels that differed from the English novel of manners. This generic term commonly referred to those works that catered to the interests and demands of the more educated and cultivated classes of readers, and specifically to readers of sentimental or domestic romances.[20] The "regular romance" referred to here by Melville, however, is a more specifically defined set of conventions which, as a version of its French predecessor, appealed to the regular or general reader of this form—mainly working-class readers. By characterizing his new work with these key words, Melville linked *Pierre* to the French sensational romance, a genre that combined social analysis with sentiment, sensation, and erotic intrigue. Midcentury reviewers in tune with these conventions easily recognized Melville's intentions in *Pierre*.

Reading the French Sensational Romance in Pierre

Sentimental language, aristocratic, economically successful characters, and a domestic setting are essential elements in the French sensational romance. Frequently in French novels, the domesticity of Home provides a context for the sensational antidomestic events that occur by establishing an air of stylized respectability, one that the sensational rhetoric and themes of the novel undermine.[21] Stories depicting the downfall of the aristocracy attracted general readers, especially low wage-earners, whose lives bore little resemblance to those of the social elite. This conventional plot formed the basis of several popular French sensational romances written by Hugo, Sand, and Sue, authors avidly read by American working-class audiences as well as politically and socially perceptive readers from the middle class.[22]

In the opening pages of *Pierre*, Melville aligns his romance to French practice. The beginning establishes the ideals of tradition, love, and Home and provides a sentimental portrait of idyllic rural aristocratic life. During a "trance-like" morning in June, Pierre emerges from the traditional "embowered and high-gabled old home of his fathers" (3). Amid romantic scenery complete with "brindled kine, dreamily wandering to their pastures" (3), Pierre visits the cottage of his love. The description contains the symbols found in the conventional rural cottage scene, a common sentimental illustration of domesticity that was popular in general magazines:

> As . . . Pierre neared the cottage, and lifted his eyes, he swiftly
> paused, fixing his glance upon one upper, open casement

there. Why now this impassioned, youthful pause? Why this enkindled cheek and eye? Upon the sill of the casement, a snow-white glossy pillow reposes, and a trailing shrub has softly rested a rich, crimson flower against it (3–4).

Pierre responds to the vine-encrusted window, the flower, and the "snow-white" pillow with all of the ardor of the typical romantic hero. He speaks in noticeably unreal but "respectable" language that reinforces the conventionality of the novel:

Well mayst thou seek that pillow, thou odoriferous flower, thought Pierre; not an hour ago, her own cheek must have rested there. "Lucy!"
    "Pierre!" (4).

Plucking and fastening the flower to his coat, Pierre departs: "I must away now, Lucy; see! under these colors I march" (4). The scene closes with Pierre, and by implication the narrative, traveling under sentimental dress.

These elements were viewed by Melville's contemporaries as the props for a sensational plot, rather than the "failed" attempts at a sentimental domestic romance that modern scholars unfamiliar with this genre commonly attribute to the author of *Pierre*.[23] Antebellum reviewers knew what to expect: "A clash and a catastrophe are foreseen at the moment," as one critic aptly noted of the opening of *Pierre* (*New York Albion*, 21 August 1852).

Like the French sensational romance, Melville plants the seeds of destruction in the depiction of his aristocratic characters. The narrator firmly endows Pierre with an elite social standing:

In general terms we have been thus decided in asserting the great genealogical and real-estate dignity of some families in America, because in so doing we poetically establish the richly aristocratic condition of Master Pierre Glendinning, for whom we have before claimed some special family distinction. (12)

Acting according to the social "rules" of the aristocracy, Mrs. Glendinning, Pierre's mother, transacts most unsentimental dealings with her only son. She approves of Lucy Tartan as a suitable wife for her son primarily on economic and social, rather than emotional, grounds: "Lucy is a delicious girl; of honorable descent, a fortune, well-bred, and the very pattern of all that I think amiable and attractive in a girl of seventeen" (56).

Reviewers readily noted Melville's intentions here. Pierre comes "from the very highest aristocracy of the country, so high one hardly knows where to look for it," asserted the reviewer for the *Boston Daily Advertiser* (7 August 1852). The *New York Albion* came closest to recognizing Melville's purpose: "If they can't speak as such men and women would be likely to speak . . . the reader cannot sympathize with them" (21 August 1852). Indeed, the deliberate "poetic" creation of Pierre's aristocratic status is much like his "infelicities" of language —both are deliberately artificial constructions. True to the intentions of French sensationalist writers, Melville urges readers to question the worldviews of his primary characters. As a symbol of the landed gentry, Pierre gradually will come to challenge the positions of the aristocracy, and he will do so first through their very language.

Pierre does not rely on superficial forms alone, and his language offers much more than sentiment. He looks *inside* Lucy to discover a new universe of existence beyond the outward hegemonic conventions that she represents:

> Thou art my heaven, Lucy; and here I lie thy shepherd-king, watching for new eye-stars to rise in thee. Ha! I see Venus' transit now;—lo! a new planet there;—and behind all, an infinite starry nebulousness, as if thy being were backgrounded by some spangled vail of mystery. (36)

In turn, the narrator, like other narrators of French sensational romances, urges the reader to look *into* rather than *at* the scenes described. As idyllic love rapidly dissolves into sensationalized "profane" love (5), disillusionment and despair undermine the ideals of tradition, intimacy, and home established in the opening passages. The author's strategy here serves two important functions of the genre: it highlights the falseness of the aristocracy through their own sentimental language, and it consequently encourages the reader to look beyond the conventional sentiment articulated by the social elite.

To emphasize the artificiality of these aristocratic speakers, Melville

deliberately creates new linguistic combinations in *Pierre*. Evert Duyckinck, an outspoken critic of French sensational fiction, as we have
seen, listed in his *Literary World* review some of the "infelicities of
expression" appearing throughout *Pierre*. He found the combinations
"human*ness*, heroic*ness*, patriarchal*ness*, descended*ness*, flushful*ness*
. . . *et id genus omne*" especially distasteful and defiant of stylistic
conventions (21 August 1852). Some reviewers, however, understood
these intentionally created linguistic "infelicities." The *Springfield Republican* aptly characterized them as "genteel hifalutin, painful,
though ingenious involutions of language," the language of an imag-
ined upper class (16 August 1852). The general reader, well tuned to
this subversion of sentiment in the sensational romances of Lippard
and Thompson, among others, knew that people do not actually
speak in the manner represented in *Pierre*. It is, in other words, a
facade to be penetrated. Unnatural language reinforces the vulnera-
bility of its speakers, a strategy not recognized by readers unfamiliar
with the French genre.[24]

Linguistic irregularities signify flaws in the notions of respectability
the language represents. Interpersonal relations appear distorted and
disreputable, and Melville exploits the sensational interest in sensuality. Pierre's "terrible self-revelation" of his feelings for Isabel is fore-
shadowed in the eroticism underlying the relationship between Pierre
and his mother. Melville sets the stage by dramatizing the powerful emotional feelings between mother and son. Through playful
language, Pierre and his mother transform their conventional relationship into "courteous lover-like adoration" (16). For Mrs.
Glendinning, Pierre is "lover enough," . . . with the homage of Pierre
alone was she content" (5, 16). Through these characterizations, Melville clearly plays on a popular interest in erotic sensationalism. As
David Reynolds has painstakingly chronicled, eroticism and overt
sexuality were some of the most popular subjects in sensational
fiction.[25]

Although Pierre originally shares his mother's worldview, the narrator continually alerts the reader to Pierre's development in another
direction. Commenting on Pierre's aristocratic pride, the narrator
asserts, "Now Pierre stands on this noble pedestal; we shall see if he
keeps that fine footing; we shall see if fate hath not just a little bit of a

small word or two to say in this world" (12). Indeed, the narrator predicts a radically different worldview for his protagonist:

> . . . and if you tell me that this sort of thing in him showed him no sterling Democrat, . . . I beg you to consider again that this Pierre was but a youngster as yet. And believe me you will pronounce Pierre a thorough-going Democrat in time; perhaps a little too Radical altogether to your fancy. (13)

In creating this role for Pierre, Melville followed the established practice of the French sensational *des roman-feuilletons,* in which aristocratic heroes become social rebels, a pervasive theme in the works of Dumas *père,* Soulié, and Sue.[26] For readers of sensational fiction, Pierre's change in perspective represents the conventional social reversal that occurs in these romances. The rebels in the romances of Sue, Dumas, Soulié, and others create new laws by reformulating conventional practices so as to consider and serve the unfortunate masses of society. In the United States, this rebellious behavior becomes transmuted into what Reynolds calls radically subversive democratic fiction.

The appearance of Pierre's illegitimate sister, Isabel, prompts Pierre to adopt ethical rather than social and economic standards. During a discussion concerning the fate of the unmarried and pregnant Delly, Pierre shows concern for her welfare. While Mrs. Glendinning insists on banishing Delly and her expected child, Pierre raises ethical considerations regarding the treatment of illegitimate children: " 'Since we seem to have been strangely drawn into the ethical aspect of this melancholy matter,' said he, 'suppose we go further in it; and let me ask, how it should be between the legitimate and the illegitimate child—children of one father—when they shall have passed their childhood?' " (101).

Furthermore, Pierre resolves to help his sister and rescue her "from her captivity of world-wide abandonment" (105). In doing so, however, he must act against the code of behavior his social and economic status prescribes. He must disavow Mother, Home, love, and social position. With this determination to choose his sister over these social institutions comes the understanding that "in the Enthusiast to Duty, the heaven-begotten Christ is born; and will not own a mortal parent, and spurns and rends all mortal bonds" (106). Pierre discovers that "all common conventional regardings—his hereditary duty to his mother, his pledged worldly faith and honor to the hand and seal of his affianced" were "thinner and more impalpable than airiest threads of gauze" (106). This ideological shift spells disaster in the social worlds of sensational literature. Pierre's decision to employ ethical, rather than socioeconomic criteria in guiding his interactions connects him strongly to the French tradition.

Male characters do not traditionally behave this way in the realistic novel of manners, a genre popular with cultivated readers. In such works, the kind of allegiance that Pierre first represents is reserved for female characters. The sentimental heroine sacrifices her rights to property, family title, inheritance, and security to act on virtuous principles. Aristocratic males, however, do not typically relinquish their family, possessions, and social rank for philosophical and ethical beliefs. Common in sensational fiction, such characters are unusual in cultivated fiction because they conventionally represent societal values instead of challenging them. In celebrating characters from the lower classes, sensational novels do not support the traditional social divisions loyally represented in cultivated fiction.[27]

Melville's treatment of the incest theme represents his most deliberate use of sensational conventions. While partially biographical, the sources for the incestuous desires between Pierre and Isabel can be traced to a variety of popular influences. Melville alludes in *Pierre* to classical instances of incest, yet he also found accounts of tales of incest in both the sensational romances of the day and in the popular magazines for the general reader.[28]

Melville clearly links Pierre's erotic attraction to his mother to his fatal attachment to Isabel. With the pledge to support Isabel, Pierre unconsciously transfers his erotic feelings for his mother to his new-found sister. He felt "an extraordinary physical magnetism" in Isabel that "seemed irresistibly to draw him toward" her. Through his "still imperfectly conscious, incipient, new-mingled emotion" for Isabel (206), Pierre discovers erotic elements in the sibling relation: "For surely a gentle sister is the second best gift to a man; and it is first in point of occurrence; for the wife comes after. He who is sisterless, is as a bachelor before his time. For much that goes to make up the deliciousness of a wife, already lies in the sister" (7).

Like the power of the intimate bond between husband and wife, Pierre "felt a still more marvelous power" in Isabel over "himself and his most interior thoughts and motions" (151). When he suggests to Isabel that they live nominally as husband and wife, Isabel reacts with "an inexpressible strangeness of an intense love, new and inexplicable." Pierre reciprocates the feelings; upon a "terrible self-revelation, he imprinted burning kisses upon her; pressed hard her hand; would not let go her sweet and awful passiveness" (192). In a climactic moment of insight, Pierre consciously acknowledges that sensual and erotic motivations contributed to his virtuous action and support of his sister:

> "Ye heavens, that have hidden yourselves in the black hood of the night, I call to ye! If to follow Virtue to her uttermost vista, where common souls never go; if by that I take hold on hell, and the uttermost virtue, after all, prove but a betraying pander to the monstrousest vice,—then close in and crush me, ye stony walls, and into one gulf let all things tumble together! (273).

Pierre cannot segregate his erotic feelings for his sister from virtuous sibling behavior. Though "never would he be able to embrace Isabel with the mere brotherly embrace," Pierre cannot act out his sexual feelings for her. The erotic bond underlying their attraction for each other cannot be realized according to conventional moral codes. Since "Fate had separated the brother and sister, till to each other they somehow seemed so not at all" (142), their unquestionable attraction for each other cannot even be sublimated by normal sibling affection. When Isabel asks why they cannot realize their love for each other, Pierre replies, "It is the law" (274). Pierre knows that he should not go beyond unalterable moral codes, but the implication exists that he does indeed violate this moral code.

From the moment of Pierre's self-revelation in the novel, *Pierre* serves as a Pilgrim's regress rather than progress. Melville depicts the psychic disintegration that occurs in Pierre as he struggles to confront the implications of his actions. Pierre's comprehension of the awfulness of his incestuous desire is so psychologically terrifying that the hero becomes transformed into an antihero and seeks self-destruction. He dies a madman, a murderer, and a suicide.

This disrobing of Pierre's psyche, the minute depiction of his disintegration, represents one of the marked conventions of the sensational romance. As Duyckinck noted in his article on French sensational romances, this "literature of desperation" depicts the "morbid anatomy of the passions." Although Duyckinck embeds his description of the plot of Victor Hugo's *Notre Dame de Paris* with a moral that may not actually represent Hugo's intentions, this description could also easily characterize Melville's *Pierre:*

> The gradual steps by which the stern and solitary priest is forced down into the abysses of crime and wretchedness, his desperate struggles to arrest his own descent, and his final fall, are all portrayed with a gloomy depth of coloring.... The scene, too, in the condemned cell ... when, the priest, goaded by the double pangs of passion and remorse, offers to sacrifice all his eternal and temporal hopes to secure her love ... his broken ejaculations ... his wild confession, his terrible appeals, like the pleading of a lost soul. (*American Review,* March 1846)

Such bleak endings close the sensational romances of many a popular writer including Melville. Hugo's hero dies a murderer and madman; Stendhal's hero of *Le Rouge et le noir* commits suicide in jail after having attempted murder; Sue's romances end with the deaths of heroes and heroines "stacked up in funereal heaps."[29] The hero of French novels, in contrast to popular English novels of the period, rejects the socioeconomic values of society and either dies or retreats.[30]

The last scene of *Pierre,* though replete with Shakespearean tragic conventions, lacks the hopeful reconciliations that Shakespeare's tragedies usually offer. The prison, the death of these young lovers, and the presence of outside observers all significantly recall images, characters, and events from Shakespearean tragedies, as many have noted.[31] But Shakespeare treats deaths as significant acts. They imply a possibility of retribution and a recovery from the imbalance that caused the tragedies to occur. In Melville's work no such hope is offered to the reader. The author focuses on the unnecessary deaths of three young people. Despite their commitment to virtue, nobility, and innocence, Pierre, Isabel, and Lucy do not survive. They never learn the survival tactics of assimilation that Hawthorne's characters, for example, adopt. The world in *Pierre* appears bleak and hopeless.

It is essential to note that in these French sensational romances—and, one may argue, in Melville's *Pierre*—it is society, not the individual, who is condemned for these deaths. The values on which society creates its identity are inimical to the dignity, concern, and ideals that many French heroes and Pierre evince. These novels present an analysis of a society that cannot and will not tolerate remodeling of its basic, socioeconomic framework, a framework that directly opposes the ideologies of the heroes.[32]

The Reception of Pierre

Contrary to modern assumptions, Melville's attempt to write a romance did not speed *Pierre's* demise among his readers. Antebellum reviewers readily acknowledged the form of Melville's romance; in fact, the romance represented one of the most widely read genres in the early 1850s. As a more popular form than the novel, the romance attracted American writers who were interested in expanding their readerships. In the preface to the 1853 revised edition of *The Yemassee*, for example, William Gilmore Simms described his work as a romance in an effort to gain a wide following for his work.[33] As Nina Baym has suggested, this interest in the general reader and the form of the romance may account for Hawthorne's famous distinction between the novel and the romance in his preface to *The House of the Seven Gables* and his alignment with the more popular form.[34]

Pierre contains the conventions found in the regular romances of the day. Its domestic setting, aristocratic characters, sentimental language, and erotic intrigue met the demands of the form for a mixture of sensation, sentiment, and adventure. Reviewers frequently referred to Melville's attempt to write in a popular vein. The *Boston Daily Evening Transcript* noted that *Pierre* was "a regular story of life and love and tragic personal adventure." The *New York Albion* recognized Melville's use of conventional heroes and heroines of romance: "Pierre is gifted with all those graces of person and mind that are usually found in heroes of romance . . . Lucy is a very charming Lucy, of course, but not differing much from some scores of Lucies in your book acquaintance, if it be extensive." The *Baltimore American and Commercial Daily Advertiser* reiterated Melville's own description of his novel by referring to *Pierre* as "a regular romance of love and its dangers and difficulties, and of bold and successful daring."[35]

These reviews indicate that Melville's understanding of this genre reflected popular formulations of the time. Attestations that Melville could not write a domestic romance merely corroborate mistaken notions of Melville's reputed remoteness from his culture, an isolation that is clearly unfounded, judging by these reviews.

Critics also noted Melville's artistic achievement in *Pierre*. The *Morning Courier and New York Enquirer* proclaimed that "passages in this book absolutely glitter with genius . . . nothing but the most extraordinary skill could execute." The *Spirit of the Times* lauded Melville's artistry, proclaiming that *Pierre* "outstrips all his former productions, and is quite equal to *Moby-Dick, or the Whale.*" *Graham's* went the furthest in its praise of *Pierre* by stating that "none of Mr. Melville's novels equals the force and subtlety and unity of purpose."[36]

Some reviewers located the artistry of *Pierre* in its style. While more artistic and literary, this newly developed style in fact marred Melville's chance for popularity. The *Springfield Republican* addressed this issue in its review of *Pierre:* "Mr. Melville has changed his style entirely . . . while the new Melville displays more subtleness of thought, more elaborateness of manner, and a higher range of imagination, he has done it at a sad sacrifice of simplicity and popular appreciation" (16 August 1852). It is precisely this combination of elements that accounts for the negative reception of *Pierre*.

Melville combines the conventions of sensationalism with his insights in a manner that uncomfortably challenged cultivated American readers. While some reviewers acknowledged Melville's "depth, passion, even genius" in *Pierre,* many found his particular blend of ethical, social, and psychological perspectives intolerable.[37] His insights into the civilized hypocrisies of society and the politics of gender expressed in the rhetoric of sensational fiction made *Pierre* almost too psychological—even too domestic—for the majority of readers and reviewers of the book.

Melville's rejection of social and moral codes seemed illogical and belligerently defiant to cultivated middle-class America. Some reviewers disapproved of Melville's deliberate allegiance to French sensationalism. "Reader," argued the *New York Albion* reviewer, "we have not been sketching a Porte St. Martin tragedy, but condensing the newest work of one of our favorite novelists" (21 August 1852). This reviewer, and reviewers in general, criticized the highly rhetorical strategies Melville employed in *Pierre*: "He drags in a bit of episodical and gratuitous seduction. . . . Would that Mr. Melville had hit upon a less Frenchified mode of carrying us through the one and bringing about the other!" The moral ambiguities concerning Pierre's inner motivations prompted critics to view *Pierre* as a too provocative example of the sensational romance.

The suggestion of deliberate, conscious, incestuous desires horrified cultivated reviewers, who felt their role was to "elevate" the tastes of their readers, a role frequently asserted throughout reviews of the period. To these critics, Melville's romance was as "horrible in its tendency as Shelley's Cenci" (*American Whig Review,* November 1852). Relationships bordering on the incestuous formed parts of the plots of some successful novels, notably Catharine Sedgwick's *Hope Leslie* and, in the year prior to the publication of Melville's *Pierre,* Susan Warner's *The Wide, Wide World.* However, it was Melville's presentation of this theme—his strategy of deliberately identifying as incestuous the relation between the otherwise virtuous siblings—that caused the critical uproar over *Pierre.* By forcing the reader to consider male protectionism of sisters and the larger issue of patriarchal dominance in an incestuous light, Melville provided unwanted insight into the psychological motivations behind patriarchal proprietary acts—behavior, we must remember, that still regulated gender relations in antebellum America. Although the "immoral *moral* of the story" reflected a theme common to many sensational and sentimental works, these reviewers condemned what they saw as the theme of

Pierre, that is, the "impractibility of virtue" (*Literary World,* 21 August 1852). Such immorality, they argued, struck "at the very foundations of society" and "every principle of virtue" (*American Whig Review,* November 1852), acts that negated their own status as literary and cultural ambassadors.

These reviewers considered the French influence inimical to their roles and thus dangerous to the reading public. To them, Melville seems to embrace attitudes of the French and previous Gothic writers who "appear to be totally unconscious of any morality at all" (*American Review,* March 1845): "The author has dressed up and exhibited in Berkshire, some of the ancient and most repulsive inventions of the George Walker and Anne Radcliffe sort—desperate passion at first sight, for a young woman who turns out to be the hero's sister, &c.& c.&c." (*New York Herald,* 29 July 1852). Reviewers blasted *Pierre* for its immoral implications. They condemned the novel for its "unhealthy" spirit (*Church's Bizarre for Fireside and Wayside,* 21 August 1852). "The whole *tone* of the work, from beginning to end," remarked the *New York Evening Mirror,* "is morbid and unnatural" (27 August 1852). Melville's analysis of the primal bonds between parents and children and siblings was almost too close to home for most reviewers: "We cannot pass without remark, the supersensuousness with which the holy relations of the family are described. Mother and son, brother and sister are sacred facts not to be disturbed by any sacrilegious speculations" (*Literary World,* 21 August 1852). For these cultivated reviewers, who had hoped Melville's work would elevate rather than corroborate what they considered the poor aesthetic tastes of readers, the pervasive French sensational plots, characters, and themes spelled disaster for *Pierre.*

Although some reviewers condemned the "morbid style" of *The Scarlet Letter, The House of the Seven Gables,* and *The Blithedale Romance,* Hawthorne's romances achieved popular acclaim. Likewise, the sensational romances of E.D.E.N. Southworth, Alice Cary, Ann Marsh, Caroline Chesebro', and Anna Sophia Stephens were also positively received. While Melville sought this popularity, he did not achieve it with *Pierre.*

By not compromising his allegiance to popular sensational forms in an attempt to assuage, Melville adopted a stance radically different from Hawthorne and other writers praised by cultivated reviewers. In its representation of an adulterous relation between two individuals, *The Scarlet Letter* ostensibly aligned itself with the French school. However, cultivated American reviewers did not compare Hawthorne's romance, as they did *Pierre,* to French sensationalism. In fact, they commended Hawthorne for "handling this delicate subject without an infusion of George Sand." [38] Despite its forbidden topic of adultery, *The Scarlet Letter* avoids "fever and prurient excitement"; no other romance writer, asserted Henry Fothergill Chorley of the *London Athenaeum,* has treated this subject "with a loftier severity, purity, and sympathy" than Hawthorne in *The Scarlet Letter.*[39] New England reviewers treated the French subject of that novel at the level of instruction rather than sensation:

> The volume may afford matter for very instructive and edifying contemplation; for, in truth, Hawthorne, in *The Scarlet Letter,* has undermined the whole philosophy on which the French school rests, by seeing farther and deeper into the essence both of conventional and natural laws; and he has given the results of his insight, not in disquisitions and criticisms, but in representations more powerful than even those of Sue, Dumas, or George Sand.[40]

Hawthorne displays an ambivalence toward his heroine, exemplified in the contrasting views of Hester in "Hester at her Needle," and the subsequent chapter, "Another View of Hester," that cultivated reviewers could not find in *Pierre.*[41] Moreover, Hawthorne presents a heroine who actually repents her behavior and chooses to live according to the dictates of society.

Whereas Melville depicts Pierre as rebellious to the end against societal strictures that have allowed the protagonist's disintegration to occur, Hawthorne offers the reader a respite from the immorality of adultery. He presents a repentant Hester who returns to the society of her crime and transforms herself from an infamous exemplar into a societal pillar. While Hester shifts roles from adulterer to angel, Pierre dies still unknown by the society that has contributed to his tragic outcome. By reconciling his heroine to society, Hawthorne links popular forms with cultivated tastes. Melville offers no cultivated antidote to Pierre's carnal desire for his sister and the erotic feelings expressed between mother and son. In addition, Hester's adultery precedes the action of Hawthorne's story; it takes place not only offstage, but before the curtain has gone up. Pierre's transformation occurs on center stage and is a drama that draws the reader inevitably into its intensity. Rather than present the conventional remorse a responsible character like Pierre should evince, Melville becomes even more rebellious and portrays a character who breaks all codes of conduct, who becomes insane and murders. By relying almost exclusively on popular forms and French influences, he repels the very critical mouths that had once fed him.

This dark portrayal of Pierre's transformation from an upright member of the aristocracy into a crazed psychotic overwhelmed reviewers who expected to find at the novel's end a redeeming light and confirmation of society, an essential ingredient of the conventional romance. One reviewer described this sense of unrelenting doom in *Pierre:* "We close the volume with something of the feeling, and just about as much benefit as we experience on awakening from a horrid fit of the nightmare." [42] The *Southern Literary Messenger* placed *Pierre* within this "morbid" school of fiction: "In its 'shocking department' we have 'supped full of horrors.' " [43] Melville creates an unmitigated sense, argued one reviewer, of "accumulated misery that overwhelms every character in the tragedy. Insanity, murder and despair sweep their Tartarean shadows over the scene." [44] This hopeless despair accounts for the difference in reception between the conventional sensational romance and *Pierre*. The "blackness of darkness" of Melville's romance was too dark for these reviewers.

Melville's New Audiences in Pierre

The question becomes why Melville would employ a form that he readily knew was condemned by cultivated reviewers. The author seemed to have anticipated a hostile reaction from his cultivated readers and reviewers who would expect a final reconciliation of the hero with society. In fact, he tried unsuccessfully, to market his romance in the tradition of the popular sensational romances of Lippard and Thompson. George Lippard had published his best-seller

Quaker City: A Romance of Philadelphia Life, Mystery, and Crime anonymously, which was the convention among many popular writers of sensational fiction. George Thompson, whose romances Melville drew on as inspiration for *Pierre*, published either anonymously or under the pseudonym Greenhorn.

Melville appears to have aligned himself to sensational practice in his request to his English publisher, Richard Bentley, who published works for both cultivated and mass audiences. The author suggested that Bentley should alter the form of publication for *Pierre:* "It might not prove unadvisable to publish this present book anonymously, or under an assumed name:—*'By a Vermonter',* say . . . or *'By Guy Winthrop'* " (*Correspondence,* 228). This request marks a distinct move away from the publication formats of his earlier novels. His works traditionally were published in expensively bound forms that catered to the more wealthy group of cultivated readers and were thus too expensive for mass readers, especially those from the working class. Yet the genre that Melville adopts in *Pierre,* coupled with his shift toward writing for popular periodicals, indicates new literary interests.

Melville's letter to his publisher regarding an alternate mode of publishing seems consistent with his use of the different genre of the sensational romance in *Pierre* and suggests a new audience for this most ideologically challenging of works. Yet his request went unheeded. Bentley, who published several sensational romances, apparently did not consider Melville's work for a mass audience. In fact, he never published *Pierre* because he wanted to alter it radically to suit the tastes of his cultivated readers. Although Harper Brothers published cheap novels ($0.25 and $0.37) for a general audience, they relied on Melville's previous reputation and produced *Pierre* in an expensive form ($1.25 muslin, $1.00 paper) purchased mainly by wealthier readers. As a work that did not compromise its condemnation of societal structures in order to assuage cultivated readers, and which clashed severely with existing conventions demanded by this audience, *Pierre* came to represent for its cultivated audience all that was immoral, asocial, anarchical, and dangerous in popular literature.

In his writing and the subsequent reception of *Pierre* Melville experienced the consciously widening gulf between cultivated and mass audiences, a process which Lawrence W. Levine has recently described as the "sacralization of American culture."[45] During the early 1850s—a period that marked the creation of what we now call the best seller—cultivated reviewers struggled and failed to "elevate" the tastes of readers. Aesthetic statesmen could not tolerate such ideological darkness and such defiant censure of a culture that they tried so determinedly to save from feared populist control. In this battlefield *Pierre*'s French armor only guaranteed its defeat.

Melville's conscious use of the popular genre of the French sensational romance as the narrative form of *Pierre* indicates his widening interest in new audiences. Knowing all too well the problems of audience associated with writing in a style unacceptable to his cultivated readers, Melville portrays with *Pierre* an author not satisfied with economic recompense and a careful attendance to the limited tastes of his previous readers. In fact, *Pierre* is yet another example of the author's almost restless need to move to other forms.

That Melville did indeed conceive of his intended audience in wider terms than before and that he was considered a "popular," though not always a "good," writer is attested to by his reception as a magazinist—and one of the more popular at that. Melville's literary direction in the 1850s indicates an author moving to new audiences, to new forms, and ultimately to a new understanding of the role between popular forms and creativity. In what have been often considered his most clear attempts at writing to satisfy an audience, Melville's short fiction works also indicate an author firmly in control of his materials, an author who creates new, exciting ways to innovate on popular practice—in short, an author who creates an equilibrium between conventions and creativity.

PART THREE

The Periodical Marketplace

CHAPTER SEVEN

Marketplace Conditions

ADVOCATES OF THE subversion model of criticism suggest that "classic" writers—intolerant and disdainful of "popular" practice—employed subversive tactics in their fiction which largely escaped the notice of their publishers, editors (many of whom were themselves authors), and even readers. Indeed, the artistry that emerges in the fiction of antebellum—particularly "classic"—writers results from, so the argument goes, their deliberate strategies of subverting popular conventions. Perhaps no "classic" writer holds more prestige as one who resisted popular practice than Melville. According to a variety of critics, the author is said to have "revolted against his readers," "quarreled with fiction," dug "beneath" and "gone under" forms dictated by a marketplace necessity.[1]

One problem with these assessments is that they posit a bifurcated, hierarchical view of antebellum literary culture, a formulation that reflects modern cultural structures more than it does the actual situation in mid-nineteenth-century America. Nina Baym, Lawrence Buell, Cathy Davidson, Lawrence Levine, David Reynolds, Jane Tompkins, and Ronald Zboray, among others, have initiated the immense project of recovering the heterogeneity of literary forms, reading habits, and audiences that help to characterize popular antebellum culture.[2] The necessity for acknowledging this diversity is integrally linked to the contrasting styles found in magazines of the period. The heterogeneity of periodical production enabled writers to choose which magazines most closely fit their own interests. Magazinists, therefore, could easily match their works to fit editorial policies and reader expectations.

The Periodical Marketplace

Recent interest in recovering the conditions of the literary market-place in mid-nineteenth-century America has focused almost exclusively on matters of book production. But the novel was not the most popular literary form of the day. As readers turned to literary magazines, periodical literature increasingly dominated the market. By 1840, a year that produced approximately forty new novels, the existence of more than fifteen hundred periodicals provided a significantly more extensive reading environment.[3]

With the magazine fervor of the 1840s and 1850s, cultivated many readers thought of periodical literature as a useless genre. Because magazines "are filled with made-up stories . . . no better than so many lies," argues a character in a *Godey's* story of 1853, "it's bad enough to read them, much worse to write them."[4] Parke Godwin, an associate editor of *Putnam's Monthly,* described the low status of American periodicals at midcentury: "We possessed some ponderous quarter-lies, like the *North American Review,* and others, mainly organs of religious denominations, but the magazine proper had scarcely risen beyond the second story back of the milliner shops."[5] As late as 1856, when Herman Melville published *The Piazza Tales,* the reviewer for the *New York Daily Times* admonished the author for writing this collection of magazine pieces. He proclaimed that "the author of *Typee* should do something higher and better than Magazine articles."[6]

Other readers, however, viewed periodical writing as a challenging new genre. Stressing its professionalism, the author of "Writing for Periodicals," published in the *North British Review,* proclaimed that magazine literature comes "by art, not by chance": "We think it only fair that professional authors should have the credit of being able to do what other people can not."[7] Like other readers of the period, George William Curtis, a popular author and editor of *Putnam's Monthly,* considered "magazinish" writing a reputable and serious literary form. Reviewing potential contributions for *Putnam's,* Curtis highly praised a story by Herman Melville that he particularly enjoyed by calling it "thoroughly magazinish," and it was subsequently published in the monthly.[8] The editors of *Harper's* went further in their praise of periodical literature and asserted that magazines contain "the ablest and the best of the great writers' productions": "A devotion to periodical writing is rapidly increasing . . . the wealth and freshness of the nineteenth-century are embodied in the pages of the Periodicals." [9] Even critics who believed in literature as an instructional and moral agent considered the short story a "more attractive medium" than the essay "to impress . . . the lessons of morality and virtue." [10]

Readers certainly turned to the monthlies. Examining the reasons for the sudden surge in periodical readership during the 1840s, William Kirkland, a literary critic of the day, explained:

> Though but a small part of what is *published* they [monthlies] constitute much of what is *read*. A large percentage of books published scarce finds a purchaser; numbers of those purchased are never read and many that *are* read, are read by one or two persons, while with periodicals the *un*-read are the exception. One has but to look into circulating libraries, reading-rooms and the like places to see that an extensive class of readers finds time or inclination for little else. [11]

This "extensive class" radically altered the literary marketplace through its increasing demand for magazine literature.

Eager for contributions from popular authors, magazines provided writers with ready outlets for their work. After nearly two decades of writing books, Washington Irving shifted over to periodicals in 1839, with this explanation:

> I am tired of writing volumes: they do not afford exactly the relief I require; there is too much preparation, arrangement, and parade in this set of coming before the public. . . . I have thought therefore, of securing myself a snug little corner in some periodical work, where I might, as it were, loll at my ease in an elbow chair, and chat sociably with the public. [12]

During the 1840s and 1850s, prominent writers such as Caroline Chesebro' (Maria Jane McIntosh), Fanny Fern (Sara Payson Willis Parton), Fanny Forrester (Emily Chubbuck Judson), Nathaniel Hawthorne, Caroline Lee Hentz, Herman Melville, Edgar Allan Poe, Catharine Sedgwick, Elizabeth Barstow Stoddard, Harriet Beecher Stowe,

E.D.E.N. Southworth, Walt Whitman, and N. P. Willis established their careers by contributing to magazines.

Many writers found the periodical marketplace more critically receptive and economically rewarding than the book market. In a period when the annual income of many popular authors amounted usually to no more than between five hundred and sixteen hundred dollars, *Godey's Lady's Book,* in its first few years, paid the popular Lydia Sigourney five hundred dollars yearly—over two hundred dollars more than the average annual wage for skilled workers—just to add her name to its list of contributors, without her actually writing anything.[13] In the 1850s, Robert Bonner, founder of the *New York Ledger,* revolutionized the salaries of magazine writers. He boasted in his paper that he paid the popular Fanny Fern "by far the highest price that has ever been paid by any newspaper publisher to any author": one hundred dollars per column and, in the case of Fern's first serialized novel in the paper, one thousand dollars a story.[14]

Yet as Irving pointed out, writing for the magazines differed significantly from writing to meet the demands of book publishers. Despite the existence of a "literary economics" which helped to shape the conditions of the book marketplace, authors experienced a great leeway in writing novels.[15] With the notable exception of John Murray, who insisted on "factual" works, houses on both sides of the Atlantic published a wide range of books and thus did not usually restrict their authors to a particular genre.[16] When Harper Brothers learned that the popular young author of *Typee* had a second manuscript, for example, Fletcher Harper instructed his employees to "take it at once" sight unseen, and this publisher accepted other manuscripts by Melville without having read them.[17] As long as a writer maintained his or her celebrity, publishers tolerated innovation. This freedom accounts for the "experimenting," as it was termed by various reviewers of the day, in different genres which many of these writers, such as Herman Melville, were so fond of doing.[18]

Magazine writing, on the other hand, required a different kind of rigor. Periodicals aimed at audiences with specific demographic characteristics and tailored their editorial policies to satisfy their targeted readers. Due to stiff competition, periodical publishers attempted to capitalize on the uniqueness of their magazines. Thus, in the 1840s a given reader would turn to *Godey's Lady's Book* for both adventure and domestic stories, to the *Democratic Review* or the *American Review* for political and analytical essays, to the *North American Review* or the *Literary World* for literary discussions, and to *Graham's* for literary and "family circle" reading.

The varied environment of the periodical marketplace provides poorly tapped—though rich—interpretive possibilities. The contrasting magazine policies and literary practices of particular journals produced a heterogeneity of outlets that encouraged creativity in individual writers. The intellectual rigor and critical analysis of a magazine like the *Democratic Review,* for example, spurred Hawthorne to produce some of his best work of the decade in its pages. Likewise, the mixture of reason and sensation in *Graham's* reflects the bivalency that marks Poe's best short fiction.

The different styles and practices in particular magazines which catered almost exclusively to the interests of middle-class audiences in antebellum America suggest a heterogeneity of literary practices and reading interests within even one stratum of this literary culture. This heterogeneity is marked more by specific conditions of production, such as established magazine styles, than by gender, as some scholars have proposed. Individual magazines provided a common environment for both male and female contributors.

The literary environments in which Poe, Hawthorne, and Melville participated have been largely overlooked. As a result, we have few studies that connect the writing strategies of these "classic" authors to the writings of fellow contributors and editorial policies, yet the magazine context can serve as an important tool in gauging the creativity of these "classic" writers. If periodicals marketed themselves through a particular policy, and writers had choices regarding where they published, authors either published stories to fit specific magazine policies or published in magazines that mirrored their own interests. In both cases, the periodical outlet provides interpretive contexts that contain insightful means through which to examine the place, stance, methods, and achievement of given authors and to reconfigure their magazine works alongside their female contemporaries.

Godey's Lady's Book

The pages of *Godey's Lady's Book* provide an incisive example of how the magazine environment linked the writings of "classic" male and "popular" female authors. Writers as seemingly different as Catharine Sedgwick, Edgar Allan Poe, Elizabeth F. Ellet, and Nathaniel Hawthorne all published in the pages of *Godey's,* and their fiction varies considerably from the stories that they each published in other journals, such as *Graham's.* Their submissions reflect a distinct *Godey's* style.

Godey's Lady's Book is usually cast as a sentimental women's magazine, a characterization that obtains from the title *Lady's Book.* In combing through a random volume from 1844, the same year *Gody's* published stories by Poe and Hawthorne, I count at least a half-dozen references in the "Editor's Table" to "moral literature." Literary historians typically equate the genre of the moral tale with a sentimental style and further link this style to the interests of a female-only audience. Such characterizations, however, have been used to diminish the actual range of the literature published in the magazine. To recover the creative applications of the moral tale that constituted the *Godey's* style, we must investigate the relation of an editorial policy that Sarah Josepha Hale described as "the advancement of sound literature and good morals" with the deliberately antisentimental and strongly sensational style of stories such as Poe's "The Cask of Amontillado" and "The Oblong Box" published in the pages of *Godey's.* Were these tales merely anomalies in a magazine that supposedly, according to the historian Frank Luther Mott, "never admitted anything to the pages of the *Lady's Book* that was not as pure as the driven snow"?[19] In answering this question, we may recover the stylistic and ideological links between male and female writing published in its pages.

Despite its title, *Godey's Lady's Book* appealed to male as well as to female readers. Herman Melville was known to read issues of his wife's (or perhaps his own) subscription, while the magazine found eager readers in the "subscription clubs" started by soldiers on the front lines in the Civil War. Some of the major "classic" American writers, together with other, male authors of the day, contributed to the magazine. The narrative strategies and forms that writers like Poe and Hawthorne employed in their *Godey's* fiction find their sources, among other places, in the writing practices of the magazine's female contributors.

Miscellaneous in nature, *Godey's* contained stories, essays, travel accounts, poetry, and reviews by the greatest and most popular male and female American authors. The subject matter of *Godey's* stories include art, sea life, immigrants, family life, and the social elite. A look through its pages reveals styles and narrative forms employed across genderlines.

Certainly readers looked to *Godey's* for what the editors called the "moral tale," but this genre assumed a variety of forms in the pages of the magazine. This diversity appealed to a growing general readership who seemed to be characterized, in the words of one antebellum critic, by a "lack of patience for investigation, and a longing after variety." [20]

In *Godey's,* the moral tale, written by both men and women, is frequently shaped by the conventions of domestic fiction and a sentimental style, which have been described elsewhere by Nina Baym, Mary Kelley, and Susan Harris. Yet the moral tale obtains well beyond the parameters of domestic fiction and the sentimental mode. Borrowing elements and forms from working-class literature, writers of the moral tale in *Godey's* also employ the form of adventure stories about characters of reputable social standing, and they often describe the sensational adventures of artists, writers, and other professionals. These stories mainly focused on action, mystery, and intrigue in exotic settings, usually European cities, and, like domestic fiction, were written by both male and female writers. Tales here appealed to the emotions through an emphasis on sensational elements.

These *Godey's* stories typically open in one of two ways. Many authors state the moral or theme of the tale at the outset. Catharine Sedgwick, one of the most popular female writers whose stories fit magazine policies, exemplifies this practice in her 1845 story "Fanny McDermot":

Invention need not be traced for incidents fitted to touch the heart, nor need they be heightened with the dyes of romance. The daily life of our own cities abounds in events over which, if there be tears in heaven, surely the angels weep. But it is not to draw tears which flow too easily from susceptible young readers that the following circumstances are related, but to set forth dangers to which many are exposed, and vices which steep the life God has given as a blessing in dishonor, misery, and remorse.[21]

Opening paragraphs in this vein introduce such motifs as the evils of drinking, behavioral maxims, "false generosity," the benefits of "severe afflictions," and in Poe's case, revenge for wrongdoing.[22]

Other pieces begin in a more conventional manner by introducing the setting, and yet in keeping with the timelessness of moral thematics, these beginnings exclude periodicity. "We were all seated in a piazza, one beautiful summer's night," begins "My Grandmother's Bracelet" by Caroline Lee Hentz. Henry William Herbert also sets his sensational yet moralistic tale "The Fortunes of the House of Foix: The Fatal Gift" in a "beautiful" setting: "It was an early hour, on a calm, beautiful morning of the first month of autumn."[23]

These adventure stories inevitably move on to mystery, intrigue, and sensation. The tales focus on subjects such as the mysterious history of a bracelet, the terror of suffocating in a cave, the secrets of a hidden drawer, the inexplicable illness of an artist, and the transmutation of a figure in a portrait into a real person. Focusing on this last subject, N. P. Willis provides a prototype for Hawthorne's "Drowne's Wooden Image" in his own story of idyllic artistic beauty coming to life.[24]

These stories are narrated in a sensational style. In "The Artist's Disappointment," for example, Elizabeth F. Ellet intersperses her story about the conflict between fame and art with overtly sensational language: "That wild look of anguish; that fevered flush; the hurried and abrupt movement; the visible emancipation of the whole frame; all these made me shudder."[25] Robert Montgomery Bird anticipates Poe's use of ironic dialogue in "The Cask of Amontillado," which augments the sensationalism of the plot. In Bird's 1843 tale "The Death Cave," the story of near suffocation and death in an underground cave, Bird describes the feeble attempts of the protagonist to beg for his life from the villain who has tricked and abandoned him in the depths of a cavern:

> Can you not conceive of the feelings that then convulsed me . . . that unparalleled villain was stealing away, to suffer me to die a death of darkness and starvation in a cave! I called after the villain; and it was with the humbled spirit and supplicating accents of a slave. I begged for my life; I promised forgiveness and silence;—nay, I pledged an oath of secrecy; I offered him the money in my saddle-bags, and not only that, but more. I would double it—quadruple it—I would beggar my wife and children and give him all I possessed, if he would only return. . . . To this piteous appeal there came an answer; it was the sound of distant laughter—such laughter that might come from the lips of a fiend, exulting over the anguish of a condemned soul. I heard the farewell laugh of the murderer; and then all was silent in my living sepulchre—and yet not silent; for I could hear the throbs of my own heart, and a ringing, roaring sound, the pulsations of my brain.[26]

In this sensational style, other stories depict "evil genius," "diabolical smiles," "stunning blows," "sensuality . . . akin to cruelty," and "vice and beggary."[27] Readers could freely indulge their thirst for sensational acts and yet be chastened by the middle-class values and morals that framed the tales.

The techniques and orientation of Poe's "The Cask of Amontillado," "The Oblong Box," and Nathaniel Hawthorne's "Drowne's Wooden Image" find a context in this *Godey's* format. These tales either begin conventionally ("Some years ago, I engaged passage from Charleston, S.C., to the city of New York," "The Oblong Box"), and in Hawthorne's case, recall other idyllic openings ("One sunshiny morning, in the good old times of the town of Boston," "Drowne's Wooden Image"), or introduce the thematic material immediately, as in "The Cask of Amontillado": "The thousand injuries of Fortunato I had borne as I best could; but when he ventured upon insult, I vowed revenge."[28]

Like many characters in *Godey's* stories, Hawthorne's and Poe's narrators are artists or specialists, and like other pieces for the magazine, they elicit sensational or mysterious intrigue. The plots move through sensational events that border on the grotesque (Montressor's mad acts of vengeance), the mysterious (the contents of the strange oblong box of Cornelius Wyatt), or the supernatural (Drowne's seeming transformation of art into life). In order to empower these sensational elements, Poe and Hawthorne, like other *Godey's* writers, subordinate character analysis to plot, which is unrelieved or qualified by thoughts, opinions, or insights of the narrator. Like the third-person but unknowing narrator of Hawthorne's tale, the reader moves through the story from one event to the next. The narrators in these tales participate in the action of the story, and they end their tales sensationally: "This fair stranger must have been the original of Drowne's Wooden Image" ("Drowne's Wooden Image"); "There is an hysterical laugh which will forever ring within my ears" ("The Oblong Box"); "Against the new masonry I re-erected the old rampart of bones. . . . *In pace requiescat!*" ("The Cask of Amontillado").[29] These stories fit in well with the fiction by other writers for the magazine and demonstrate Poe's and Hawthorne's understanding and conscious use even of *Godey's* conventions.

Graham's Magazine

The very different tales that Poe and Hawthorne wrote for *Graham's* clearly illustrate the fidelity of these authors to magazine policies. *Graham's Magazine* represented perhaps the most literary of the periodicals of the 1840s. Among its impressive list of contributors were Park Benjamin, Caroline Chesebro', Willis Gaylord Clark, James Fenimore Cooper, Fanny Forrester, Nathaniel Hawthorne, James Russell Lowell, Joseph C. Neal, James Kirk Paulding, E. A. Poe, Catharine Sedgwick, Lydia Maria Sigourney, Bayard Taylor, and N. P. Willis. Most of these writers contributed regularly. The magazine published a different Poe story almost monthly for over one year, and Cooper's novel *Rose Budd* occupied *Graham's* pages for more than two years.

Graham's stories avoid the classically styled openings of *Godey's* by beginning with an essaylike discourse or examination of the controlling idea of the piece. This approach imparts the tales with a less sentimental and more philosophical tone. *Graham's* supported a fiction where the intellect dominated over the emotions. By blurring the distinctions between the fictional tale and the essay, this convention served the needs of the middle-class family audience who remained suspicious in the 1840s of the seductive nature of fiction and who required stories that expressed a cultural preference for literary realism.[30]

Unlike the stories in *Godey's*, which deal almost solely with individuals, *Graham's* fiction reaches out into society and grapples with educational, social, political, and gender issues. This orientation is found throughout the variety of genres published in the monthly. Henry Danforth's ocean adventure "Getting to Sea" deals with the treachery of the British and the determination of the Americans to fight political injustice during the War of 1812. Catharine Sedgwick's urban tale "A Contrast" examines the disparities within society: the dangers of ethnic stereotypes, the importance of socioeconomic status, the hopelessness of poverty, and inequities between the sexes. In "Bending the Twig," Fanny Forrester portrays with devastating acuity the demeaning and psychologically destructive methods employed by parents in socializing their children, especially girls.[31]

While *Graham's* tales often treat social and political issues, they ultimately seek solutions in individual rather than societal action. "Harry Cavendish—A Pirate" concludes not with societal measures to eradicate burglary, rape, and murder, but with personal revenge.[32] In "A Contrast" the narrator offers individual goodness as the solution to the problems raised.[33] The message of "Bending the Twig" moves remarkably even further from a societal response and posits a personal imaginary world as an escape from the cruelties of gender stereotypes.

A look at the tales of Hawthorne and Poe in light of these conventions reveals the interest of these authors to write in the *Graham's* style. While ostensibly different, Hawthorne's "Earth's Holocaust" and Poe's "The Imp of the Perverse" share common techniques with other tales published in this magazine.[34] Both stories are highly philosophical rather than action-filled. Through the conversations between the narrator and a "grave . . . looker-on," Hawthorne dedicates considerable space to discussing the philosophical implications of the mob's actions in burning various elements and representations of "civilized society." While the various sensational acts in which the mob engages could have easily been the focus of a *Godey's* story, within the pages of *Graham's* Hawthorne emphasizes the opinions and thoughts of his two major characters. Poe begins "The Imp of the Perverse" with a two-page essay on psychological impulses, much in the vein of Sedgwick's "A Contrast." This initial essay both instructs the reader how to approach the tale proper and reduces the sensationalism of human perverseness by stressing the story's intellectual component. Both tales deal with matters of society and behavior common to humankind. Like the typical endings of other *Graham's* tales, Poe seeks the solution in the individual—the psyche. Hawthorne, too, concludes his savage criticism of civilization and what seems like an impossible search for a solution to society's ills by suggesting a cure in "what, but the human heart itself!"

While most assessments of Hawthorne's and Poe's magazine fiction argue for an opposition between these "classic" writers and the popular literary culture of their day, this view strongly contradicts both authors' formulations of artistic genius and their examples.[35] With their definitions of genius as a necessary mixture of popular cultural forms and personal insight, these writers not only endorse popular practices, but make them central to their own compositional acts by adhering to specific editorial policies and practices.[36]

The 1850s Marketplace

The changing conditions in the periodical marketplace of the 1850s provided environments which encouraged the kind of personal creativity that characterizes the magazine writing of the best periodical writers of this decade: Fanny Fern, E.D.E.N. Southworth, and Herman Melville. During the 1850s, some magazines reached mass circulation, much like the phenomenon that was occurring in the selling of some popular novels, where copies sold extended into the tens of thousands and some, like Susan Warner's *The Wide, Wide World*, Maria Cummins's *The Lamplighter*, and Harriet Beecher Stowe's *Uncle Tom's Cabin*, into the hundreds of thousands. Harper Brothers started its initial run of *Harper's Magazine* in June 1850 with 7,500 copies; by December of that year readership had increased dramatically to 50,000, and by January 1854, 130,000 issues reeled off the presses monthly.[37] Robert Bonner created the best-seller of periodicals with his *New York Ledger*. By hiring best-seller writers, most notably Stowe, Southworth, and Fern—whose *Fern Leaves* in 1853 and *Ruth Hall* in 1855 sold 70,000 and 50,000 copies, respectively—his readership quickly surged to more than 400,000 readers weekly. Increasing dramatically within two decades, American periodical audiences now controlled the marketplace.

The enormous success of magazines stemmed from their own particular and heavily advertised editorial policies. As long as the contributors to Bonner's *Ledger* adhered to the editor's demand for a style that was "pure in morals, honest and noble in sentiment, simple in diction, plain in construction, and thoroughly adapted to the taste and comprehension of the people," writers such as Fern and Southworth could freely treat a variety of topics including crime, women's rights, adventure, and social issues.[38] Both Fern and Southworth creatively combined Bonner's editorial policy with their own literary concerns and styles, and they consistently produced some of their best writing in the pages of the *New York Ledger*. Southworth's most popular (and many would proclaim her best) novel, *The Hidden Hand,* was serialized three different times in the *Ledger,* while the weekly articles of Fanny Fern produced a sensation almost unheard of among antebellum readers.[39]

When we turn to Melville—a writer who is said to have produced great short fiction almost in spite of reader expectations and magazine practices—we discover in his magazine fiction particularly instructive examples of a creative reliance on editorial policies.[40] Like Poe and Hawthorne before him, and alongside Fern and Southworth who aligned their tales to specific magazine practices, Melville traded in this popular market by tailoring his submissions to adhere to the policies and stances of two monthlies that vied for top ratings, *Harper's Magazine* and *Putnam's Monthly.*

Magazine writing offered Melville the opportunity to earn a prescribed and steady income, a reason commonly cited for his switch from the novel form. However, more than financial gain was at stake. For the first time in his career, he discovered large audiences receptive to his literary interests. These interests have been overlooked by the modern reader who does not place Melville's fiction within the context of these magazines. Modern scholars miss these differences when they treat the sixteen magazine works collectively. It is common practice to discuss these short stories in terms of their order of composition and to divide them into three chronological groups. These discussions locate forms and themes specific to stories composed at the same time.[41] This chronological model underscores controlling characteristics that link stories from a given compositional period at the expense of analyses of technique and style in each of the stories. In other words, chronology alone lifts Melville's work out of its cultural context. Thematic analyses, when unilaterally applied, tend to misconstrue the specificity of Melville's interest in representing cultural attitudes through the contrasting requirements of *Harper's* and *Putnam's*.

When Melville turned to magazine writing in 1853, he participated in the two distinct literary environments of *Harper's* and *Putnam's*. Melville's magazine writing, together with his novels of the fifties, exhibit the author's deep concern over a wide range of social issues including poverty, homelessness, slavery, industrialization, and sexism. As we shall see, the particular articulation of these themes reflects the author's deference to their publishing contexts, the stylistic conventions that distinguished *Harper's* and *Putnam's*. Considering the larger environment of what I am calling the periodical marketplace of antebellum America provides insight into the motivations that might have encouraged the author of seven novels to move to magazine fiction.

CHAPTER EIGHT

Creative Reliance:
Periodical Practices in the
Magazine Fiction

M ELVILLE SUBMITTED seven tales, roughly half of his entire short fiction output, to one of the most politically conservative and sentimental monthlies of the decade, *Harper's Magazine.* Although periodicals such as *Putnam's* and even *Holden's Dollar Magazine* provided the author with more heterogeneous environments, and *Putnam's* paid him the same high rate per page (five dollars), Melville continued to submit to *Harper's.*[1] The particular type of social critique found in tales such as "The Fiddler," "Jimmy Rose," "Cock-a-Doodle-Doo!" and "The Paradise of Bachelors and the Tartarus of Maids," all published in *Harper's,* has been considered covert autobiographical reflections about "going under."[2] Yet these reflections are not limited to and defined by a personal strategy of the author. Often treated as allegories of Melville's despair over lost fame and "failure," the themes of social alienation and obscurity in Melville's *Harper's* stories form part of a larger tradition in *Harper's* fiction.[3] In fact, Melville's reserve illustrates a conscious use—and even endorsement—of magazine conventions. The author's stylistic techniques in the seven tales published in *Harper's* are directly linked to the editorial policies and magazine practices of the popular sentimental monthly.

The deliberateness of Melville's practices and his keen awareness of the contrasting magazine styles becomes clear in the distinct fiction he wrote for *Putnam's*. The liberal philosophy of *Putnam's* editors encouraged Melville to include some of his most sophisticated formulations of political, social, and aesthetic themes in the fiction that he submitted to this magazine. Not solely a characteristic of Melville's prose, richly symbolic language and a heterogeneous style became the trademark of *Putnam's* essays and stories.

Melville carefully considered this stylistic approach and orientation when writing for *Putnam's*. Some of the author's best shorter works and indeed the stories included in the collection *The Piazza Tales* (1855), such as "Bartleby, the Scrivener: A Story of Wall Street," "Benito Cereno," "I and My Chimney," and "The Encantadas" were initially written for and published in *Putnam's Monthly*. These submissions contain unabashedly realistic appraisals of socioeconomic, racial, and gender inequities. While the stories in *Harper's* treat social issues through sentimental rhetoric that is suggestive, the author's stories for *Putnam's* criticize sentimental views that soften social and political realities.

Writing for these two major literary monthlies of the 1850s, which differed significantly in ideological perspectives and literary styles, required, from Melville, a stylistic heterogeneity and creativity that modern readers have come to associate with him. The author's continued submission to both monthlies indicates his interest in working within the different magazine policies. The challenge for *Harper's* contributors to empower the sentimental image alone—the signified —with potentially different levels of signification remained for Melville an artistic challenge, as his later stories for *Harper's* demonstrate. At the same time, the task of *Putnam's* writers in directly criticizing pervasive uses of abstracted sentiment in literary narratives through the use of heterogeneous, multileveled texts represented a kind of writing intimately related to the style of the author of *Moby-Dick*.

Examining Melville's magazine fiction in its socioliterary context reveals how literary economics, marketplace realities, and subversive rhetoric—factors that informed the practices of both the writer and the literary magazines—stimulated rather than dissuaded literary creativity. By understanding how the author employs forms expected by readers in each of the magazines, we can see how Melville "revolts" *with*, rather than against, his readers.[4]

Nonpartisan Sentiment in *Harper's*

Started in 1850, *Harper's Magazine* became one of the century's most widely read magazines, with a circulation surpassing one hundred thousand by 1860. Its overwhelming popularity stemmed largely from its editorial policy of aiming to please all segments of the middle class —to reach "the great mass of the American people" ("A Word at the Start," *Harper's*, June 1850). Since the "great mass" of middle-class readers held different and at times opposing political views, the monthly discouraged controversy: "The Magazine . . . will provide . . . the most perfect freedom from prejudice and partiality of every kind" (June 1851). It accomplished this feat by strictly maintaining what they considered a nonpartisan stance on politics, social issues, and religious topics. *Harper's* catered to the taste of a mixed reading public through a stylistic mode that hoped to assuage more than to criticize.

Forerunner of Saturday night radio programs listened to by American families nationwide a century later, the "parlor" literature of *Harper's Magazine* favored family-oriented, entertaining, and moralistic fiction.[5] This emphasis on entertainment and nonpartisanship in turn provided a needed outlet for a more critically oriented journal that would offer social analysis for those readers interested more in social issues than in entertainment.

With their determination to remain a magazine of "light" literature aimed at "parlor" readers, the *Harper's* editors preferred a sentimental style. This narrative mode, while employed in thematic treatments of an array of topics including domestic, social and political issues, subordinated analysis of events to an emphasis on the emotional response of narrators, characters, and readers. Sentimental fiction in *Harper's* cast the motifs of suffering, abuse, poverty, and exploitation —social problems that plagued American society in the 1850s—into stylized portraits of moral fortitude. This sentimental style was employed to emphasize the abilities of characters, always the poor, unempowered, and the marginalized, to find contentment through the hardships they encounter by transforming the social problems their existence embodied into a celebration of the moralistic principles of toleration and acquiescence. Such thematized messages, rather than focus on the issues themselves, attempted to demonstrate that "diffi-culties are the tutors and monitors of men placed in their path for their best discipline and development" (January 1852, 212). In this light, the fiction of *Harper's* loosely corresponds to the genre David S. Reynolds has called conventional reform literature, a genre popular with the middle-class antebellum readers who constituted the audi-ence for the monthly.[6]

The emphasis on class in *Harper's* fiction reflects the larger social distancing that was occurring between working-class people and the burgeoning new middle classes. Aloof, spectator-narrators represent-ing the privileged middle class isolate themselves from the events they relate and use their status to observe less fortunate characters from above on the ladder of success. Celebrating the economic success of middle-class readers, *Harper's* tales relegate the stance of acquiescence and toleration to the lower classes, who are the subjects, rather than the narrators. In this way, middle-class narrators displace in their fiction the very people whom the stories ostensibly chronicle. While narrators allude to the misery of poverty and alienation, they deflect the reader's empathy from the despair vividly portrayed to themselves by disengaging themselves from the environments of their unfortu-nate characters. Instead of explicitly expressing opinions regarding misspent lives, *Harper's* narrators resort to a conventional response, usually culminating in a final sentimentalized exclamation, such as that ending "The Chateau Regnier": "May he die in peace!" (June 1853, 221–38). Such endings indirectly laud the good-willed nature of the narrator without directly grappling with the unresolved social problems that the stories raise. This abstract representation of social issues, coupled with emphasis on the emotions, philanthropy, or simply the good fortune of the narrator, enabled writers to support the *Harper's* commitment to a perspective that supports raising timely issues, but stops at implication.

This process of displacing the working class, immigrants, African Americans, and Native Americans to the margins—and beyond—of society mirrors the actual displacement and subjugation that such peoples experienced as the new middle class empowered itself through a self-conscious centering of their new class base. This strat-egy, recently labeled by Laura Wexler as the "imperialist project of sentimentalization," needed, in order to create an existence for the middle class, to assign other groups to lower ranks.[7] Thus, in the case of *Harper's* the "cultural work" in which the form engages is work that reproduces itself culturally, reinforcing itself even through ostensibly focusing on the socially disadvantaged.

Certainly allegiance to this sentimental "overplot"—a term borrowed from Nina Baym and popularized by Susan K. Harris—does not preclude an author's subversive treatment of it, as feminist scholars have pointed out.[8] Jane Tompkins and Cathy Davidson, as well as Baym and most recently Harris, have discovered in the sentimental novels of the period a structural overplot that contains ideological contradictions and what Harris calls "radical possibilities" for the perspectives endorsed by the overplot.[9] Applying Jacques Derrida's argument that any form contains its own contradictions and ideological gaps, these scholars suggest that the subversive strategies female writers employed actually emerged from within the form, and were not imposed from outside. These recent recoveries of the writing strategies of female sentimental writers suggest an alternative view of subversive practices. Rather than embed elements in a reputedly organic—and superficial—form, writers such as Susan Warner, Fanny Fern, and Harriet Beecher Stowe emphasize the alternative ideological perspectives that emerge in the sentimental formula for their own social, political, and aesthetic ends.

This insight into the heterogeneity of the sentimental form provides the context within which we should consider Melville's compositional practices in his fiction for *Harper's*. Contrasting different kinds of lifestyles, Melville's stories adhere closely to the magazine's stylistic demands. The author focuses on social issues of the day, including reversed fortunes and economic status. Yet in the fashion of the magazine, Melville's narrators both chronicle and distance themselves from their tales of the "unfortunate": "ruined" men ("The Happy Failure," "Jimmy Rose"), loss of fame ("The Fiddler"), poverty ("Cock-a-Doodle-Doo!" "Poor Man's Pudding and Rich Man's Crumbs"), and social inequities ("The Paradise of Bachelors and the Tartarus of Maids"). In addition, they support the ideology that poverty and obscurity are ennobling virtues ("Cock-a-Doodle-Doo!" "The Happy Failure," and "The Fiddler").

Although Melville suggests social criticism in his titles and images and provides alternative possibilities to the ideological structures his tales seem to support, they avoid the direct critical analysis of the earlier novels and contemporaneous stories written for *Putnam's*. They end on the same sentimental note found in the other pages of the magazine: "God grant that Jimmy's roses may immortally survive!" ("Jimmy Rose"), "Heaven save me equally from the 'Poor Man's Pudding' and the "Rich Man's Crumbs,' " "COCK-A-DOODLE-DOO!—OO!—OO-OO!" "Praise be to God for the failure!" ("The Happy Failure"), and "Oh! Paradise of Bachelors! and oh! Tartarus of Maids!" Although Melville creatively employs this formula, as did female sentimental novelists, his use of the sentimental mode also supports the tastes and expectations of his readers.

A cursory look at Melville's fiction and other stories published in *Harper's* reveals the links between the author's tales generically and stylistically to the larger magazine tradition. Two stories published in the monthly anticipate the orientation and theme of "Cock-a-Doodle-Doo!" as well as the author's use of the diptych. In the anonymous "Better than Diamonds," a typical *Harper's* story, a middle-class narrator observes the tribulations of a poverty-stricken family (March 1853, 501–2). Though he chronicles their sorrow, this teller remains distant from the subjects of his story, and he remains the focal point, an emphasis repeated in Melville's tale. Another *Harper's* piece, "Success in Life," illustrates the sentimental approach to life's miseries by demonstrating that "the true test of success in life is character" (July 1853, 238–39). This theme parallels the belief of Melville's character Merrymusk that a poor man can be richer in contentment than a man with "mere gold or acres."

In "Poor Man's Pudding and Rich Man's Crumbs," Melville's narrator offers views of the lives of poor and rich men, and he continually reminds the reader of his own superior position, much like the privileged narrator of "Better than Diamonds." This stance distances him from the lives of the impoverished peasant family whom he depicts with amused condescension. This teller reacts with embarrassment and horror at being considered one of the masses who hungrily consume the remnants of a royal feast. Though chronicling the misery associated with poverty, the narrator retreats into the typical noncommittal, sentimentalized concluding statement of many *Harper's* narrators: " 'Now, Heaven in its kind mercy save me from the noble charities of London,' sighed I, as that night I lay bruised and battered on my bed; 'and Heaven save me equally from the "Poor Man's Pudding" and the "Rich Man's Crumbs" ' " (*Piazza Tales*, 302). This seeming dichotomy actually refers in both cases to the poor and thus extricates the narrator from truly sympathizing with the impoverished. This ending, like so many others in *Harper's* tales, reinforces the teller's identification with the favored upper classes. While Melville may indeed have borrowed his dichotomous subject and form from Catharine Sedgwick's *The Poor Rich Man and the Rich Poor Man* (1838), as several critics have suggested, both works, together with the fiction in *Harper's*, reflect the stylistic conventions of the larger tradition of conventional reform literature.[10]

Two other stories from the pages of *Harper's* anticipate Melville's method in "Jimmy Rose." In "The Chateau Regnier," the narrator relates the tragic life story of Heinrich (June 1853, 121). He refrains from offering solace, expressing concern, or providing help; he merely chronicles Heinrich's tragedies and final disappearance: "I never saw him again. From time to time I hear about him"(121). In "Four Sights of a Young Man," a story that may have provided Melville with one of the formal models for his 1854 diptychs, the narrator divides his chronicle of the downfall, ruin, and resolution of an individual into four separate sketches or "sights." The title suggests a depiction of the dissolution of this young man. By deliberately breaking up the narrative into separate scenes, the narrator retreats from the intrinsic horror and tragedy of his subject. The nondiscursive narrative distances the reader from the story and prevents empathy with the character. Like the narrator in Melville's "Jimmy Rose," this teller expresses little emotion regarding the misfortunes of his friend. Rather, he retreats from his narrative through sentimental rhetoric: "I trust the poor lad was mad; but that was my last sight of William Hardy" (December 1853, 68).

Melville adopted these subjects and methods in his own chronicle of the downfall of an individual in "Jimmy Rose." The narrator distances himself from the tragedy of Jimmy Rose by restricting his role to impassive observer. Though not as structurally obvious as the author of "Four Sights of a Young Man," who divides his narrative into disparate scenes, Melville presents a disjointed narrative which minimizes empathy for Jimmy Rose. The narrator, and by extension, the reader, remains outside the confines of the noncommittal, sentimental rhetoric of "Poor, poor Jimmy—God guard us all—poor Jimmy Rose!" (*Piazza Tales*, 345), which, with each reoccurence, distances the narrator (and the reader) from Jimmy Rose's tragedy.

Melville's creative yet deferential employment of *Harper's* practices can be observed in "The Paradise of Bachelors and the Tartarus of Maids." Considered one of the best and most subversive of Melville's stories, this tale demonstrates just how closely the author depended on *Harper's* conventions, and like many of the sentimental novels of the day, it emphasizes the ideological gaps inherent within the sentimental formula. By understanding Melville's particular manipulations of the sentimental form, we can better gauge the creativity that emerges.

"The Paradise of Bachelors and the Tartarus of Maids"

One way to approach this tale is to place the diptych form into its generic context. The diptych, with its corresponding allusions to social inequities and problems, represented a popular strategy found in mid-nineteenth-century magazines and novels. Maria Jane McIntosh, for example, employed this technique in her sentimentalized view of Southern life in *The Lofty and the Lowly; Or, Good in All and None All-Good*, a novel published one year prior to the publication of Melville's tale.[11] The bifurcated title, a common practice in sentimental fiction, often refers to the stark discrepancies in the moral, social, or socioeconomic levels of the main characters.

Godey's Lady's Book, one of the most sentimental magazines of the day and one to which the Melville household not only subscribed, but which in 1850 had also advertised Melville as a forthcoming contributor, frequently employed this form. The January 1853 number opens with a provocative illustration of an elegant boudoir where a rich, young, beautiful woman adorns herself in a gilt mirror on the left, while the right side depicts an impoverished one-roomed cottage in which a poor, exhausted, older, woman slumps over her sewing. The title to this illustration, "Pin Money: How It Is Spent; Needle Money: How It Is Earned," points to the discrepancy between these lives.[12] The disjointed title, coupled with the illustration, seems to depict the tragedy of this imbalance. Significantly, the story that accompanies the *Godey's* illustration then seeks to negate this imbalance. It glosses over the social implications of the pairing, sentimentalizing and ideologizing the scenes in a chronicle about how the rich woman aids the poor woman. The story does not discuss the social context that has forced the woman to live in poverty, but concludes only with "however, the poor are helped by the rich."[13]

Melville participates in this practice by creating a fragmented tale of socioeconomic and gender differences through his contrast of the ample paradise of bachelors and the impoverished tartarus of maids. At one level, the contrast of gender here—an obvious difference to readers of the 1850s—would have been easily interpreted by his readers as the paradise of bachelor*hood*, a state popularized by Ik Marvel's (Donald Mitchell's) *Reveries of a Bachelor*, which had been serialized in *Harper's*.[14] Likewise, the tartarus of maids could just as easily have represented the isolated state of remaining unmarried, a popular topic in sentimental magazines. Indeed, this level of interpretation is borne out in the story (if women would marry, they would not be forced to work in the factories).

Melville's use of the diptych form both underscores the polaric worlds encountered by his narrator and creates a middle-class niche for him. Like other *Harper's* narrators, Melville's teller pokes fun at but identifies with the affluent. Contrasting the exhausting routine and stark work environment of the worn, conformist, virgin workers at the paper mill with the carefree lives of bachelor professionals at the Templars, he relates in a tone of rapture his evening with these elite bachelors. He clearly aligns himself with their attitudes and lifestyle: " 'Sir,' said I, with a burst of admiring candor—'Sir, this is the very Paradise of Bachelors!' "[15] Mirroring the practices of other writers for *Harper's*, Melville creates a narrator who, although he sketches in detail the lives of women enslaved by industrialized labor, remains distant from these socially, economically, and (to the mind of his narrator) sexually impoverished women.

Unlike the *Putnam's* stories in which minority voices emerge, sound, and ultimately supplant the hegemonic perspective of the narrator, no voice speaks for the mill girls in *Harper's* fiction. Just as the narrator of the anonymous "Slate and its Uses" retreats from intolerable mill conditions: "The noise in the mill is so horrid that we cannot stay; but a glance is enough," Melville's narrator hurriedly retreats from the dismal paper mill "wrapped in fur and meditations," thoughts which he could share with his readers but does not. He concludes instead with the same kind of noncommittal and senti-mentalized statement found in "Poor Man's Pudding and Rich Man's Crumbs," "Jimmy Rose," and other stories in *Harper's:* "At the Black Notch I paused, and once more bethought me of Temple-Bar. Then, shooting through the pass, all alone with inscrutable nature, I ex-claimed—Oh! Paradise of Bachelors and oh! Tartarus of Maids!" [16] The ending highlights the successful narrator who, remaining ambiv-alent toward the horrors of the social realities portrayed, extricates himself from social ills and criticism—the very issues upon which Melville's *Putnam's* stories focus.

While eternal stares from the eyes of Babo's mounted head, the endless prayers of Don Cereno, and even the continued rumors and explanations of Bartleby's previous work lives retain voices long after the accounts of the narrators end in Melville's *Putnam's* stories, "The Paradise of Bachelors and the Tartarus of Maids" offers only circular-ity—the recursive voice of the narrator, who in coming to the end of his tale, merely starts again at the beginning. The narrator extricates himself, but the circularity that is offered as an ending prohibits action on the larger issues of social inequities and gender raised in the story. The reader is left with both unreconcilable social discrepancies and an escape through the circular arguments of sentiment. Both the unwillingness of the narrator to reflect beyond the diptych structure —and the attempt through the circular ending to restrict the reader's interpretation of that structure to a tale celebrating middle-class sta-tus—demonstrates Melville's deference to the *Harper's* style. This reserve reinforces the editorial policies of *Harper's.*

Yet the circular insight of the middle-class narrator and the act of conjoining privileged and under-privileged characters can function as acts of subversion. The conflation of economics, social status, and gender in the story title indicates Melville's interest in alternative possibilities. The very juxtaposition of the bachelors and the maids provides a highly unlikely mixture that challenges the structural framework—and by extension societal structures—which allows for this volatile combination to exist. Melville's depiction moves from a rigid socioeconomic paradigm to the problems of gender, status, industrialization, and alienation, themes all raised in the story. In this manner, the policies and conventions of the magazine form a basis as well as a context for subtle criticism and the creativity that inevitably ensues in the hands of this author, a strategy employed in some of his other *Harper's* tales such as "The 'Gees." [17]

The question is whether to consider the social criticisms that Melville's *Harper's* stories raise as subversive acts. The term *subversion* implies (and has been interpreted by many critics to mean) a reluctant deference to literary economics, reader tastes, or publication necessities. Yet Melville chose to write for *Harper's*, a choice that was not guided by economic necessity or even literary popularity, since he received the same pay for publishing in *Putnam's* and whose audience readily lauded Melville's stories in its pages. As we have seen, Melville constantly embraced the reader throughout his works by encouraging an interaction between text and reader. This openness to the reader suggests a different way to consider Melville's purposes in writing for *Harper's*. Some critics have posited that the author exhibited ambivalent attitudes toward radical and conservative beliefs, an idea that could be supported by Melville's continued interest in writing for the conservative *Harper's*. But Melville's writing provides a more insightful approach to his reasons for contributing to *Harper's*. His tales can be seen as attempting to reach out to and instruct the reader on the limitations of the sentimental approach to treating social issues in fiction. In this light, Melville attempts to change his readers' attitudes regarding the most appropriate style for thematizing social issues. Thus, subversive strategies of the author can be seen as instructional, not hostile, acts. This interest *in* the reader, rather than *beyond* the reader, as commonly implied in criticism that labels Melville's achievements in *Harper's* as subversive, locates and explains both the author's deference to and his creative use of essentially conservative magazine conventions.

But a central point in understanding Melville's particular compositional strategies here is that his *Harper's* tales differ significantly from the methods employed in contrasting the lives of the slaves and the Spanish sailors in "Benito Cereno," for example, or of Bartleby and the attorney in "Bartleby, the Scrivener." In these stories, oppositional perspectives fully participate in the drama. In "The Paradise of Bachelors and the Tartarus of Maids," however, the worlds of the bachelors and the maids remain fragmented rather than interactive. The narrator offers only discordant slices. While these discordancies challenge and criticize newly formed middle-class attitudes toward social stratification, they also simultaneously reflect those views. Melville's treatment of middle-class complacency stops with the images presented, challenging but not offering alternatives to *Harper's* readers.

In writing for *Harper's,* Melville necessarily restrained the thoughts and actions of his narrators—a restraint that some have argued characterizes the author's ambivalence toward authority, acquiescence, politics, and revolution. His endorsement of a rhetoric that goes only so far may indeed reflect a personal as well as a national dialectical struggle.[18] By co-opting oppositional implications, Melville's *Harper's* stories, together with other pieces written for *Harper's,* mirror American middle-class tastes and the types of thematic articulations found in the magazine fiction of the decade.[19] The isolated *Harper's* narrator represents the economically successful and socially respectable individual. By celebrating the cleverness of the narrator in disassociating himself from the lower classes, *Harper's* sentimental rhetoric displaces the social problems that comprise the plots.

This is not to say that the sexual, political, and social innuendos which twentieth-century readers have ascribed to the story do not exist. Melville's *Harper's* stories are always richer than their surface forms indicate. The point is that Melville consciously adheres to the *Harper's* dictum for a sentimental structure in crafting his own message. His interest in questioning or even challenging the ideological views supported by both the magazine and the sentimental form had to be relegated to the substrata of his *Harper's* tales. Although overlapping themes can be found in the stories written for *Putnam's* during the same period, this deference to a sentimental rhetoric that stops at implication clearly distinguishes Melville's *Harper's* fiction from the stories submitted to *Putnam's.*

Liberal Language in *Putnam's*

Putnam's Monthly started in 1853 as a critical commentary on the times and as a direct contrast to the political conservatism and sentimentalism of *Harper's Magazine*. Rigorously analytical, *Putnam's* appealed to a more intellectual, politically liberal, and thus smaller audience that ranged from two thousand to twenty thousand subscribers, averaging around sixteen thousand readers monthly.

Putnam's promised American commentary on national and international affairs. In his first editorial, Charles Briggs asked, "In what paper or periodical do you now look to find the criticism of American thought upon the times?" (January 1853, 2). Answering his own question, Briggs promised to collect "the results of the acutest observations, and the most trenchant thought, illustrated by whatever wealth of erudition, of imagination, and of experience" that American writers possess (2). By emphasizing "trenchant thought" and "erudition," rather than just the popularity of their writers as was the custom in *Harper's,* the editors conveyed the rhetorical style to which they aspired.

The monthly treated social, political, and literary themes from a perspective markedly different from the nonpartisan, non-analytical stance of its competitor. Articles, essays, and stories analyzed and evaluated the variety of perspectives that comprised a particular issue. Unlike its competitor, *Putnam's* strongly condemned the popular rhetoric of sentiment, a mode of writing that, according to the editors, tried to assuage and cover more than it directly challenged and uncovered. *Putnam's* editors rejected sentimental rhetoric as a tool for representing the times, because it glossed over reality and "paints only the gentle, the grieving, the beautiful" (February 1854, 223). The sentimental style of *Harper's* fiction, argued *Putnam's* editors, severs the link between social problems and the teller's emotional response to them by highlighting abstracted sentiment. The antisentimental stance implied a dissatisfaction with the consistently "clear, true, and transparent" prose of sentimental writing (*Putnam's,* February 1853, 77) and endorsed a deliberately ambiguous, multilayered text.

A look at how editorial policies on sentimental rhetoric at *Putnam's* were articulated in fiction illustrates how closely Melville's strategies reflected general practices in the magazine. George William Curtis, a best-selling author in addition to being one of the magazine's editors, subverts sentimental conventions in "The Potiphar Papers." The story contains a setting commonly employed in domestic fiction. The author reinforces this domesticity by including a traditional activity, home decorating. In the conventional sentimental tale, the adventures of the decorator would dominate the story. A male narrator, disturbed at the refurbishing attempts of his wife and family determines to undermine their efforts. Melville's story "I and My Chimney" reproduces a similar situation. The similarity of these two tales helps to explain Curtis's thorough enjoyment of Melville's story. These narrators contrast strongly with the sentimental bachelor in Ik Marvel's *Reveries of a Bachelor,* who dreams of domesticity. While the *Putnam's* stories adhere to a common rigorous antisentimentalism, Marvel's bachelor—highly praised by the sentiment-loving reviewers of *Harper's*—epitomizes the sentimental rhetoric.

The antisentimental stance of *Putnam's* pervaded even the more nonfictional forms. While a frequent use of superlatives and exclamations marked *Harper's* sentimental travel literature, *Putnam's* travel writings provided acute political analyses of the places under discussion and questioned conventional views. A writer in *Putnam's* described *Harper's* travel writers as the "worn-out debauchees of Europe who travel to get rid of themselves or to find a new sensation." *Putnam's* travel writers, on the other hand, "estimate [all novelties] at their true value with an unerring practical sagacity." (review of *The Homes of American Authors, Putnam's,* January 1853). While J. Ross Browne and others published travel pieces in *Harper's* that simply cashed in on readers' conventional expectations, Melville, Thoreau, Curtis, and Stephens published in *Putnam's* acute analyses of the areas and people under their scrutiny.

Putnam's included travel articles that rhetorically supported the liberal political positions of the magazine. The ostensibly innocently placed travel article on Hawaii in the July 1853 seems innocuous enough. It assumes much greater significance, however, in the context of the serious political discussions that dominated public opinion regarding government formulation of a policy regarding annexation. As the article reveals, many people believed that support for annexing

Hawaii stemmed purely from potential American economic gain, rather than from ideological concerns. The allusion to "the many rumors afloat last week of the filibustering intentions of some of the San Francisco visitors," a visible enough threat in the culture, is couched in an apparently naive explanation for the "insane" behavior of the islanders that the tourists observe. It implies that with the threat of an American takeover, "a revolution, at the very least" would ensue on the part of the islanders.[20] Beneath the celebratory narrative of Hawaiian culture lurks the warning of political chaos and revolution resulting from American economic greed and annexation.

In an article titled "Salt Lake and the New Saratoga" in the September 1853 issue, the author anticipates a "marketplace" mentality in the minds of commodity-driven individuals who would seek to exploit the natural splendor of the scenery. He warns his readers that he writes for a much different purpose and urges them to alter their exploitative motivations:

> It is not the intention of this article to alarm the hotel proprietors of Saratoga by this impeding stampede in fashionable life. Nor would the present writer counsel them (just now) to curtail their outlays for improvements to sell their plate, to lessen the retinue of their servants, or neglect the stocking of their wine cellars. But they are provident men. They will keep an eye on the future. They will take care that their investments can at any moment be transferred to meet the changed face of these shifting times.[21]

In this way, travel writing in the pages of *Putnam's* served as a medium for debating societal and ideological issues.

These practices are evident also in Thoreau's travel account of his expedition to Canada, "An Excursion to Canada," which was serialized for three issues in the first volume of *Putnam's* in 1853.[22] Thoreau uses his essay as a medium to criticize religious conventions. Observing some Canadian troops enter a church in Sault Sainte Marie, he compares their actions to cattle: "One and all kneeled down the aisle before the high altar to their devotions, somewhat awkwardly as cattle prepare to lie down. . . . It is as if an ox had strayed into a church and were trying to bethink himself."[23] He extends the metaphor to include all religious people who blindly follow religious traditions. Thoreau's description then encompasses the natural world: "The church . . . was a great cave in the middle of the city and what were the altars and the tinsel but the sparkling stalactites, into which you entered in a moment, and where the still atmosphere and the still light disposed to serious and profitable thought."[24]

Through this strategy, Thoreau offers a deeper layer of meaning to what had seemed like a simple, clear, and transparent description of natural scenery. By suggesting nature as an alternative to the need for churches as buildings and as institutions, he adds to his description both pragmatic and pantheistic ideologies. From this point in the account, Thoreau's narrative encompasses a larger experiential arena than physical description. Thoreau's strategy provides the reader with the opportunity to navigate through the narrative to discover alternative social assessments.

Though related in topic to J. Ross Browne's "Adventures in the South Seas," a narrative serialized in *Harper's,* which we will consider shortly, Melville's travel tale, "The Encantadas," mirrors the antisentimental approach of "An Excursion to Canada" and other *Putnam's* travel writings. Through his antisentimental rhetoric, Melville clearly distinguishes "The Encantadas" from former sentimental travel descriptions.

Although Melville employs the same method of portraiture he used in his sentimentalized and romantic descriptions of previous works, his language in "The Encantadas" signals a change. As in *Moby-Dick,* where Melville describes the effect of ocean waves on the individual by evoking an image more immediately recognizable to his land-locked readers—the "billowing waves of grasses upon the plains—he employs natural scenery from the environment of his readers as a means for them to imagine more clearly the Encantadas.[25] The very suggestion that black "cinders" "*dumped* here and there" in a "city lot" could possibly evoke the image of South Pacific islands clearly demonstrates Melville's conscious use of antisentimental language and encourages the reader to consider this travel description to be of a radically different nature from accounts written in a sentimental mode.

Melville immediately dispels any conventionalized preconception

the reader might bring to the "Enchanted Isles": "A group of rather
extinct volcanos than of isles; looking much as the world might, after
a penal conflagration" (*Piazza Tales,* 126). As Carolyn L. Karcher has
noted, the various sketches of "The Encantadas" provide the reader
with different ways to consider these isles.[26] With sketch one, "The
Isles at Large," Melville offers a startling view of islands whose name,
Las Encantadas, or the enchanted ones, should connote sentiment
and romanticism. He shifts such preconceived notions of "enchanted" to mean "evilly enchanted" (*Piazza Tales,* 131). Such an
approach to description in "The Encantadas" carries on the *Putnam's*
tradition established by Thoreau and other travel writers.

Putnam's travel articles attempt to alter preconceived notions that
readers bring to their texts. Like Thoreau in "An Excursion," Melville
intends his lesson on reading to extend beyond natural description.
He instructs the readers to consider what he describes from different
perspectives. Within the graphic description of island scenery, for
example, Melville reveals thoughts on slavery and freedom. Karcher
has demonstrated how Melville "unflinchingly exposes the ugliness of
slavery and the brutality of the master class" in this story.[27]

"The Encantadas" does not stop at challenging reader preconcep-
tions. It offers a solution to the apparent discrepancy between
thought and reality: "Sackcloth and ashes as they are, the isles are not
perhaps unmitigated gloom" (130); similarly, the tortoise, with its
"most ugly shapes and horrible aspects, dark and melancholy on its
back, still possesses a bright side" (131). This stress on possessing a
complete picture of a situation or an idea aligned "The Encantadas"
with *Putnam's* conventions. Just as his individual sketches of the
islands do not suffice in providing an informed understanding of the
isles, so Melville's accounts of these various political states are not
meaningful in isolation. Unlike his former travel descriptions, "The
Encantadas" urges the reader to consider previous notions and
the relation between surface and implication.

Subversive Sentiment in "Bartleby, the Scrivener"

The first story that Melville submitted to *Putnam's,* "Bartleby, the
Scrivener: A Story of Wall Street," (1853), demonstrates his use of the

heterogeneous narrative style available within the literary environ-ment of the magazine. The common stance of *Putnam's* writers against sentimental rhetoric and their commitment to challenge hegemonic values goes far in accounting for the strategies that Mel-ville employed in "Bartleby, the Scrivener," one of his best and most stylistically challenging stories.

In "Bartleby, the Scrivener" the author employs a sentimental style as a methodological weapon against itself, and in doing so, reinforces the *Putnam's* editorial stance. Partially sentimental, this story portrays the devastating effects of Wall Street on those "pallidly neat, pitiably respectable, incurably forlorn" individuals like Bartleby, and yet the overall manner is more in keeping with the heterogeneity of *Putnam's* than the sentimentalism of *Harper's* (*Piazza Tales*, 19). We need to understand Melville's strategy here.

In order to represent the sentimental perspective, Melville creates a narrator who resembles the detached narrators of *Harper's*. In some ways, "Bartleby" follows the pattern of a story from the December 1852 issue of this magazine, a source heretofore unexamined. In "My Client's Story," a lawyer describes an encounter that culminates in the disintegration and ultimate death of the client (December 1852, 48–52). He foreshadows the eventual outcome of this doomed individual: "He seemed a broken-down man: gray-haired, thin-visaged—and cadaverous" (48). From the outset, the narrator distances himself emotionally from his client. He constantly retreats from establishing a clear relationship between them: "We were once companions—almost friends . . . we had been intimate without altogether having been friends" (48). Furthermore, the narrator reacts to his client's emotionally moving confession with a chilling coldness: "It was proper to consider the matter coolly for there was such a thing as an over-sensitive conscience" (50). Throughout his sketch of the other man's decline, the narrator remains aloof, unsympathetic, and un-willing to become emotionally involved.[28]

The narrator of "Bartleby" also stresses his lack of involvement with others: "All who know me, consider me an eminently *safe* man" (*Piazza Tales*, 14). This lawyer engages not in defending the rights of others: "I seldom . . . indulge in dangerous indignation at wrongs and outrages" (14). He chooses rather, "in the cool tranquility of a snug retreat," to conduct "a snug business among rich men's bonds and mortgages and title-deeds" (14). This specific contextual link between Melville's lawyer-narrator, the attorney in "My Client's Story," and the larger tradition of spectator-narrators in *Harper's* tales clarifies the controversial motivations behind Melville's particular characterization of his narrator that have plagued what Dan McCall has recently called the "Bartleby Industry."[29]

Like so many of the narrators in *Harper's* stories, this teller ultimately detaches himself from the lives of his more unfortunate employees. Preferring the walls of his office to "what landscape painters call 'life,' " the narrator retreats behind a "folding screen" that separates him from his staff. The screen serves as a metaphor for the distance of authority that enables him to demand submissive behavior from them (18–19), and it also suggests the sentimental distancing devices of the *Harper's* formula.

Yet the narrative method in "Bartleby" differs significantly from Melville's *Harper's* fiction. By examining the methods of social involvement and retreat adopted by individuals in the workplace, Melville allies his tale with the editorial concerns of *Putnam's*. This subject was of particular interest to the monthly since, from its first issue, it encouraged analyses of the world of work.[30] Passages such as the following by George William Curtis portrayed the despair of the industrial worker: "I knew that men had been hard at work since sunrise—since daybreak—toiling heavily at labor that should not end until their lives ended; confined in close and noisome places, in which the day was never very bright, and their hopes grew daily darker."[31] Curtis's depiction of the dehumanized worker anticipates Melville's chronicle of Bartleby's attitudes toward survival in the world of business.

Melville conflates the magazine editors' concern for the effects of industrialization on the individual worker with their—and his own —arguments for a narrative style that can represent individual perspectives. The narrator assumes the dual role of lawyer and narrator, and his relation to his literal and narrative subject, Bartleby, conveys a double story: the tale of the lawyer's involvement with his employee Bartleby and the tale of the narrator's relation to his subject. Through this paradigm, Melville cleverly employs the magazine's concerns about Wall Street's exploitation of the individual worker as a means to examine the periodical marketplace's demands on the writer for a sentimental style.

In Melville's chronicle the conflicting ideologies of employer and employee serve as a paradigm for different narrative styles. The narrator's role as employer limits his social awareness. He involves himself in the work lives of his staff in order to demonstrate his own superior abilities in surviving within the world of Wall Street by wielding authority over others. Yet the narrator's "method" turns back on himself. While the other employees acquiesce "with submission," Bartleby "prefer[s] not to" (20). The scrivener's behavior emphasizes the need for a different type of social involvement—the survival of the individual caught within the rigidly structured financial world— and, by extension, a different narrative style. The tale analyzes and ultimately questions the narrator's "method," both as an employer in a position to aid discontented employees like Bartleby and as a narrator in a position to account for Bartleby's tragic story. The title highlights the multitextual layers of the tale: "Bartleby, the Scrivener: A Story of Wall Street" relates the narration of the story of Bartleby to the story of the narrator's Wall Street.

In this *Putnam's* tale, Melville emphasizes upon alternative perspectives—views that ultimately relate to the different modes of narration. The narrator of "Bartleby" emphasizes method in the opening paragraph. He contrasts the approaches to narrative method and brags to the reader how he could provide a sentimental sketch: "if I pleased, [I] could relate divers histories, at which good-natured gentlemen might smile, and sentimental souls might weep" (13). While these "good-natured gentlemen" and "sentimental souls" represent the general or conventional reader, as Michael Gilmore suggests, the narrator's concerns and emphasis here are not on the readers, but on his own narrative approach and method in relating his tale.[32] Deliberately discarding the sentimental mode for his narration of Bartleby, he consciously reserves it for the account of his *own* story. He proudly depicts himself as calculating and conservative: "The late John Jacob Astor, a personage little given to poetic enthusiasm, had no hesitation in pronouncing my first grand point to be prudence; my next, method" (14). Method, of course, is a double tip-off to the narrator's methodical approach to Bartleby as well as to this teller's narrative method in his tale.

The narrator sentimentalizes not Bartleby's story but rather his own narration. He defines himself in sentimental tones. Melville's revisions to the story sharpen his analysis of the rhetorical power of sentiment. By changing the "wasted" form of Bartleby from a Christlike figure "stretched on a blanket" to a regressive fetal position, Melville shifts the emphasis from the actual tragedy to the narrator's reaction to it.[33]

To sentimentalize the story of Bartleby would be to sanctify him at the expense of the narrator's own authority and respectability that he wields as narrator. In this respect, Melville's examination of class relations extends into and includes the classes of author-narrators and subjects, a central link that modern readers, intent on restricting Melville's insights to socioeconomic relations have overlooked.[34] The reader would directly empathize with a portrait of Bartleby as a tragic victim of Wall Street. Sanctification of this employee would directly castigate the narrator since he, as the employer, would be largely responsible for the tragedy. By extracting sentimental rhetoric, he deflects Bartleby's tragedy and reduces its impact. As a result, he remains the focal point and maintains narrative control and superiority over his subject. Uttering the words "with kings and counsellors" (from Job 3) upon discovering the death of his former employee, the lawyer chooses "superior sadness" rather than lament, as Hershel Parker has noted.[35]

The narrator relates his intense feelings of revulsion toward hearing that a man like Bartleby "by nature and misfortune prone to a pallid hopelessness" was forced to work as a subordinate clerk in the dead letter office: "Dead letters! does it not sound like dead men?" (45). He does gain insight into Bartleby's "pallid hopelessness"—too late to aid this employee, but not too late to provide a sympathetic rendition of the tragedy (45). Even so, the lawyer retreats from his insight into deplorable working conditions and their detrimental effects on workers. He chooses instead to retreat behind the conventional sentimental stance: "Ah Bartleby! Ah humanity!" (45).

Rather than console, this sudden, final retreat of the narrator disturbs. It points out the limitations of sentimentalism. We see the irony of the narrator's method in relating his stories: the story of *his* Wall Street and the story of Bartleby's dissolution within the narrator's world. The lawyer's account of Wall Street chronicles the compromises of individual self-respect that must occur in this world as it is constructed by the narrator. Given the irreconcilable results that have stemmed from this situation, the narrator must vindicate himself through sentimentalism in order to survive the dehumanization of the workplace.

The sentimental stance and "method" of the narrator, and by implication the popular practice of sentimental writing, is at stake in this story. This central point of the tale is overlooked by even those critics who see the "Victorian sentimentality" of the narrator, or in McCall's case, attack prevailing views of the narrator's "Victorian gush." [36] The narrator's ending statement appears in this context as no "vague sentimentality," as Allan Emery once argued. [37] It reveals, instead, a deliberate, precise sentimentality, and this is exactly the point that Melville raises by employing such language. It is more instructive to consider the subversive tactics that Melville employs here in relation to the particular narrative style that the author so cleverly and critically raises, rather than in connection with the author's alleged indignation at being forced to write for the populace he resented.

This sentimentalist retreat of the narrator points to the confines of narrative perspective in "Bartleby." We wonder at the beginning of the story exactly why the narrator writes the story of Bartleby when he states clearly that "no materials exist for a full and satisfactory biography of this man" (13). We look in vain for explanations from the narrator of Bartleby's behavior. By constructing the story in this manner, Melville demonstrates that his narrator's sentimental approach to narrative is a means of extracting himself from a highly challenging situation that would necessitate an ideological change, a shift this comfortable narrator is clearly unwilling to consider.

Melville's mixture of sentiment and social analysis serves dual functions in this tale. It poignantly depicts the depersonalization that occurs in the money-making professions, while stopping short of sentimentalizing the stories of individuals like Bartleby. At the same time, it sentimentally portrays the attempts of employers like the narrator to aid their employees, while simultaneously pointing out that narrator's ineffectualness in changing the nature of the work-place. The story of Bartleby and the story of Wall Street conjoin through social critique and separate through the diffusing screen of sentiment.

By conflating the attitudes of *Putnam's* editors toward the prob-lems of industrialization and toward narrative method, Melville rep-resents and yet transcends magazine conventions. The more favorable policies of *Putnam's* provided this author with a context that encour-aged creativity. "Bartleby, the Scrivener" blends sentiment and social critique in such an effective manner that it rekindled the writer's popularity with flagging supporters. His depiction of the power strug-gles involved in the complex relations between employer and em-ployee, narrator and narrative, contributed to the story's popularity and fascination for *Putnam's* readers. In a letter to Evert Duyckinck, Richard Henry Dana proclaimed that " 'Bartleby' . . . shows no com-mon insight."[38] Indeed, Melville's insights into the literary uses of magazine conventions and their impact on readers' perspectives of society, as well as into the nature of narrative itself, produced one of the most widely read and discussed tales in American literary history.

Israel Potter: Or, Fifty Years of Exile

The unusual compositional history of *Israel Potter* illustrates how Melville altered his style when writing for *Harper's* and for *Putnam's*. Of all the author's periodical fiction, this narrative of a Revolutionary War "hero" remains the only work by Melville that, on rejection from one magazine, was reconceived to meet the editorial policies of its competitor. These radically different environments provide clear con-texts for the author's orientation, methods, and his own treatment of historical canonization in *Israel Potter*. They shed new light on what has been viewed as the "elaborate free fiction" of Melville's only serialized novel, *Israel Potter, Or, Fifty Years of Exile: A Fourth of July Story*.[39]

On 25 May 1854 Melville wrote to *Harper's* in an attempt to solicit interest in a "Serial in your Magazine, supposing you had one, in prospect, that suited you."[40] The proposed serial—presumably *Israel*

Potter—received either no response or a rejection from the editor at *Harper's*.[41] Turning to the politically progressive *Putnam's* on 7 June, Melville submitted his "sixty and odd" pages of manuscript originally intended for *Harper's*.

Here the periodical context helps to clarify what have appeared to be compositional and textual ambiguities in *Israel Potter*. The "sixty and odd" pages of manuscript correspond roughly to chapters 1 through 6. Of those chapters, all but chapter 1 (a geographical description of the Berkshire region) represent what Walter Bezanson (editor of the historical notes to the Northwestern-Newberry edition of *Israel Potter*) has called "a virtual paraphrase" of Henry Trumbull's *Life and Remarkable Adventures of Israel R. Potter* (1824). While these early chapters—and presumably the manuscript—parallel their historical source, the remainder of the finished serial (and book) move markedly from the source to the point of calling into question the practice of paraphrased biography which the early chapters—and narrative style—appear to endorse.

Overlooking the periodical context as an explanatory source for textual discrepancies, or at least what look like changing intentions of the author, some Melville scholars have attributed the very different stylistic modes of narration employed in the early chapters (and manuscript) and later chapters to a lack of compositional planning on the part of the author.[42] But placed within the context of the conflicting stylistic practices of *Harper's* and *Putnam's,* the shift in stylistic modes in *Israel Potter* suggests an awareness on Melville's part of the different magazine environments.

A surviving, but incomplete transcription of a letter to G. P. Putnam which accompanied the submitted sample offers insight into the composition of *Israel Potter.* In this letter Melville attempts to clarify the purpose of his enclosed manuscript: "The manuscript is part of a story called 'Israel Potter,' concerning which a more particular understanding need be had."[43] This letter represents the only known clarification or "understanding" of one of his magazine works. Why would Melville have needed to explain his manuscript to the editors at *Putnam's* unless the writing sample did not appear to reflect the interests of the editor, of general editorial tastes, or of magazine practices?

The subject of a Revolutionary hero would easily have spurred interest from a magazine that consistently displayed a keen preference for politically charged material. *Putnam's* had published not only several politically oriented articles and sketches per issue, but also a short serial on the history of one "Founding Father," George Washington. Since *Israel Potter* was to contain its own treatment of a "Founding Father," Benjamin Franklin, something other than the actual subject matter of the proposed serial required clarification. In other words, perhaps there was something that Melville thought *Putnam's* might find questionable regarding the treatment of his subject.

One hypothesis suggests that Melville tried to demonstrate that his sample would not challenge what he called the "tender consciences of the public" or "shock the fastidious."[44] Melville scholars have long thought that the 7 June letter represents the author's reaction to the magazine's rejection of "The Two Temples," a tale that the author had submitted the previous month. The letter of 7 June does employ language that recalls Melville's references to the rejected story in a letter of 16 May.[45] Some weeks prior to the submission of the *Israel Potter* manuscript, Melville had overestimated the editorial claim to "criticize the times." The editors at *Putnam's* regretfully rejected Melville's theologically critical story "The Two Temples" for this reason:

> I am very loth to reject the Two Temples as the article contains some exquisitely fine description, and some pungent satire, but my editorial experience compels me to be very cautious in offending the religious sensibilities of the public, and the moral of the Two Temples would array against us the whole power of the pulpit, to say nothing of Brown, and the congregation of Grace Church.[46]

The fact that the publisher of the monthly, Charles Putnam, took it upon himself to write an additional letter to Melville to reassure him of the monthly's interest in and strong support of his ideologically challenging fiction indicates the high status that Melville's tales held for the editors of *Putnam's*.

However, Melville ended his 7 June letter by claiming that his new work would not breach the monthly's commitment to silence on the subject of religion: "I engage that the story shall contain nothing of any sort to shock the fastidious. There will be very little reflective writing in it; nothing weighty. It is adventure" (*Correspondence*, 265). While this promise certainly refers to the religious issues raised in his previous correspondence with *Putnam's*, since the magazine's editors had not expressed hesitation over the homelessness and starvation of Bartleby, or the violent slave revolt and the grotesque image of Babo's decapitated head impaled on a pole, the letter also strongly implies that the submitted sample did not contain any "weighty" material.

If the submitted sample corresponds to chapters 2 to 6 (the only portion of *Israel Potter* that closely paraphrases Trumbull's biographical narrative of Israel Potter), and challenges few if any social or political attitudes, then why did Melville feel the need to explain his manuscript? Because the "particular understanding" which Melville had provided has been deleted from the transcript, we can only surmise its contents. Thought to be an explanation of the proposed book as a "virtual paraphrase" of Trumbull's *Life and Remarkable Adventures of Israel Potter*, this supposition supports only the contents of the submitted manuscript, what Melville called "some sixty and odd pages"—corresponding to chapters 2 to 6, which represented material originally written for *Harper's*.[47]

Melville could easily have discerned from reading and from writing for *Putnam's* editorial disapproval of "paraphrased" biographies, a policy that was favorable, however, with *Harper's*. Since he had consistently displayed through his magazine submissions a clear understanding of the differences in literary conventions and styles between *Harper's* and *Putnam's*, it seems at least questionable that the author "did not yet know that he would abandon sustained use of the *Life* in the next batch of manuscript," as Bezanson has suggested.[48]

On the contrary, Melville's need to explain a manuscript that paraphrased an existing biography must have required, on the author's part, a commitment—and thus a conscious decision—to move rapidly away from this narrative mode to a nonsentimentalized, critical treatment of a historical subject. To market material previously aimed at *Harper's* readers, Melville would have needed to sell his *Harper's* tale to the editors at *Putnam's* and to explain to George Palmer Putnam how he would develop his proposed serial. In light of the changed publishing context, Melville's letter to Putnam suggests that the author tried to interest the new magazine in his serial by proposing a more detailed account of the novel than the sample indicated, as the excerpt of his letter implies. Biographical stories in *Harper's* differed considerably from those published in *Putnam's;* to understand the extent to which Melville shaped his *Israel Potter* serial, we must examine further the practices of the competing monthlies.

Approaches to Sentiment and Biography in *Harper's* and in *Putnam's*

Two articles on the same topic which appeared within one month of each other in the pages of *Harper's* and *Putnam's* indicate the different orientations and styles of these magazines. In March 1853 *Harper's* published excerpts from J. Ross Browne's "Crusoe-Life; A Narrative of Adventures in the Island of Juan Fernandez." In this account, Browne exploits the associations of the island with Defoe's famous character and recounts in a sentimental style his exploration of the reputed home of Robinson Crusoe:

> Never shall I forget the strange delight with which I gazed upon that isle of romance. . . . Think then, without a smile of disdain, what a thrill of delight ran through my blood, as I pressed my feet for the first time upon the fresh sod of Juan Fernandez! Think of it, too, as the realization of hopes which I had never ceased to cherish from early boyhood; for this was the abiding place, which I now at last beheld, of a wondrous adventurer, whose history had filled my soul years ago with indefinite longings for sea-life, shipwreck, and solitude! Yes, here was verily the land of Robinson Crusoe. (March 1853, 306)

The story is dotted with illustrations of scenes from Defoe's novel, while the author recounts his exploration of all the popular events and characters from the tale that he claims to have met with in his imagination and in his ramblings over the island. Central to understanding *Harper's* practice is the point that Browne both emphasized his narrator's emotional response to the scenes described and appealed to the emotions of sentiment and melancholy so popular in *Harper's* stories. Adapting the style of Ik Marvel's famous *Rever-*

ies of a Bachelor, well known to *Harper's* readers because it was serialized for over a year in the pages of the monthly, Browne employs the sentimental mode as he murmurs to his readers: "What pleasant sadness was it that weighed upon my heart?" Browne's account contains references to the past, to childhood, dreams, visions, fancy, adventure, and longings, all motifs characteristically found in *Harper's* sentimental fiction. The emphasis on melancholic emotions and reveries through employing a sentimental style parallels the characterization that *Putnam's* made of this leading conventional style in *Harper's.* J. Ross Browne was certainly capable of writing more "realistic" narratives, as his 1846 *Etching of a Whale Cruise* testifies, and the sentimental narrative style of his contributions to *Harper's* suggests an understanding, on Browne's part, of the particular practices that marked the literary environment of the magazine.

In a note in the February 1854 issue, Briggs recalled the beginning of what he referred to as the "Sentimental school." Reviewing the success of *Reveries of a Bachelor,* he lists the conventional topics of sentimental writing:

> Ik Marvel founded a school of *litterateurs,* whose peculiar characteristics are, much sentimentality, and a little thought about nature and the poetic side of every-day life, expressed in the form of the soliloquy, although occasionally breaking into the colloquial, the author addressing his words to some imaginary hearer. . . . Reveries, thinkings, memories, mysteries, shadows, and death—old times, voices from the past, stars, moonlight, night winds, old homesteads, flowing rivers, and primeval forests, filled the pages of the new books, and the columns of the daily papers. Ik Marvel delighted the readers of the morning paper with a deer, a dog, and a dead girl, served up in every conceivable style of sorrow, sadness and sighs, for a whole year, at least once a week.[49]

Another article augments the list of conventional motifs written in the sentimental mode:

> A mother weeping over the grave of her son of fifteen summers; a husband stealing with soft step, modulated voice, and imprisoned agony, round the death-bed of his young wife; a

love scene between a youth and a maiden, where passion ex-
hales itself into a dreamy mist, enveloping them both and
softening their outlines to our vision til they melt away in a
cloud of splendor, and leave us pleased but unsatisfied.[50]

This sense of disconnected emotion dissatisfied *Putnam's*, whose editors preferred an openly critical style.

A travel article, also about Robinson Crusoe, in the March 1853
issue of *Putnam's* reflects the different approach of *Putnam's* writers.
Entitled "Robinson Crusoe's Island," this anonymous piece (as all
works were in *Putnam's*) exploits not the conventional views of Defoe's character for sentimental effects, as Browne does so effectively in
his *Harper's* story, but rather problematizes the question of historical
accuracy:

> It is a remarkable fact in literary history, or, perhaps, we should
> rather say, in literary criticism, that for more than a hundred
> years an unquestioned connection has been maintained in
> popular opinion between Robinson Crusoe and Juan Fernan-
> dez . . . while yet the slightest examination of an unabridged
> copy of *Robinson Crusoe* will show that it contains no refer-
> ences whatever to Juan Fernandez, but that, on the contrary,
> a very well-defined locality in another part of the Western
> Hemisphere, is assigned to the imaginary island. (March 1853,
> 275–76).

"Robinson Crusoe's Island" compares the story of Selkirk, Defoe's
reputed source for island information, to that of the narrative of Peter
Serrano and argues that the latter's experience on a Caribbean island
provided Defoe with the material for the island home of Robinson
Crusoe. Through this critical approach the author deconstructs the
sentimentalized myth popularized by Defoe. This attempt to challenge conventional attitudes and folkloric knowledge is found
throughout the pages of *Putnam's* and represents the orientation and
policies of the analytical monthly.

Perhaps the most marked difference between the practices of the
two magazines—and one fundamental to the styling of *Israel Potter*
—is evident in their biographical stories. With the flexible boundaries
between historical and literary narratives that existed in mid-

nineteenth-century American writing, biographical tales in both magazines adhered to Aristotelian dictates for narrative structure (the most revered mode at midcentury).[51] That is, the narrator does not stop at reciting facts, but also incorporates the biographical facts, incidents, and stereotypes into a plot-driven, dramatic narrative.

Harper's biographical stories reiterate biographical and autobiographical accounts of a famous life. Jacob Abbot, for example, supplied *Harper's* with fictionalized accounts of the lives of Benjamin Franklin and Napoleon.[52] Factual in orientation, these pieces supported popular views of cultural heroes. In "Benjamin Franklin," Abbot briefly mentions in the introductory paragraphs that he based his present account on Franklin's *Autobiography*. Throughout the remainder of his piece, Abbot paraphrases Franklin's own story and writes it as if he, Abbot, were the actual informational source.

In *Harper's* the factual recounting of incidents creates the tone of the biography as history. But as in most stories published in this magazine, biographies are exploited for their sentimental and moralistic value. The biographical story is narrated not for its intrinsic values, but rather for "the picturesque and almost romantic interest which attaches itself to the incidents of his personal history," Abbot mentions in "Benjamin Franklin."[53] *Harper's* supported popular romantic pictures of life, love, and history, and writers employed a sentimental style which celebrated and emphasized popular knowledge and folklore surrounding a famous life. By glossing over disconcerting facts and realities, the sentimental approach underscored the predictable. *Harper's* practice reinforced conventional, conservative views instead of providing direct critiques, analyses, and insights, which are nevertheless often found as subtexts in sentimental works.[54]

The facts of a life in the pages of *Harper's* do not speak for themselves as biographical facts but reinforce an emphasis on morality:

> A Quaker lady came to him [Franklin] one day, on board the vessel in which he was sailing to New York, and began to caution him against two young women who had come on board the vessel at Newport, and who were very forward and familiar in their manners. . . . When they arrived at New York the young women told him where they lived, and invited him to come and see them. But he avoided doing so, and it was well

that he did, for a few days afterward he learned that they were both arrested as thieves. If Franklin had been found in their company he might have been arrested as their accomplice. (January 1852, 153)

Like their more literary counterparts in *Harper's*, biographical stories ultimately represent an ideological principle fundamental to the middle classes. They act as ideological metaphors: "His public life, in fact, began and ended with the beginning and the end of that great protracted struggle by which the American nation was ushered into being. His history is then simply the history of the establishment of American independence" ("Benjamin Franklin," *Harper's*, February 1852, 309). Perhaps because this orientation expressed the larger tradition of *Harper's* writing, biographies occupied a disproportionately large space as well as front matter of the monthly's pages and seem to have been a genre quite popular with *Harper's* readers.

In contrast to the all-knowing, omniscient tone of the *Harper's* narrator, who appropriates a biography and retells it as his own, the biographical narrator in *Putnam's* adopts the role of an interpreter and evaluator of the reputed facts of a life. In the opening paragraph of "Washington's Early Days," the narrator introduces his method and approach: "We shall make use of all authorities within our reach, not even rejecting tradition, which is often the vehicle of important truth where character is to be estimated" (*Putnam's*, January 1854, 1). Narrators referred openly to the various biographical sources on which they relied, and these references surface throughout. In this magazine, known biographical "facts" were not exploited for their ideological potential, but were analyzed, questioned, and probed in keeping with the overall policies of the management.

Conventional views of heroes, such as Washington's reputed powers of self-control, are challenged: "For the temperament of Washington was impetuous, and his passions were fiery, though we are little accustomed to think so" (6). Through this approach, *Putnam's* writers challenge the truth of "facts" and treat them as literary embellishments:

We must allow Mr. Weems the praise of a good narrator, and his generous enthusiasm makes him an inspiring one. As to the

facts, we must first accept them as honestly believed by a
gentleman and a clergyman; and many of them can claim the
benefit of internal evidence. If not literally true, *"Ils meritent
bien de l'etre."* . . . It is not difficult to recognize the warm
poetic fancy of the narrator in this sketch, but we are quite
willing to accept it, even as "Imaginary Conversations" of old
times. (4, 6)

Writers of these more analytical and critical biographical tales highlight the fictional elements of the genre and thus call attention to the
difficulty of absolute truth in the historical narrative.

Putnam's *Practices and* Israel Potter

As a potential serial for the pages of *Harper's, Israel Potter* would have
needed to seem as factual as possible to conform with the styles of the
biographies of Franklin and Napoleon. As Bezanson has pointed
out, Melville's early chapters closely resemble the factual tone of
Trumbull's text.[55] More than 50 percent of Melville's manuscript contains transcribed words and phrases from Trumbull. This virtual
paraphrase—or appropriation—of the material of a previous biogra-
pher exactly reflects *Harper's* tradition. But it is central to understanding Melville's compositional methods in—and his reliance on
—magazine practice that the majority of these appropriations are
found in chapters 2 to 6, the sections that most likely constituted the
manuscript originally intended for *Harper's.* In their chronicling of
the life and loves of a historical figure, chapters 2 to 6 belong to the
genre of biographical stories popular with *Harper's* readers. Melville's
interest in preserving this established tradition contextualizes the
close paraphrasing in the chapters representing the submitted manuscript.

But *Harper's* biographical stories, as we have seen, underscored
sentiment, and writers provided highly romantic accounts of amo-
rous events in the lives of historical figures. In this vein, Melville's
early chapters parallel this use of sentiment. Israel's doomed love for
a neighborhood girl frames chapter 2, which concludes in a manner
closely aligned to the sentimental style in *Harper's* stories: "But if
hopes of his sweetheart winged his returning flight, such hopes were

not destined to be crowned with fruition. The dear, false girl, was another's" (*Israel Potter*, 11). The short-lived romance of Israel Potter is only referred to once after chapter 6. While this abrupt end of the romance supports Bezanson's conjecture that chapters 2 to 6 represent the original manuscript sent to the magazines, it also demonstrates the implications of writing for *Putnam's*. Because this antisentimental magazine would have had little interest in a sentimentalized biographical romance, it seems logical that Melville dropped the episode.

Why did he not omit it altogether? Though including such material seems more in line with the policies of *Harper's*, Melville exploits the possibility of simultaneously representing and criticizing a sentimental style. *Putnam's* prided itself on criticizing sentimental topics for their limited insight. Melville had employed this strategy in both "Bartleby, the Scrivener" and "Benito Cereno," stories published in *Putnam's* prior to the serialization of *Israel Potter*.[56]

After closing chapter 2 with the sentimental exclamation about lost love, Melville begins chapter 3 by dashing all hopes for a sentimental biography. Mentioning various romantic exploits, the omniscient narrator clearly warns the reader of the antiromantic and mostly realistic nature of this narrative: "But if wandering in the wilderness; and wandering upon the waters; if felling trees; and hunting, and shipwreck; and fighting with whales, and all his other strange adventures, had not as yet cured poor Israel of his now hopeless passion; events were at hand for ever to drown it" (12). This move from sentimentalized response to its critique exemplifies Melville's ability to make conventional forms more complex and multitextual as well as suggests a conscious affinity to *Putnam's* practice.

But *Putnam's* did not rest in criticizing popular use of the sentimental mode; the larger orientation of the magazine was political. Melville's additions and changes indicate his attempt to gear his *Harper's*-oriented manuscript to the conventions of *Putnam's*. One significant parallel between the ideological orientation of *Putnam's* and Melville's tale lies in the nationalism inherent in celebrating the Yankee character, in chapter 3, for example, at the expense of the English. Since *Putnam's* prided itself on being strictly an American magazine that rebuffed all English influence, these additions would

have been lauded by the editors of *Putnam's*. *Harper's*, which sought
to model itself on English literary tastes and contained a large proportion of English literature, would clearly have found Israel's rebellious
attitude toward English culture antithetical to their orientation. The
American national pride pervading these early chapters represented
the hallmark of *Putnam's*.

The political analysis that dominates *Israel Potter* reflects most
directly Melville's use of *Putnam's* policies. The author introduces in
his prefatory lines the theme of political rebellion, which complements his exploitation of the Yankee theme dominating the remainder of the submitted manuscript pages. He dramatizes the politically
rebellious spirit of Yankees in chapters 5 and 6, where he significantly
lengthens Trumbull's scene of the encounter between Israel and the
British king. Melville's innovation of the Trumbull manuscript here
may imply the nature of the modifications he ultimately made when
tailoring his story for the pages of *Putnam's*, for it patently opposes
the practice of *Harper's*. Without the manuscript this suggestion remains conjecture; however, in light of Melville's treatment of political
institutions and themes of rebellion in other stories for the monthly,
Israel Potter echoes the author's style in *Putnam's*.[57]

Transforming the manuscript and plans for *Israel Potter* into a
Putnam's piece required major stylistic revision. At a deeper level,
chapters 2 to 6 differ markedly from Trumbull's text and *Harper's*
practice.[58] One of the most significant changes is in the point of view.
The biographical stories in *Harper's* were narrated in first person (as
was Trumbull's narrative) to enhance the authenticity of the narrator-
author. Melville shifts from first-to third-person narration. This significant act alters the nature of biographical narrator to reflect the
tone of *Putnam's*, where the specific use of third person constantly
highlights the genre as a tale told by someone of questionable authenticity. Melville's own prefatory discussion in *Israel Potter* concerning
the nature of biography, the narrative method used, and the adoption
of the role as "editor" follows the general practices in *Putnam's* of
problematizing narrative representation.

Since *Putnam's* did not share *Harper's* interest in publishing serialized biographical accounts of historical figures, it seems logical that
Melville would supplement his submitted sample with a description

and promise of analysis, travels, and characterizations more in keeping with *Putnam's* conventions. His changes to the Trumbull narrative in chapters 2 to 6, coupled with his reputed "restlessness" and conscious move to "elaborate free fiction" after chapter 6, indicate his commitment to a fictionalized, literary treatment of political anomalies in keeping with *Putnam's* editorial policies.[59] The investigation into the nature of a hero and the ambivalence of a government which allows soldiers to die in poverty points to this journal's commitment to questioning, analyzing, and criticizing destructive political policies and institutions.

Putnam's American commentary on European culture provided unflinching analyses of the differences between the politically powerful and weak. "How They Manage in Europe," an article in the April 1853 issue, concluded with this devastating opinion of political conditions in Europe:

> This, then, is the way they manage to govern the people in Europe. By the skilful use of patronage, of the church, and of education; by the denial of the press, of free-locomotion, and the rights of the trade; and by the distribution of standing armies, they bamboozle, delude, suppress, and constrain, until the wretched people, impoverished, ignorant, separated and set at enmity with each other, are reduced to a slavery from which it seems almost madness for them to hope to escape. (436)

Melville expresses these attitudes not only in condemning the tyranny of the English king, but also in equating poverty with slavery. In "Israel in Egypt," Israel Potter considers his miserable situation and reiterates themes presented in "How They Manage in Europe":

> Sometimes, lading out his dough, Israel could not but bethink him of what seemed enigmatic in his fate. . . . here he was at last, serving that very people as a slave, better succeeding in making their bricks than firing their ships. To think that he should be thus helping, with all his strength, to extend the walls of the Thebes of the oppressor, made him half mad. Poor Israel! well-named—bondsman in English Egypt. (*Israel Potter*, 157)

Melville also provided more complex portraits of famous heroes than found in the pages of *Harper's*. "Seeking here to depict him in less exalted lights," he offered the readers of *Putnam's* a more unsentimentalized and analytical depiction of the famous American personality than could have been found in the pages of *Harper's* (*Israel Potter,* 48). The undercutting of sentimentalized portraits of American heroes—as seen in Melville's analytical treatments of Franklin, Ethan Allen, and John Paul Jones—locates this work as a distinctively *Putnam's* production.

Perhaps the most *Putnam*-like characteristic of *Israel Potter* was its "American" spirit. Throughout the serialization, reviewers in various papers and magazines commented on this quality. Praising the first issue in July, a New York paper declared *Israel Potter* "an original American romance," and indeed, its original subtitle, "A Fourth of July Story," invited such a response (*New York Commercial Advertiser,* 3 July 1854). This American spirit was formulated as a direct, honest style, a quality that Melville's characterization of Israel continually exemplified. The author's writing style complemented the character-ization of his American hero. Reviewers of the serialization praised *Israel Potter* for its "manly, direct, and clear" style (*Morning Courier and New York Enquirer,* 29 July 1854). Colonel Greene of the *Boston Post* praised *Israel Potter* for its "curt, manly, and independent tone."[60] These reviews imply a contrast between a "manly, direct" tone and a nationalist political ideology.

Putnam's editors hoped for precisely such independent and direct writing from their contributors. Melville's story of a rebellious hero whose life dramatizes the contradictions inherent in commonly held ideologies of the founding fathers reflected the politics of the maga-zine's policies perfectly. Through his innovative manipulations of magazine conventions in *Israel Potter,* Melville displays his mastery of form as well as his "geniality" toward editorial policy—and politics.[61]

Some Melville scholars have pointed out that *Putnam's* itself seems to have criticized Melville for not following Trumbull's biographical tale more closely. It is important to remember that *Putnam's* changed hands in the spring of 1855, just before Melville's serial finished. Thus, the editorial that criticized Melville's performance in *Israel Potter* indicated the views of a new editor and a new management. This changed perspective would soon drastically alter the editorial policies of *Putnam's* and transform the once analytical monthly into a mirror image of its competitor, *Harper's*. This example underscores the necessity for acknowledging the complexities inherent in given magazine environments, contexts frequently altered through changes in management policies, reader expectations, literary shifts, and cultural developments.

Editorial Politics and "Benito Cereno"

Of all of Melville's shorter fiction, "Benito Cereno" represents the author's most creative use of magazine policies, popular forms, literary sources, and personal thematic concerns. Melville's engagement with editorial politics in *Putnam's Monthly* suggests a mutuality between author and publishing context that is often overlooked in textual studies of Melville's tales. The political opinions debated by *Putnam's* editors throughout numerous articles, essays, and stories on the questions of racial equality, the institution of slavery, and expansionism find thematic and ideological analogues in "Benito Cereno." A clear affinity exists between Melville's probing study of the nature of political hegemony in the Americas and the editorial politics of the monthly.

This link provides a context that significantly enhances interpretation of the tale. When removed from its publishing context, "Benito Cereno" has appeared to many readers as an ambiguous—even ambivalent—story of revolution.[62] The act of placing this tale, written for one of the most intellectual and politically progressive magazines of mid-nineteenth-century America, into its original context elucidates for modern readers the intertextuality, traces, and resonances inherent in "Benito Cereno." Contextual analysis reconfigures Melville's reputed ambivalence—or racism, as some scholars have asserted—into an unequivocal indictment of racial inequality.

Putnam's promised American commentary on both national and international affairs. The publisher, George Palmer Putnam, the chief editor, Charles F. Briggs, and the contributors were closely aligned to the antislavery movement. Briggs, popularly known as Harry Franco, was an outspoken critic of slavery and a staunch supporter of various abolitionists. Writers such as Richard Burleigh Kimball, Parke Godwin (from the radical *Democratic Review* of the 1840s), and Frederick Law Olmsted, (one of the founders of the extant, liberal weekly paper *The Nation*) consistently spoke out against poverty, slavery, racial bigotry, and expansionism. Godwin proclaimed that *Putnam's* was "profoundly stirred by these agitations of the outer world. For the first time in the history of our higher periodicals, its managers had stepped down from their snowy pedestals to take part in the rabble and scuffle of the streets.[63]

So powerful—and convincing—were these writers that they contributed significantly by the end of the decade to changing the political stance of their competitor, *Harper's*. George William Curtis, who eventually switched editorial positions to become the political editor of *Harper's,* was instrumental in changing the orientation of that politically conservative monthly to reflect the liberalism of the by-then defunct *Putnam's*.

The political views expressed in *Putnam's* were enormously influential. As Thomas Bender has noted, the progressive attitudes regarding racial equality, slavery, and racism shaped what would by the early 1860s represent Northern political opinion as well as formed the platform of the new Republican party.[64] The political essays and articles on American interventionism and racial equality written by Kimball, Olmsted, and Godwin were referred to in popular literary culture through the end of the century.

Even the new publishers, Dix and Edwards, who took over in 1855 after financial problems forced Putnam to sell the magazine, committed themselves, despite a real need to boost Southern circulation, to the editorial politics of racial equality. Olmsted, one of the new editors with the change in management asserted in a letter to Godwin: "We shall be prepared and willing to lose 1000 Southern subscribers if the article commands the attention and respect that most of your articles have."[65] The essay to which Olmsted referred, "Uncle Tom at Home," rigorously criticized sentimental views of African Americans as dependent children, views that promoted the idea of racial inferiority and as a result helped to sustain slavery.

Yet *Putnam's* did not merely editorialize a particular stance. Articles, essays, and stories analyzed and evaluated the variety of perspectives that comprised a particular issue. Parke Godwin, author of more than thirty pieces in *Putnam's,* employed this analytical style in his political essays. For example, in "Our Parties and Politics," Godwin first describes the different parties and platforms that were currently active in the mid-fifties. But in discussing the ideological implications of these platforms, he points out and often severely criticizes the contradictions in, for example, believing in individual liberty but reserving it for whites only.

Putnam's editors established their progressive political stance by leading the first number of the magazine with a highly controversial plea against current American foreign policy. In "Cuba," Richard Burleigh Kimball vividly depicts the set of relations that underlie American intervention, a paradigm based on a practice of appropriation and exploitation, which Melville employed as a thematic construct in "Benito Cereno":

> It is, however, a poor excuse for the unlawful seizure of the territory of a friendly power, or for an unwarrantable interference with their rights, to raise, in avoidance of the charge of robbery or oppression, this plea of "manifest destiny"; for the proposition is as good on the part of the highwayman, as that of a power which shall take to the high road of nations, and armed with more resistless energies, prey upon the weak or distracted.[66]

The majority of articles on manifest destiny supported Kimball's opposition.[67] *Putnam's* presented through these articles a clear denunciation of an American foreign policy that would support government intervention and expansionism, themes repeated in "Benito Cereno."[68]

In addition to foreign policy matters, the editors also avidly participated in separate debates over racial equality, although the issues of annexation and racial policies are closely linked. During the early fifties, claims that the various "races" descended from different species received popular attention. *Putnam's* severely criticized this theory. In several articles, writers argued for the humanity of African Americans and their right to be treated on equal footing with other races.[69] In a review of Josiah Nott's *Types of Mankind,* which the

magazine ran on the first page of the July 1854 issue, Godwin dedicates fourteen pages to discrediting Nott's racist theory.[70] Since reviews almost never appeared on the first page in this magazine, this
particular notice serves a larger rhetorical purpose than just book
reviewing. The entire first page does not even discuss the book's
thesis, but instead offers the egalitarian view that all humans have the
same ancestors. Godwin reiterated this stance on racial equality in a
subsequent article, published in the 1855 issue, entitled "Are All Men
Descended from Adam?" which argued for the "moral, religious, and
physical unity of the races."[71]

In an effort to complicate the analytical stance of the magazine,
writers offered multiple perspectives. In "Hayti and the Haytians,"
Kimball contrasts his uninformed views of people of African descent
with his enlightening experiences in Haiti, by asserting, for example,
that Afro-Haitian women were better mannered than white American
ladies: "I never have seen in any city of the Union ladies of more
cultivated and accomplished *manners,* than some I have seen in Port
au Prince."[72] With a subtle ambiguity and pointed satire which underscores the subjective, hypocritical, and irrational bigotry inherent
in the proslavery perspective, Kimball remarks on the dissolution of
racial barriers that people experienced on the island, even visitors
from the Southern states: "A gentleman from Alabama, who spent
some weeks on the island, remarked as he was about leaving, that he
should have to be very careful when he reached home, or he should
find himself tipping his hat to every negro he met on his plantation"(58). At the same time, however, Kimball attributes what he
terms "savage" qualities to the Haitians: "I have already alluded here
to the fact that there is a strange blending of Parisian refinement
and civilization, with native African barbarism and morals" (59). Yet
Kimball does not use such a description to discount the humanity of
people of African descent and their right to be treated on an equal
footing with other races, themes also repeated in "Benito Cereno."

Writers who attempted to offer alternative views that undermine
racial stereotypes usually portrayed people of color as human beings
imbued with both civilized and what travelers referred to as "native"
or "barbaric" qualities, the same characteristics attributed to white
people whose actions were the subject of criticism in the pages of the

magazine. The author of "African Proverbial Philosophy" discusses the reason why some African groups had women warriors, such as two warring peoples, the Dalhomians and the Yorubas. He describes the Yorubas with all the attributes usually reserved for Anglo-Saxons: "They are a people active, keen, commercial, ingenious, affectionate, moral." At the same time, he notes that women occupied the front lines of the Dalhomian invasion. The fighters "were chiefly women, who are always placed in the foremost of their battles, as more to be depended on,"[73] an idea that Melville might have borrowed for his multiple depiction of African women in "Benito Cereno." Throughout these *Putnam's* articles, writers continually pointed out the problems with stereotypical and biased views.

Melville continued the practices of Godwin, Kimball, Briggs, and Curtis by submitting a series of tales to the monthly, particularly "The Encantadas," "Benito Cereno," and "The Bell-Tower," which questioned, probed, and ultimately challenged sentimental depictions of political interventionism as brotherly assistance and slavery as paternal nurturing. In "Benito Cereno," the author subtly examines these pressing political and social issues that faced the United States in the mid-fifties by playing off sentimental views, represented in the character of Amasa Delano, against the political criticism of the progressive magazine. Melville portrays and criticizes an American ideology that is based on "piratical" appropriation of an enslaved people for "material gain," dramatized both through Benito Cereno's relation to the ship's "cargo" and Amasa Delano's sentimentalized attitudes toward slavery. The author's articulation of America's economic impetus for expansion corroborates the perspective offered by Kimball's articles on the Caribbean, editorials by Briggs, and essays by Curtis and Godwin. In light of this magazine context, studies that depict Melville's political views as antithetical to his culture and his literary environment ignore the author's role in representing and supporting *Putnam's* positions on social and political issues.[74]

In fact, *Putnam's* policies on ethnicity, race, and interventionism help to clarify a narrative structure and voice that some have seen as ambiguous at best. In addition, the practices of *Putnam's* provide a solid context and a source for Melville's rigorous condemnation of slavery in "Benito Cereno" and thus corroborates the already solid interpretations of this issue.[75] In this multivalenced tale, Melville weaves a complex web of editorial stances on social and political theories with his own concerns for multilayered writing.

"Benito Cereno"

In "Benito Cereno" (published in three installments from October to December 1855), Melville creatively dramatizes the perspectives of the magazine on race and imperialism by changing the name of Amasa Delano's ship from the *Tryal* to the *San Dominick*. This change reflects the author's intent to embed a signifier with multiple layers of meaning, a process characteristic of Melville's best style. The name *San Dominick* both recalls the order of Dominicans, the "Black" Friars, and evokes the Santo Domingo slave revolt. In the context of *Putnam's*, Melville's direct allusion to this famous revolt suggests a solidarity with the political opinions regarding the uprising which were frequently expressed in the magazine.[76]

Beyond an affinity with editorial politics, "Benito Cereno" reflects the magazine's concern with method. An article that chronicled the series of events from colonialism and slavery through rebellion and a reversal of political power may have provided Melville with a thematic structure for his political tale. In "Hayti and the Haytians" Richard Burleigh Kimball depicts the tragic outcome of colonialism, slavery, and rebellion, all issues dramatized in "Benito Cereno."[77] He condemns France's dictatorial policies toward its subjects, and he describes the reversals that occur as a result of this shift in power. Kimball posits that the act of basing a set of relations on the unequal positioning of oppressor and oppressed only encourages revolt and ultimately a reversal of positions and further tyranny.

In "Benito Cereno" Melville refashions the original narrative of Amasa Delano regarding the slave revolt aboard the *Tryal* by apparently repeating Kimball's schema. "Benito Cereno" chronicles the same sequence of events as in Kimball's account: colonialism, tyranny, slavery, revolt, and violence, followed by further suppression. Through this paradigm, Melville dramatizes the conflicting perspectives toward American expansionism and its clear link to slavery, creating a deeply probing tale of human behavior. By employing

Delano's original narrative he examines the nature of interpersonal relations that encourage the violence and brutality exhibited in all of the major characters. Through the volatile memories of slave revolts, Melville examines in this ingeniously crafted tale the underlying assumptions regarding the racial and economic superiority on which policies of imperialism and slavery are based.

The tale's narrator emphasizes the process of perception. The contrast of different legal, imperialist, and sentimental perspectives that together perpetuate the inequality and oppression in the tale—and by extension in society—serves as the foundation for the author's theme. Melville suggests through this emphasis on process that a careful sorting of the possibilities is necessary to understand and overcome the ironic reversals that are intrinsic to institutional practices such as slavery and expansionism. It is precisely this analytical probing of surfaces that the magazine and Melville's tale urge.

Melville reconfigures political issues into a literary study of the underlying paradigms of power that create such human drama as that depicted in "Benito Cereno." For this reason, Melville does not restrict the forces of evil and brutality to one group, either to the African slaves or to the Spanish sailors. Rather, the narrator presents the conflicting behaviors of the major characters in the story, contrasting the behavior of Atufal as slave and Atufal as enslaver. He also presents the ferocity that the "gentle" Amasa Delano exhibits once he adopts the role of the avenging authoritarian, and the striking difference between the Spanish sailors as meek victims and as ruthless vindicators.

As Carolyn Karcher and Michael Rogin have argued, Melville dramatizes the differences in perception regarding the primacy of patriarchal institutions, and the idea that African American "children"—the slaves—needed white "fathers"—plantation owners—to care for them.[78] In this way Melville, like other writers for *Putnam's*, attempts to humanize the stereotypes of people of African descent. In accentuating the ferocity of the Africans subjected to repression, Melville certainly means to show that they react as any individual might to the tyranny of enslavement. Through this context, he forces the reader to consider the reasons for each extreme alteration in behavior, and it is this method, an effort to engage the reader in perceiving the underlying reasons behind political and racial attitudes and acts, that closely ties "Benito Cereno" to magazine practices of *Putnam's.*

Melville's narrator displays no surprise in the sequence of events that have occurred on the *San Dominick:* "But, under the circumstances, precisely this condition of things was to have been anticipated" (*Piazza Tales,* 51–52). Melville's tale criticizes Delano's limited American perspective and, indeed, every perspective on the impossible subject of slavery. By contrasting the various positions in society —the oppressed, the naive, the exploiters, and the legal authorities— he points out the severe limitations in each of these views. The ending provides the reader with two possibilities: the ominous suggestion to also "follow the leader," or the unstated choice offered by the larger story (and by the larger magazine environment) to find literary, political, and ideological alternatives to these limited and dangerous viewpoints.

The parallels between editorial policies and the particular structures, styles, and themes of not only "Benito Cereno" but also Melville's other contributions to *Putnam's Monthly* suggest a clear link between text and context.[79] The conditions of the periodical marketplace as well as individual magazine practices provide valuable insights into the nature of literary creativity as well as clear interpretive communities for the act of reading.

It is Melville's uncanny ability to conflate political, social, and ideological issues with literary concerns that contributes to the artistry of "Benito Cereno." One of the author's greatest innovations of magazine practices is to suggest that the exploration of multiple views requires a multileveled structure: "Hitherto the nature of this narrative, besides rendering the intricacies in the beginning unavoidable, has more or less required that many things, instead of being set down in the order of occurrence, should be retrospectively, or irregularly given" (*Piazza Tales,* 114). Melville innovates magazine practices of liberalism, critical analysis, and multiple perspectives by employing them as a paradigm for literary method. His expertise at "making literary" (to borrow a term from Russian formalism) a variety of views, practices, and forms from this magazine environment points to the particular nature of his creativity.

Melville's choice to publish simultaneously in two magazines so radically different from one another in political, social, and literary scope indicates the author's interest in creatively relying on magazine practices. In writing for *Harper's*, Melville assumed the thematic and artistic challenge of employing the sentimental mode both to represent and to change conservative middle-class views in what appears to be an attempt to instruct readers. Since *Putnam's* readers expected critical treatments of political, social, and ideological positions, Melville creatively engaged in magazine practices by blending his own interests with those of his readers. Melville's reliance on editorial policies, then, reflects an effort to reach, rather than to trick, the reader. In the end, the author's magazine fiction extends beyond personal strategies and rationalizations—beyond technique, style, and literary economics—to the reader, a relation that Melville appears to have considered positively and creatively.

PART FOUR

New Audiences, New Forms

CHAPTER NINE

Writing the American Novel:
The Confidence-Man

WHEN MELVILLE STARTED *The Confidence-Man: His Masquer-ade* in the spring of 1855, he was still submitting stories such as "Benito Cereno" and "The Apple-Tree Table" to the editors of *Putnam's*, the monthly where he had been enjoying an enthusiastic following among its readers. Throughout the reviews of *The Piazza Tales*, a collection of Melville's *Putnam's* stories, critics commonly referred to the "great attention" the tales had generated among that audience.[1] The reviewer for the *New York Dispatch* recalled the surging popularity of Melville's stories in various issues of the journal. When "The Encantadas" appeared, he recalled, "the chapters were universally considered the most interesting papers of that popular Magazine, and each successive chapter was read with avidity by thousands."[2] Melville's tales were so popular with *Putnam's* readers that the author's work became the trademark for the magazine. The *American Publishers' Circular* maintained that Melville's *Putnam's* stories "were, in no small degree, instrumental in raising that journal to its present proud position—the best of all American Monthlies."[3]

Melville crafted his new work, *The Confidence-Man*, with this strong readership in mind. Though the letter written to the publisher of the journal has not (yet) been found, Melville apparently proposed *The Confidence-Man* for both serialization in the monthly and subsequent book publication.[4] His allegiance to *Putnam's* conventions prompted some reviewers of *The Confidence-Man* to assert that Melville's work had first appeared as a serial in the pages of the monthly.[5]

One issue repeatedly discussed in *Putnam's* concerned the lack of what the editors thought of as a truly *American* novel. They often lamented that "our first novel of society has yet to be written."[6] In an article entitled "Novels: Their Meaning and Mission," published in the October 1854 issue of *Putnam's*, the editors argued that a "national novel" is not possible in a society so riddled with sectionalist rhetoric as America in the 1850s:

> America has no national novel for the very good reason that there is no such thing as American society. Particular portions, indeed, and particular sides thereof have found interpreters. Western and Indian life has a Cooper; Southern, a Kennedy; and New England, a Hawthorne and a Sedgwick; but her "idea" has never yet been embodied—her pulse, the state of it, has never yet been recorded; for the reason that arterial circulation has hardly yet commenced; her "mission" has not yet quite got itself evolved; and *the* American Novel, like her "Coming Man," is only a "coming."[7]

The Confidence-Man can be read as Melville's response to this charge. This work flows with American traditions, conventions, institutions, and people. Both the author's motivation and his strategy of interweaving the popular folk type of the confidence man with the magazine's concern for a truly American novel provide interpretive insights into the frequently misunderstood structure and highly auditory qualities of *The Confidence-Man*. By recovering the cultural attitudes and nationalistic hopes of the magazine, ideas that Melville treats in *The Confidence-Man,* we will discover an author in tune with the interests of the magazine and its readers.

Far from expressing a "mood of Timonism" in *The Confidence-Man*, Melville creates from popular forms and critical concerns a highly artistic work. Through his chronicle of a voyage to the heart of America, the author charts the course of his own artistic development, a growth resulting from the remarkable creativity inherent in his creation of the American novel.

Confidence Men and *Putnam's* Tradition

Evert Duyckinck described the notion of the confidence man as "an original American idea,"[8] and it is with the folk heritage of this persona that we must start in our study of Melville's motivations and artistry in *The Confidence-Man.* An article in the Albany (or Springfield) papers regarding the reappearance of the confidence man William Thompson in April 1855 was partly responsible for prompting Melville to start work on *The Confidence-Man.*[9] The term *confidence man* was first coined in 1849 by a writer in the *New York Tribune* who recorded the events surrounding the swindling activities of this William Thompson. A *Literary World* review of the production of William E. Burton's 1849 farce, "The Confidence Man" characterized the confidence man as a "new species of the Jeremy Diddler," a name Melville refers to in his work.[10] By the mid-1850s, stories of confidence men swept the country, and the image became common in popular literary culture.[11]

As a regular reader of many of the period's magazines and newspapers, Melville had undoubtedly encountered the several published literary accounts of confidence men in the 1850s in these magazines. We underestimate Melville's interest in literary artifacts of his day by asserting, as the editors of the Northwestern-Newberry edition have done, that "however much or little of the 'original confidence man' that Melville was aware of in 1849, it was the 1855 newspaper item that moved him to write something suggested by the confidence man's career."[12] As David Reynolds has recently demonstrated, Melville's stance as "an attentive culture watcher" almost certainly enticed the writer to cater to the general public's fascination over the "likeable criminal" in creating his own confidence man.[13] In writing for *Putnam's* readers, Melville took great care in composing *The Confidence-Man* according to *Putnam's* editorial policies. By 1855, for example, the journal provided satires in their popular "Cursive and Discursive" column where the editors poked fun at magazine writers, editors, publishers, politicians, and various public personalities. *The Confidence-Man* mirrors this practice through its lightly veiled satirical portraits of Horace Greeley, Bayard Taylor, Fanny Kemble, Emerson, Poe, and Hawthorne, among others, all of whom were easily identified and lauded by *Putnam's* readers and reviewers.[14] Likewise, the economic greed and "freebooting" attitudes of individuals portrayed in Melville's depiction of American society echo the themes and sentiments found in several articles and stories in *Putnam's* during the winter and spring of 1856.[15]

A review of G.H. Lewes's *The Life and Works of Goethe* in the February issue of *Putnam's* may have reinforced ideas that Melville discovered in his own readings of Goethe and Thomas Carlyle. This review illustrates themes presented in Goethe's *Faust* that also form the basis to Melville's *The Confidence-Man*. Both works treat as their themes the "social effects" of "an incoherent society." In his work Melville employs the same metaphors for society and prevailing attitudes governing individual behavior that Goethe had used in *Faust*, who had presented society "as one vast masquerade, where the spokesman are fools, and the only recognized nexus—money—a stupendous paper lie."[16]

This notion of society as a deceptive institution where its members participate in and favor economic appropriation informs other articles and stories in *Putnam's*. The appearance of "The Compensation Office," a story published in the May 1855 issue of *Putnam's*, may have served as the impetus for Melville's beginning work on *The Confidence-Man* in May 1855, along with the newspaper account on William Thompson.[17]

With its repetitious plot, its depiction of the confiding and beguiling public, and its reputed "swindler" protagonist, *The Confidence-Man* strikingly resembles "The Compensation Office." The latter tale concerns a man who runs a "compensation" business. In this dialogue-driven story, various individuals appear who demand compensation for faulty financial, emotional, and social investments that they have made. The merchant tests these customers to determine whether they have faith in themselves and in others.

These individuals also appear in Melville's *The Confidence-Man*. A "philosophical man" who specializes in "truth" serves as a prototype for Melville's man from the "Philosophical Intelligence Office" (114).[18] Another individual plans to extract money from unwitting victims for the "widows and orphans," paving the way for Melville's swindler of "widows and orphans" (37). A "young man" who "thinks" for a living anticipates the young gentleman who reads Tacitus in *The Confidence-Man* (25–27). The "self-possessed" compensation merchant with "burning eyes" seems intimately related to the "self-possessed" confidence-man of Melville's work (194).

Another story that appears to have served as a model for Melville is "Elegant Tom Dillar," published in the May 1853 issue of *Putnam's*.[19] Some characters in *The Confidence-Man* find their analogue in this story. Tom Dillar, a wealthy man, becomes a victim to a confidence game in which an alleged friend persuades him to speculate in the "Pottawatamy Coal Stock," an incident that closely parallels Melville's confidence game concerning the "Black Rapids Coal Company" (22; 47). Penniless, Tom Dillar poses as a "Black minstrel" in order to earn a living, a situation that also appears in *The Confidence-Man* through the character of Black Guinea, a character who sings and exploits the conventionally white stereotypes of African Americans in order to survive economically (10–17).[20]

Like the various characters in *The Confidence-Man,* Tom Dillar is urged to "trust."[21] By the end of this story, the reader discovers that society, not the disguised Tom Dillar, is not to be trusted. The theme is the same central question on which "The Compensation Office" turns: Who swindles whom? Only one of the customers displays any confidence in the compensation merchant. One by one, they question his integrity and accuse him of being a swindler and an impostor. When the customers attempt to extract compensation from the merchant without having justly earned it, they project their own confidence games on him: "Without much confidence in his profession . . . she was sure he was an imposter."[22] By the conclusion of the story, however, it is obvious that the swindlers are "the swindling public who partakes" in confidence games. Like "The Compensation Office," "Elegant Tom Dillar" depicts a society that is intrinsically "dishonest."[23] Those who lack faith in themselves and depend instead on compensation and appropriation succeed only in swindling themselves.

Melville provides a clue to this motif in the first sentence of *The Confidence-Man,* which encourages the reader to consider the confidence man in a benevolent light. Melville compares the first appearance of the figure to the sudden appearance of "Manco Capac at Lake

Titicaca" (3). Readers of *Harper's* could easily recognize this allusion to the man who came from God and civilized a barbaric people. In the June 1853 issue, the author of "Ancient Peru" discussed Manco Capac's role in "civilizing the natives" of Peru on his sudden appearance among them.[24]

By comparing the "man in cream-colors" with Manco Capac, Melville implies that the confidence man intends to redeem the people.[25] This is substantiated by the figure's first guise as the man in cream colors who assumes a Christlike character in an effort to teach the people charity.[26] But as in Goethe's *Faust,* the protagonist finds himself in the midst of greed and deception.

Considered within the context of its sources in "The Compensation Office," Melville's novel reveals an ambiguous personage who tries to educate "the natives of all sorts":

> Men of business, and men of pleasure; parlor men and back-woodsmen; farm-hunters and fame-hunters; heiress-hunters, gold-hunters, buffalo-hunters, bee-hunters, happiness-hunters, truth-hunters, and still keener hunters after all these hunters. Fine ladies in slippers, and moccasined squaws; Northern speculators and Eastern philosophers . . . Sante Fé traders in striped blankets, and Broadway bucks in cravats of cloth of gold; fine-looking Kentucky boatmen, and Japanese-looking Mississippi cotton-planters; Quakers in full drab, and United States soldiers in full regimentals; slaves, black, mulatto, quadroon; modish young Spanish Creoles, and old-fashioned French Jews; Mormons and Papists; Dives and Lazarus; jesters and mourners, teetotalers and convivialists, deacons and blacklegs; hard-shell Baptists and clay-eaters; grinning negroes, and Sioux chiefs solemn as high-priests. (9)

Like the compensation merchant in "The Compensation Office," Melville's confidence man attempts to teach and to test the charitableness and the integrity of his customers.

By appropriating characters, guises, ruses, and themes from other *Putnam's* stories concerning confidence games and men, Melville easily alerted his audience to the tricks used in his own work. When Evert Duyckinck discovered that Melville's latest work concerned the exploits of popular confidence men, he commented on the rhetorical implications of this topic, declaring it "a fine playful subject for a humorist philosopher." He expected Melville to treat this conventional character critically: "It is a grand subject for a satirist like Voltaire or Swift . . . it might be made to evolve a picture of our life and manners. We shall see what the sea dog philosophy of *Typee* makes of it." [27]

Melville's reviewers understood the nature of the depiction in *The Confidence-Man.* The reviewer for the *Boston Evening Transcript* saw satirical and metaphysical implications in the presence of such a conventional character as the confidence man: "It is not to be wondered at, therefore, that the subject caught the fancy of Herman Melville—an author who deals equally well in the material description and the metaphysical insight of human life." [28] The *Albany Evening Journal* noted the novel's thematic layers and declared the book an "apologue": "The incidents and characters are chosen with a view to convey a theoretic moral, not a vivid delineation based on real life, like 'Typee' or 'Omoo.' " [29]

Stories in *Putnam's* that criticized society, institutions, and common ideologies did not employ the conventional plot-driven narrative. Instead, such works were composed as sketches in order to focus on the morals, themes, or attitudes proffered. A *Putnam's* reviewer had praised *Clouds and Sunshine,* though "there is no progression and the last page is an echo of the first." The importance of the book came from its structure which was a "series of conversations upon human life and destiny, in which three persons take part, one representing faith, another speculation, and a third skepticism." [30]

Like "The Compensation Office," and *Clouds and Sunshine, The Confidence-Man* indicates its orientation through its nondevelopmental structure. Melville forces the reader to consider the rhetorical implications of keeping the plot predictable by repeating the same sequence of encounters. He deliberately chooses a story line that is firmly grounded in and determined by popular traditions and knowledge. Insofar as a writer must use popular conventions, and these conventions, in turn, determine the course of the narrative, the plot is the least original element of a literary work. Melville emphasizes in *The Confidence-Man* the writer's ability to work imaginatively within the constraints of conventions. He directs the reader to character and style.

Throughout the novel, Melville alludes to the identity of the confidence man as an author. From the first appearance of the figure, people perceive him as a writer whose "writing was much the same sort" (4). The theme of the writer as a deluder, one who deludes his audience into believing what he says through his use of conventional forms, is found in the pages of *Putnam's.* In "The Genius of Charles Dickens," published in the March 1855 issue of *Putnam's,* the author describes the role of the novelist in terms repeated in *The Confidence-Man:*

> The novelist might suggest the accomplished modern magician, who presents himself in ordinary dress, and without any of the *claptrap* of jugglery, even with the confessed purpose of deception, and by his adroitness and dexterity deludes and perplexes the keenest vigilance of our senses.[31]

The novelist resorts to games in order to produce the intended effect.

In this context *The Confidence-Man* depicts the plight of the writer who repeats the same story to the point where the public dismisses his writing as "much the same sort" (4). The artist or writer who succumbs to this situation becomes a confidence man in the sense that he swindles himself of the opportunity for literary development. Through its conventionalized tricks and forms that delude readers into believing in its originality, the literary work itself is a confidence game.

Melville suggests that the creation of character is one of the writer's outlets for literary creativity in a work determined by popular conventions. In chapter 14, his first chapter on the nature of fiction, Melville justifies his conventionalized plot and moves to the importance of celebrating the author's expression or depiction of characters: "The grand points of human nature are the same today as they were a thousand years ago. The only variability in them is in expression, not in feature" (71). *The Confidence-Man* celebrates the author's power of depiction through highlighting the characters.

Melville's attitudes toward character development echo sentiments in "The Genius of Charles Dickens," where the author discusses the consistency of characters in the novels of Dickens and in literary works in general. He argues that "whether good or bad, noble or mean, to the poet's eye, men are true to their own kind." [32] Melville rephrases this notion in *The Confidence-Man*. He supports the idea that an author presents characters as they act, which in itself determines their consistency. Characters do not need to be consistent because in real life they are not: "Is it not a fact, that, in real life, a consistent character is a *rara avis?*" (69).

Chapter 43, a chapter that Melville may have added late in the composition of the novel, could have been prompted by an article in the August 1856 issue of *Putnam's*.[33] "Literary Imitations" discusses the want of originality in even the best works of poetry and prose.[34] The author argues that modern readers cannot discern originality from imitation: "Imitation meets us everywhere, in books, and most in those one would think most original." [35] What readers commonly consider original in a work of fiction is actually appropriated from some previous work: "The reader will remember a hundred other instances in which our best books of poetry and imagination show themselves indebted to preceding works, and greatly diminish the boast of originality among the moderns." [36]

Melville reiterates the assertion that few original characters exist in literature. Characters are "novel, or singular, or striking, or captivating, or all four at once," but not original (238). Though an author finds his characters "in the town, to be sure" (238), an *original* character is a product of the individual's creation, and a rare occurrence. Melville indirectly extols the original character of the confidence man that he has created in this conventional story: "In nearly all the original characters, loosely accounted such in works of invention, there is discernible something prevailingly local, or of the age; which circumstance, of itself, would seem to invalidate the claim, judged by the principles here suggested" (239).

By stressing the style, characters, and language of his work, Melville highlights the writer as creator, as artist. This orientation of *The Confidence-Man*, the celebration of the artist and the self, parallels the celebratory rhetoric of the Walt Whitman's *Leaves of Grass*. As we shall see, Melville's work also shares the nationalistic themes of Whitman's work. *The Confidence-Man* represents Melville's attempt to write *the* American novel of American society.

The Great American Novel

In a review article of the works of two of *Putnam's* most celebrated writers, Melville and George William Curtis, Fitz-James O'Brien declared *The Confidence-Man* "a thoroughly American story."[37] Since *Putnam's* readers knew that American stories entailed critiques of society, they understood the implication of O'Brien's assertion. J. E. A. Smith of the *Berkshire County Eagle* also described *The Confidence-Man* as a "picture of American society . . . though slightly distorted."[38] The *Worcester Palladium* saw "nineteenth-century notions" depicted in Melville's novel.[39]

Melville employs conventional American symbols that represent the nation as a whole. Reviewers, especially the British who were not immersed in American sectionalism, readily noted these "bright American touches . . . scattered over the perspective—the great steamboat deck, the river coasts, the groups belonging to various gradations of New World life."[40] The *Westminster and Foreign Quarterly Gazette* declared the American steamboat, *Fidele,* to be "that epitome of the American world.[41] Mirroring the image of the Mississippi as the great American artery described in the *Putnam's* article, Melville's Mississippi unites "the streams of the most distant and opposite zones, pours them along, helter-skelter, in one cosmopolitan and confident tide" (9).

The image of the confidence man was so associated with native originality that Melville's readers immediately recognized it as a deliberate American icon. The reviewer of the *Boston Evening Transcript* considered the confidence man an American folk character:

> One of the indigenous characters who has long figured in our journals, courts, and cities, is "the Confidence Man"; his doings form one of the staples of villainy, and an element in the romance of roguery. Countless are the dodges attributed to this ubiquitous personage, and his adventures would equal Jonathan Wild.[42]

The notion of a type of individual, commonly called a "cosmopo-lite" (or "cosmopolitan") pervaded popular literary culture during the 1850s. *Putnam's* had published a review entitled "History of a Cosmopolite" that described the stereotypical cosmopolitan.[43] This type was considered sophisticated, worldly, cunning, frequently shrewd, but above all *American*. By equating the "cosmopolite" with the confidence man, Melville creates a representative American character.

Melville's cosmopolite embodies characteristics that complement both popular attitudes and the author's particular formulation of American identity. As a blend of various customs and cultural ideolo-gies, he "federates, in heart as in costume, the various gallantries of men under various suns" (132), an idea originally introduced in *Moby-Dick*: "Isolatoes federated along one keel."[44] This formulation repeats the same rhetoric employed in describing another central American symbol, the Mississippi. The "one cosmopolitan and con-fident tide" (9), then, fuses the American character with the land and establishes the orientation of the novel. *The Confidence-Man* is a portrait of American society and its representative American at their best and worst.

Melville depicts the highly oral character of American culture. One reviewer described *The Confidence-Man* as a work "made up of 45 conversations."[45] In its presentation of American society as a group of individuals who interact with one another, *The Confidence-Man* assumes an audience of listeners, rather than readers. Throughout the novel, the audience must listen to the conversations that occur be-tween various characters. People speak in a variety of dialects, which encourages the reader to consider how they talk. Impressions and adulatory descriptions of various aspects of American society are conveyed in rhythm. This concept of audience as listener shapes the form of the novel. By capturing the diversities among American dialects and transforming them into literary dialogue with a distinct American tune, *The Confidence-Man* represents Melville's great con-tribution to the concept of an American novel.

From the first sentence in the novel, Melville draws the reader's attention to the rhythmic power and auditory quality of the language:

> At sunrise on a first of April,
>   there appeared,
> suddenly as Manco Capac
>   at the lake Titicaca,
> a man in cream-colors,
>   at the water-side
> in the city of St. Louis. (3)

He describes the man in cream-colors by employing poetic syntax: "His cheek was fair, his chin downy, his hair flaxen, his hat a white fur one, with a long fleecy nap" (3). This use of poetic syntax creates a cadence to the description that warrants recitation instead of plain reading.

Melville forces the reader to think of the language as spoken, rather than written. Chapter 2 opens with a page-long series of comments from various people:

> "Odd fish!"
> "Poor fellow!"
> "Who can he be?"
> "Captain Hauser."
> "Bless my soul!"
> "Uncommon countenance." (7)

When Melville conveys an impression, he often resorts to highly rhythmic language. Alliterative language lulls the reader with the peaceful rhythm just as the movement of the ship lulls the man sleeping peacefully aboard the boat:

> like some enchanted man in his grave,
> happily oblivious of all gossip,
> whether chiseled or chatted,
> the deaf and dumb stranger
> still tranquilly slept,
> while now the boat
> started on her voyage. (8)

While Melville had previously employed poetic language in *Mardi* and *Moby-Dick,* he had not related it to thematics as he does in *The Confidence-Man.*

In extolling the beauty of natural scenery, Melville relies on poetic form. Chapter 16 opens with a highly poetic passage:

> The sky slides into blue,
>   the bluffs into bloom,
> the rapid Mississippi expands:
>   runs sparkling
>   and gurgling,
>   all over in eddies;
> one magnified wake of a seventy-four.
> The sun comes out,
>   a golden huzzar,
>   from his tent,
> flashing his helm on the world.
> All things,
>   warmed in the landscape,
> leap.
> Speeds the daedel boat as a dream. (77)

This use of poetic form as the medium for recording impressions originates both in the author's growing interest in the genre and in attitudes regarding the rhetorical power of description discussed in *Putnam's.*

The magazine had fused the concept of American identity with the concept of the poetic. Americans are "born with poetic perception amid the stateliest natural forms—forests, mountains, rivers, plains —that seem to foreshadow a more imperial race."[46] Melville embodies this concept of American as poet by employing poetic forms in writing the American novel, once again reflecting the nationalistic themes and poetic techniques that Whitman employed in *Leaves of Grass.*

Melville seems to have adopted a suggestion from a *Putnam's* article that relates the poetic to artistic creativity. In "The Genius of Charles Dickens," the author discusses the role of poetry in a work governed by conventions. He suggests poetic form as a means for the writer to add a personal, creative element to established tradition:

> Since, in the actual condition of things, the arrangements of society, the jostling of other characters, or their own cowardice

and folly, check and distort the normal growth of men, poetry opens to them the range of the ideal, and supplies such circumstances and relations as shall minister to their completeness.... For the ideal characters which poetry requires, the actual personages of history can furnish but traits and outlines, but genius can complete and animate them or import directly from the realms of the imagination angels and men of larger mold than have lived on earth.[47]

The author justifies the use of poetic rhythm within conventional forms. He suggests that the use of this poetic form signals to the audience the author's original contribution: The 'fine frenzy' of the poet, communicated to his readers through the measured movement of language, readies them to the medium of his own passion.[48]

Throughout Melville's novel, the confidence man frequently refers to the poetic mode and discusses the role of the poet. When considered in light of the poetic forms in the novel, these statements serve as Melville's personal defense of the poetic form in *The Confidence-Man.* "Charity, like poetry, should be cultivated," proclaims the confidence man (156). In chapter 29, Frank Goodman, the cosmopolitan, describes an unusual but appealing form of poetry. He defines the form of the "panegyric on the press": It is a kind of poetry, but in a form which stands in something of the same relation to blank verse which that does to rhyme. A sort of free-and-easy chant with refrains to it (165).

In a defense of Egbert's work, the cosmopolitan presents the following defense of poetry: For poetry is not a thing of ink and rhyme, but of thought and act, and, in the latter way, is by any one to be found anywhere, when in useful action sought (199). Through this rhetoric, Melville bridges the gap between fictional and poetic form. When challenged on this poetic form, the cosmopolitan proclaims, "I cheerfully concede to the indefinite privileges of the poet" (168). One of these privileges, Melville implies, is the freedom to create poetic form within larger traditional constructs.

Melville's shift of emphasis from plot to an increased interest in literary form has prompted a variety of surmises. Q. D. Leavis sees Melville's use of the "circular movement" in *The Confidence-Man* as an adoption of a new "technique for self-protection and emotional survival."[49] Edgar A. Dryden has noted the development of form in *The Confidence-Man:* rather than plot development, *The Confidence-Man* "develops into a higher form."[50] The assessment of James E. Miller, Jr., best summarizes the debate. He suggests that "Melville was simply seeking a new form."[51] A master of literary forms, Melville characteristically sought further development through exploring yet another literary form.

CHAPTER TEN

The Move to Poetry

T WO WEEKS AFTER the appearance of *The Confidence-Man*, Melville's publishers declared bankruptcy. This inevitably had a severe impact on their magazine, *Putnam's Monthly*. When Miller and Curtis took over the publication in July 1857, they radically changed the foundation on which Putnam had built the monthly. New publishers, new editorial policies, and new readers radically altered the former existence of the "best of American monthlies." On the back cover of the July edition, the editors stated their new policy:

> The new proprietors of the Magazine beg to announce that it will hereafter be much enlarged and conducted upon a more popular basis. A larger space than heretofore will be devoted to miscellaneous and entertaining literature. . . . The object of this arrangement is, to make the best possible Family Magazine . . . the friend of sound morals, and the ally of cheerfulness and humor.[1]

The socially discerning literary environment of *Putnam's* had encouraged Melville to write what Q. D. Leavis calls his most mature prose and "some of his most interesting thinking."[2] In 1857 the new editors of *Putnam's* traded in the very audience central to Melville's *Putnam's*-oriented fiction in the hope of securing a more economically remunerative market majority, the general reader of sentimental fiction. From this moment, Melville no longer had a vehicle—either a critical magazine or a perceptive publisher—for reaching those readers who most appreciated his work.

Yet this end of an era only partially accounts for Melville's move away from novel writing. Textual evidence suggests an evolved sense of literary form in *The Confidence-Man*. In this work, Melville had extended the concept of audience to include both reader and listener, and this formulation was to inform his work for the next twenty years.

Melville apparently planned to implement the suggestion of the last line of *The Confidence-Man:* "Something more may follow of this masquerade" (286). In his *Journal of a Visit to Europe and the Levant*, the author alluded several times to a sequel to his novel.[3] Upon his return from the Levant, he discussed the idea of transforming his journal and travel notes into a work entitled "Frescoes of Travel by Three Brothers."[4] Many of the topics of Melville's lectures come from this travel material.[5]

Melville's much-quoted but ambiguous statement to his brother-in-law that he "is not going to write any more at present," does not stipulate just what exactly Melville is not going to write.[6] Indeed, this could have been a response to whether he planned to write any more stories, or even a sequel. While the topic itself suggests a possible travel book, Lewis Mumford proposes that Melville intended to write a book of poetry that would serve as the prototype for *Clarel*.[7]

Melville's journey to the Mediterranean and the Levant prompted the writer to consider aesthetic questions. During this trip, he seems to have developed more than a general interest in aesthetic and poetic form, an interest already sparked in *The Confidence-Man*.[8] This evident interest in poetry contributed to Melville's decision not to continue with fiction. The celebration of the self, the understanding of the individual's creative role in the literary process, and the notion of writing for oneself encouraged Melville to move to a literary form more personal and more creative, allowing for an infinite variety of expression. In this sense, *The Confidence-Man* serves as the author's apology for moving to other literary forms.

Melville's 1857 lecture, "Statues in Rome," provides an answer to this seemingly inexplicable change in direction. Describing the Vatican, Melville alerts us to an evolved understanding of form:

> If one stands a hundred feet in front of St. Peter's and looks up, a vast and towering pile meets his view. High, high above

are the beetling crags and precipices of masonry, and yet higher still above all is the dome. The mind is carried away with its very vastness. But throughout the Vatican it is different. The mind, instead of being bewildered within itself, is drawn out by the symmetry and beauty of the forms it beholds.[9]

As John Allison has suggested, Melville distinguishes "massive" form that inhibits from "symmetrical" form that generates thought. While these two forms "coexist" in Melville's later work, they also clarify the relation between structure and theme in *The Confidence-Man*.[10] As in his later poetry, where a static design controls and yet provides symmetry, the static plot of the confidence man's intrigues remains a constant and controls *The Confidence-Man*. Yet it also offers expansion in the form of personal artistic creativity—the bridging of prosaic and poetic forms. In the next years, Melville employs a solid poetic structure whose simplicity provides clarity and yet sparks enough curiosity to encourage "something more"—that is, creativity, innovation, art.

We misperceive the relation of Melville to his culture when we present his heterogeneity as evidence of a personal creative genius alone. But we gain considerable insight into his actual compositional practices and the nature of his creativity when we place his works in the context of his culture. The decision of a writer such as Melville to employ radically different forms provided him with the opportunity to create the heterogeneity that marks his writings. As his formulation of genius indicates, Melville was a master at reading and innovating, not creating, forms. In this light, we can think of this author as a responsive genius who employed popular forms to reflect back on his world, and it is in this context that Melville's concept of a correspondent coloring assumes meaning.

Notes

Preface

1. Melville, review of Hawthorne's *Mosses from an Old Manse*, *Literary World*, 17 August 1850, 126.
2. Nathaniel Hawthorne, *Mosses from an Old Manse* (New York: Wiley and Putnam, 1846), 4; Edgar Allan Poe, *Graham's*, 1847.
3. Hans Bergmann, *God in the Street: New York Writing from the Penny Press to Melville* (Philadelphia: Temple University Press, 1995), 13–14.

1. Cultural Contexts

1. *Columbian Magazine*, June 1847; *National Anti-Slavery Standard*, 27 May 1847; *New York Sunday Times and Noah's Weekly Register*, 2 May 1847.
2. See Meade Minnigerode, *The Fabulous Forties, 1840–1850: A Presentation of Private Life* (Garden City, N.Y.: Garden City Publishing Co, 1924), 211, 225; Carl Bode, *The Anatomy of Popular Culture, 1840–1861* (Berkeley: University of California Press, 1959); James D. Hart, *The Popular Book: A History of America's Literary Taste* (Berkeley: University of California Press, 1961), 90–94; William Charvat, "James T. Fields and the Beginnings of Book Promotion, 1840–1855" and "The People's Patronage," in *The Profession of Authorship in America, 1800–1870: The Papers of William Charvat*, ed. Matthew J. Bruccoli (Columbus: Ohio State University Press, 1965), 168–69, 313–17; Cathy N. Davidson, *Revolution and the Word: The Rise of the Novel in America* (New York: Oxford University Press, 1986); Ronald J. Zboray, "Antebellum Reading and the Ironies of Technological Innovation," in *Reading in America: Literature and Social History*, ed. Cathy N. Davidson (Baltimore: Johns Hopkins University Press, 1989), 180–200; and Ronald J. Zboray, *A Fictive People: Antebellum Economic Development and the American Reading Public* (New York: Oxford University Press, 1993). This last work quotes from the 1855

speech by George Palmer Putnam to the Association of New York Publishers, in which he provides a different calculation of books published in America: "The records of American publications, for the twelve years ending in 1842, show an aggregate of 1,115 different works. Of these, 623 were original, and 429 were reprinted from foreign books. . . . In the year 1853, there were some 733 works published in the United States . . . 420 were original American works—thus showing an increase of about 800 per cent in less than twenty years"(3).

3. Stuart Blumin, *The Emergence of the Middle Class: Social Experience in the American City, 1760–1900* (Cambridge: Cambridge University Press, 1989), 9–10.

4. David S. Reynolds, *Beneath the American Renaissance: The Subversive Imagination in the Age of Emerson and Melville* (New York: Alfred A. Knopf, 1988), 24–25, 199, 206, 277–89, 313, 352–57, 373–74. This description of antebellum readerships expands the delineations offered by Nina Baym in *Novels, Readers, and Reviewers: Responses to Fiction in Antebellum America* (Ithaca: Cornell University Press, 1984). She posits two categories of readers: middle-class and working-class readers. She refers to the first group as "a small group of cultivated, discreet, intelligent, educated, tasteful, thoughtful readers who wanted something more than, but not incompatible with, the tastes of the ordinary readers," who were defined as those " 'mere' readers looking for pleasure and reading for story" (47). But reviewers of the period, themselves members of the middle class, referred to the divisions of readers within this class itself, as I have recounted.

5. Terrence Martin, *The Instructed Vision: Scottish Common Sense Philosophy and the Origins of American Fiction* (Bloomington: Indiana University Press, 1961).

6. See Kathleen Tillotson, *Novels of the 1840s* (Oxford: Clarendon Press, 1954), 13–16, for a discussion of the period's suspicion of fictional works. (The Trollope account is quoted on 16.) See also George Paston, *At John Murray's: Records of a Literary Circle, 1843–1892* (London: John Murray, 1932), 24–39.

7. See John Limon, *The Place of Fiction in the Time of Science: A Disciplinary History of American Writing* (New York: Cambridge University Press, 1990), and Robert Scholnick, ed., *American Literature and Science* (Louisville: University Press of Kentucky, 1992).

8. Zboray, *A Fictive People.*

9. Review of Charles Darwin, *Darwin's Voyage of a Naturalist, Graham's,* June 1846.

10. For classifications of the travel narrative in American literary history, see Mayle F. Cedarstrom, "American Factual Voyage Narratives, 1815–1860," Ph.D. dissertation, University of Wisconsin, 1932; Jarvis P. Stout, *The*

Journey Narrative in American Literature: Patterns and Departures (Westport, Conn.: Greenwood Press, 1983), 36–78; and Martin Green, *The Great American Adventure* (Boston: Beacon Press, 1984). See also D. J. Hall, *English Medieval Pilgrimage* (London: Routledge and Kegan Paul, 1965); Boise Penrose, *English Travelers in the Renaissance, 1420–1620* (1914; rpt. New York: Bert Franklin, 1968); Samuel Eliot Morison, *The English Discovery of America*, 2 vols. (New York: Oxford University Press, 1971–74); and Percy G. Adams, *Travel Literature and the Evolution of the Novel* (Lexington: University Press of Kentucky, 1983), 38–80.

11. These statistics are based on my own calculations.

12. See George Palmer Putnam, *American Facts: Notes and Statistics Relative to the Government, Resources, Engagements, Manufactures, Commerce, Religion, Education, Literature, Fine Arts, Manners and Customs of the United States of America* (London: Wiley and Putnam, 1845), 81; Samuel G. Goodrich, *Recollections of a Lifetime, or Men and Things I Have Seen: In a Series of Familiar Letters to a Friend, Historical, Biographical, Anecdotal, and Descriptive* (New York Miller, Orton and Co., 1857), 2:379–93.

13. For an elaboration of this convention in eighteenth- and nineteenth-century travel narratives, see Janet Giltrow, "Speaking Out: Travel and Structure in Herman Melville's Early Narratives," *American Literature* 52 (1980): 118–32.

14. Charles R. Anderson, *Melville in the South Seas* (New York: Columbia University Press, 1939), 191; T. Walter Herbert, *Marquesan Encounters: Melville and the Meaning of Civilization* (Cambridge, Mass.: Harvard University Press, 1980), 162.

15. For a summary of the conventions of the travel narrative, see Richard Slotkin, *Regeneration through Violence: The Myth of the American Frontier, 1600–1860* (Middletown, Conn.: Wesleyan University Press, 1973), 243–47; William C. Spengemann, *The Adventurous Muse: The Poetics of American Fiction, 1789–1900* (New Haven: Yale University Press, 1977), 6–67; Adams, *Travel Literature and the Evolution of the Novel*, 110–46; Giltrow, "Speaking Out"; and Robert Roripaugh, "Melville's *Typee* and the Frontier Literature of the 1830s and 1840s," *South Dakota Review* 19 (winter 1962): 46–64.

16. Horatio Bridge [Nathaniel Hawthorne] *Journal of an African Cruiser* (New York: Wiley and Putnam, 1845); Eliot Warburton, *The Crescent and the Cross; or, Romance and Realities of Eastern Travel* (New York: Wiley and Putnam, 1845)—I quote from the English edition (London: Ward, Lock, and Co., 1845).

17. Herman Melville, *Typee, or A Peep at Polynesian Life* (Evanston: Northwestern University Press and the Newberry Library, 1968). See all of chaps. 20, 21, 25, 27, 29, 30, 31, and sections in chaps 17, 119, 24, 26, 28.

18. Frederick Marryat, "How to Write a Book of Travels," in *Pacha of Many Tales* (London: G. Routledge and Sons, 1841), 177–89.

19. Charles S. Stewart, *A Visit to the South Seas, in the United States Ship Vincennes, during the Years 1829 and 1830*, 2 vols. (New York: John P. Hoven, 1833), 2:11.

20. William Ellis, *Polynesian Researches* (London: Fisher, Son and Jackson, 1831), 1:264–65.

21. Warburton, *The Crescent and the Cross*, 26.

22. Letter from Herman Melville to John Murray, 6 December 1845, in Melville, *The Letters of Herman Melville*, ed. Merrell R. Davis and William H. Gilman (New Haven: Yale University Press, 1960), 283.

23. Charles Anderson hypothesizes that Melville employed materials from travel narratives because of his inexperience as a writer and his cursory acquaintance with Marquesan life. See Anderson, *Melville in the South Seas*, 126, 191. Hershel Parker responds to the belief that Melville "filled out" his fictionalized story with factual information at the request of his publisher who insisted on veridicality. He provides evidence that the author included appropriated material from other travel accounts before his future publisher read the manuscript. This strategy reflects precisely the general habits of travel writers who, as I have discussed, frequently and openly borrow from other travels works. See Hershel Parker, "Evidence for the 'Late Insertions' in Melville's Works," *Studies in the Novel* 7 (1975): 407–24.

24. For an evolutionary history of the travel narrative, see Eric J. Leed, *The Mind of the Traveler: From Gilgamesh to Global Tourism* (New York: Basic Books, 1991); John Samson includes a brief history of travel literature in *White Lies: Melville's Narrative of Facts* (Ithaca: Cornell University Press, 1989), 25–27.

25. Alfred Russell Wallace, *The Malay Archipelago* (London and New York: Macmillan, 1869), 282, 475, quoted in Leed, *The Mind of the Traveler*, 209.

26. David S. Reynolds has written extensively on the ideological basis of Oriental fiction in *Faith in Fiction: The Emergence of Religious Literature in America* (Cambridge, Mass.: Harvard University Press, 1981), chaps. 1 and 2; see also idem, *Beneath the American Renaissance*, 37–53.

27. Ellis, *Polynesian Researches*, 1:189; Charles S. Stewart, *Journal of a Residence in the Sandwich Islands in the Years 1823, 1824, and 1825* (London: H. Fisher and Sons and P. Jackson, 1828), chap. 3. See also George Borrow, *The Bible in Spain* (London: John Murray, 1843), the precursor to Melville's *Typee* in Murray's Home and Colonial Library Series, in which Borrow consistently deprecates native life. For an analysis of Borrow's methods, see Michael Collie, *George Borrow: Eccentric* (Cambridge: Cambridge University Press, 1982), and David Williams, *A World*

of His Own: The Double Life of George Borrow (Oxford: Oxford University Press, 1982). See especially Reynolds's discussion of the different attitudes in travel accounts, in *Beneath the American Renaissance,* 47–49.

28. Nathaniel Ames, *Nautical Reminiscences* (Providence: William Marshall, 1832), 58, quoted in Reynolds, *Beneath the American Renaissance,* 48.

29. See Stewart, *A Visit to the South Seas,* 1:330; John Coulter, M.D., *Adventures in the Pacific* (Dublin: W. Curry, Jun. and Co., 1845), 189; and Ellis, *Polynesian Researches,* 3:233.

30. Stewart, *Journal of a Residence in the Sandwich Islands,* 1:335; Coulter, *Adventures in the Pacific,* 185; Ellis, *Polynesian Researches,* 3:238; William C. Bryant, *Letters of a Traveller* (New York: G. Putnam, 1849), 123; Bayard Taylor, *Views A-Foot* (New York: Harper and Brothers, 1846), 243. See also Walter Allen, *Transatlantic Crossing* (New York: Random House, 1979), 56, 60, and Nathalia Wright, *American Novelists in Italy: The Discoverers: Allston to James* (Philadelphia: University of Pennsylvania Press, 1965).

31. Anderson, *Melville in the South Seas,* 178, and Lawrence Thompson, *Melville's Quarrel with God* (Princeton: Princeton University Press, 1952), 53.

32. See J. Ross Browne, "Etchings of a Whaling Cruise," *American Review,* September 1845, 231.

33. James E. Miller, Jr., *A Reader's Guide to Herman Melville* (New York: Noonday Press, 1962), 33.

34. Paston, *At John Murray's,* 38–40.

35. Frederick Burwick, book review, *Nineteenth-Century Fiction* 39 (1984): 213.

36. Two recent biographies of Borrow discuss the writer's colorful life: see Collie, *George Borrow,* and Williams, *A World of His Own.*

37. Charles R. Anderson, "Melville's South Sea Romance," *Eigo Seinen* 115 (1969): 565.

38. See, for example, William Ellery Sedgwick, *Melville and the Tragedy of the Mind* (Cambridge, Mass.: Harvard University Press, 1944), 28; Milton R. Stern, *The Fine-Hammered Steel of Herman Melville* (Urbana: University of Illinois Press, 1957), 29–65; Edgar A. Dryden, *Melville's Thematics of Form: The Great Art of Telling the Truth* (Baltimore: Johns Hopkins University Press, 1968), 33–46; John Seelye, *Melville: The Ironic Diagram* (Evanston: Northwestern University Press, 1971), 11–28; William B. Dillingham, *An Artist in the Rigging: The Early Work of Herman Melville* (Athens: University of Georgia Press, 1972), 9–30; Thomas P. Joswick, "*Typee:* The Quest for Origin," *Criticism* 17 (1975): 335–54; Faith Pullin, "Melville's *Typee:* The Failure of Eden," in *New Perspectives on Melville,* ed. Faith Pullin (Edinburgh: Edinburgh University Press, 1978), 1–28.

39. Herbert, *Marquesan Encounters;* Mitchell Breitweiser, "False Sympathy

in Melville's *Typee*," *American Quarterly* 34 (1982): 396–417; Samson, *White Lies*, 22–56.

40. Samson, *White Lies*, 22–56.

41. Herbert, *Marquesan Encounters*, 158.

42. Michael Paul Rogin, *Subversive Genealogy: The Politics and Art of Herman Melville* (New York: Alfred A. Knopf, 1983), 44.

43. Reynolds, *Beneath the American Renaissance*, 48, 169–211.

44. Review of Joel T. Headley, *The Alps and the Rhine* [New York: Wiley and Putnam, 1846], in *Graham's*, April 1846, September 1845, 143–44.

45. See the romantic description of native manners in Captain David Porter, *Journal of a Cruise Made to the Pacific Ocean, in the U.S. Frigate Essex in the Years 1812, 1813, and 1814* (Philadelphia, 1813), 86, 121, and Benjamin Morrell, *A Narrative of Four Voyages to the South Seas, North and South Pacific Ocean, China Sea, Ethiopic and South Atlantic Oceans, Indian and Antarctic Oceans from the Years 1822–1831* (New York: J and J Harpers, 1832). See also Ellis, *Polynesian Researches*, 1:249–50, and Stewart, *A Visit to the South Seas*, 2:339–40. Charles Anderson and T. Walter Herbert discuss the romantic tone of these travel writers; see Anderson, *Melville in the South Seas*, 121–35, and Herbert, *Marquesan Encounters*, 189. George Borrow liberally employed sentimental and sensational effects; see Borrow, *The Bible in Spain*, vi, and chap. 3. Samuel Stiles recounts Borrow's popularity in *A Publisher and His Friends: Memoirs and Correspondence of John Murray* (London: John Murray, 1911), 2:240–45.

46. Nina Baym discusses the rise of "highly wrought" fiction in Baym, *Novels, Readers, and Reviewers*, 207–9. Patrick Brantlinger offers an analysis of sensational fiction in "What Is 'Sensational' about the 'Sensation Novel'?" *Nineteenth-Century Fiction* 37 (1982): 1–28. See also Hart, *The Popular Book*, 100–102.

47. Ellis, *Polynesian Researches*, 2:254.

48. *New York Evening Mirror*, 21 May 1847.

49. *Graham's*, August 1845.

50. *Godey's*, March 1844; *Knickerbocker*, January 1844.

51. *Graham's*, March 1847; *Knickerbocker*, April 1844; and *Arthur's Magazine*, November 1844.

52. See Paston, *At John Murray's*, 47–48.

53. For an examination of how sentimental writers complicated the formula, see Jane Tompkins, *Sensational Designs: The Cultural Work of American Fiction* (New York: Oxford University Press, 1985), 149.

54. Emma C. Embury, "The Transplanted Flower: Or, The Florence Bride," *Columbian Lady's and Gentleman's Magazine*, January 1844, 41.

55. See Frank Luther Mott, *A History of American Magazines* (Cambridge: Cambridge University Press, 1948), 1:309, 546. I have not found any

discussion in the literature of the strong sensational elements in these reputedly sentimental magazines. The increasing element of sensation throughout general family and domestic magazines of this period goes far to explain the overt sensationalism in the best-sellers of the 1850s.

56. *Godey's*, July 1849.

57. Poe somewhat unfairly made the following claim about many of these magazines: "They are so nearly alike that if the covers were changed it would not be easy to distinguish one from the other. They nearly all have the same contributors and the same embellishers" (*New York Broadway Journal*, 25 January 1845, 60).

58. See Thomas Philbrick, *James Fenimore Cooper and the Development of American Sea Fiction* (Cambridge, Mass.: Harvard University Press, 1961), 168–202.

59. Melville's first sketches published in the *Lansingburgh Herald* conform to sentimental and sensational conventions of the day. See William H. Gilman, *Melville's Early Life and Redburn* (New York: New York University Press, 1951), 108–22, and appendix B, 264–71.

2. Typee: *(Re)Making the Best-Seller*

1. John Bryant, *Melville and Repose: The Rhetoric of Humor in the American Renaissance* (New York: Oxford University Press, 1993), 131.

2. Letter from Herman Melville to John Murray, 15 July 1846, in Melville, *Correspondence*, ed. Lynn Horth (Evanston and Chicago: Northwestern University Press and the Newberry Library, 1993), 56.

3. Andrew Delbanco, "Melville in the '80s," *American Literary History* (winter 1992): 723.

4. William Spengemann, *The Adventurous Muse: The Poetics of American Fiction, 1789–1900* (New Haven: Yale University Press, 1977). For Melville's early readings, see William H. Gilman, *Melville's Early Life and Redburn* (New York: New York University Press, 1951), 108–22, 264–71, and Thomas Philbrick, *James Fenimore Cooper and the Development of American Sea Fiction* (Cambridge, Mass.: Harvard University Press, 1961), 168–202.

5. Wilson Heflin, *New Light upon Melville's Cruise in the Charles and Henry* (Glassboro, N.J.: Melville Society, 1977).

6. Gansevoort Melville, *Journal*, 24 January 1834, in Jay Leyda, "An Albany Journal by Gansevoort Melville," *Boston Public Library Quarterly* 11 (1950): 336, referred to in Gilman, *Melville's Early Life*, 77.

7. Nathaniel Parker Willis, unsigned review, *New York Home Journal*, 24 November 1849.

8. Gilman, *Melville's Early Life*, n. 83, 327.

9. Ibid., n. 162, 317, and letter from Helen to Augusta Melville, 1845, New York Public Library. I am grateful to Laurie Robertson-Lorant for this last reference.

10. Gilman, *Melville's Early Life*; Bryan C. Short, *Cast by Means of Figures: Herman Melville's Rhetorical Development* (Amherst: University of Massachusetts Press, 1992); Bryant, *Melville and Repose.*

11. Gilman, *Melville's Early Life*, 108.

12. Nina Baym, *Women's Fiction: A Guide to Novels by and about Women in America, 1820–1870* (Ithaca: Cornell University Press, 1978).

13. N. P. Willis, review of *Mardi*, in *New York Home Journal*, 28 November 1849.

14. For the misappropriation of the term *romance* by contemporary scholars as a term of classification for mid-nineteenth-century fictional works, see Nina Baym, *Novels, Readers, and Reviewers: Responses to Fiction in Antebellum America* (Ithaca: Cornell University Press, 1984), 225–35.

15. Short, *Cast by Means of Figures*, 33.

16. Poe, review of *Barnaby Rudge*, in *Graham's*, February 1844, 99.

17. Ibid.

18. William Ellis, *Polynesian Researches* (London: Fisher, Son and Jackson, 1831), 1:342; Charles S. Stewart, *A Visit to the South Seas, in the United States Ship Vincennes, during the Years 1829 and 1830*, 2 vols. (New York: John P. Hoven, 1833), 413; George Bennett and Daniel Tyerman, *Journal of Voyages and Travels*, ed. James Montgomery (Boston: Crocker and Brewster, 1832), 1:306–7.

19. See Captain David Porter, *Journal of a Cruise Made to South Pacific by Captain David Porter in the United States Frigate Essex, in the Years 1812, 1813, and 1814* (New York: Wiley and Halsted, 1822), 124; Ellis, *Polynesian Researches*, 1:264–65; Bennett and Tyerman, *Journal of Voyages*, 1:306–7; John Coulter, M.D., *Adventures in the Pacific* (Dublin: W. Curry, Jun. and Co., 1845), 204–14; and Georg H. von Langsdorff, *Voyages and Travels in Various Parts of the World, 1803–1807* (London, 1813), 1:117–22.

20. Letter to Mrs. Peabody, in Eleanor Metcalf, *Herman Melville: Cycle and Epicycle* (Cambridge, Mass.: Harvard University Press, 1953), 91.

21. James E. Miller, Jr., *A Reader's Guide to Herman Melville* (New York: Noonday Press, 1962), 30. For thematic interpretations of the dual narratorial voice, see Newton Arvin, *Herman Melville* (New York: William Sloane, 1950), 83. Lawrance Thompson questions how the narrator could leave the paradise he idealized, in Thompson, *Melville's Quarrel with God* (Princeton: Princeton University Press, 1952), 53. William B. Dillingham offers a full thematic analysis of this apparent conflict between horror and romanticism in Dillingham, *An Artist in the Rigging: The Early Work of Herman Melville* (Athens: University of Georgia Press,

1972), 9–30. See also T. Walter Herbert, *Marquesan Encounters: Melville and the Meaning of Civilization* (Cambridge, Mass.: Harvard University Press, 1980), 149–75. Michael Clark analyzes the aesthetic sensibility that informs Melville's work in an attempt to discern "what makes the facts come alive," in Clark, "Melville's *Typee*: Fact, Fiction, and Esthetics," in *Critical Essays on Herman Melville's Typee*, ed. Milton R. Stern (Boston: G. K. Hall, 1982), 211–26. See also Mitchell Breitweiser, "False Sympathy in Melville's *Typee*," *American Quarterly* 34 (1982): 396–417.

22. Herbert, *Marquesan Encounters*, 158.

23. Dillingham, *An Artist in the Rigging*, 17.

24. *Godey's*, May 1846; *Graham's*, May 1846; *New York Tribune*, 4 April 1846; *New York Morning Courier*, 17 April 1846; *New York Illustrated Magazine*, April 1846; see also *Merchant's Magazine and Commercial Advertiser*, 4 April 1846. For discussions of the critical response to Melville's *Typee* by his contemporaries, see Charles Robert Anderson, "Contemporary American Opinions of *Typee* and *Omoo*," *American Literature* 9 (1937): 1–25; Watson G. Branch, *Melville: The Critical Heritage* (London: Routledge and Kegan Paul, 1974), 1–50; Hugh W. Hetherington, *Melville's Reviewers, British and American, 1846–1891* (Chapel Hill: University of North Carolina Press, 1961), 20–65; and Thomas J. Rowntree, ed., *Critics on Melville* (Coral Gables, Fla.: University of Miami Press, 1972).

25. *The American Review: A Whig Journal*, April 1846; *Knickerbocker*, May 1846; *New York Gazette and Times*, March 1846; *New York Mirror*, 4 April 1846; Nathaniel Hawthorne, *Salem Advertiser*, 25 March 1846.

26. *Literary World*, 8 May 1841, 319; *Washington National Intelligence*, 26 May 1847.

27. George Palmer Putnam, *George Palmer Putnam: A Memoir, Together with a Record of the Earlier Years of the Publishing House Founded by Him* (New York: G. P. Putnam's Sons, 1912), 153.

28. The major exception to these small sales was Bayard Taylor's *Views A-Foot*, which, according to the memoirs of George Palmer Putnam, sold approximately fifty thousand copies within five years of its publication in 1847; see ibid., 152.

29. Baym, *Women's Fiction*, 300–301.

30. See Henry Fothergill Chorley, *London Athenaeum*, 21 February 1846, and *Eclectic Review*, April 1846; see also *John Bull*, March 1846.

31. *London Times*, 6 April 1846.

32. *London Critic*, 14 March 1846.

33. Melville, *Correspondence*, 56.

34. Richard Brodhead, *Hawthorne, Melville, and the Novel* (Chicago: University of Chicago Press, 1976); see also Clark, "Melville's *Typee*," 212.

3. Reader Expectations and Innovation in Omoo *and* Mardi

1. Gordon Roper, "Historical Note," *Omoo: A Narrative of Adventures in the South Seas* (Evanston and Chicago: Northwestern University Press and the Newberry Library, 1968), 319.
2. William H. Gilman, *Melville's Early Life and Redburn* (New York: New York University Press, 1951), 220.
3. Nathaniel Ames, *A Mariner's Sketches* (Providence: Cory, Marshall and Hammond, 1830) and *Nautical Reminiscences* (Providence: W. Marshall, 1832); Robert Montgomery Bird, *The Adventures of Robin Day* (Philadelphia: Lea and Blanchard, 1839); Richard Henry Dana, Jr., *Two Years before the Mast* (Boston, 1840; rpt. New York: Airmont Publishing, 1965); James Fenimore Cooper, *Ned Myers: A Life before the Mast* (Philadelphia: Lea and Blanchard, 1843); Charles Briggs, *Working a Passage: Or, Life in a Liner* (New York: John Allen, 1844).

   For a discussion of the trend toward realism in the nautical fiction of the early 1840s, see Thomas J. Philbrick, *James Fenimore Cooper and the Development of American Sea Fiction* (Cambridge, Mass.: Harvard University Press, 1961), 166–202; Bert Bender, "*Far Tortuga* and American Sea Fiction since *Moby-Dick*," *American Literature* 55 (1983): 230–33; Jeanne-Marie Santraud, *La Mer et le roman américain dans la première noitié du dix-neuvième siècle* (Paris: Didier, 1972); W. H. Auden, *The Enchafèd Flood, Or, The Romantic Iconography of the Sea* (New York: Random House, 1950); Richard Poirier, *A World Elsewhere: The Place of Style in American Literature* (New York: Oxford University Press, 1966); and Gilman, *Melville's Early Life*, 170–72. James Hart discusses Melville and Dana in "Melville and Dana," *American Literature* 9 (1937): 49–55, arguing that they differed dramatically in temperament and writing style. Robert F. Lucid discusses Melville's indebtedness to Dana in *White-Jacket,* but does not refer to his allegiance to Dana in *Omoo;* see Lucid, "The Influence of *Two Years before the Mast* on Herman Melville," *American Literature* 31 (1959): 243–56. Perry Miller discusses Melville's indebtedness in *Redburn* to *Working a Passage;* however, neither he nor anyone else that I can determine has noted Melville's debt to Briggs in *Omoo.* See Miller, *The Raven and the Whale* (New York: Harcourt, Brace, 1951), 55–57.
4. James Fenimore Cooper, *The Pilot* (New York: C. Wiley, 1823). For Smollett's influence on the realistic and often sordid fiction of Frederick Marryat, see Robert Gidding, *The Tradition of Smollett* (London: Methuen, 1967), 158–61. See the analysis of sea imagery in Robert Montgomery Bird's *Robin Day* in Philbrick, *James Fenimore Cooper,* 177–90. Though not strictly a nautical reminiscence, *The Narrative of Arthur Gordon Pym* follows in the tradition established by Smollett and his

followers. See Philbrick's discussion of Poe's work in *James Fenimore Cooper*, 168–77.

5. The metaphor "sea-bird on the wing" is from Charles J. Peterson, one of the few romantic sea writers of the 1840s; see Peterson, *Cruising in the Last War* (Philadelphia: Lea and Blanchard, 1839).

6. Charles F. Briggs, *The Adventures of Harry Franco: Or Tales of the Panic* (New York: Saunders, 1839); Bird, *The Adventures of Robin Day*; Cooper, *The Pilot*, 13–14; Dana, *Two Years before the Mast*, 59. For an analysis of Bird's novel, see Curtis Dahl, *Robert Montgomery Bird* (New York: Twayne, 1963), 106–12.

7. Dana, *Two Years before the Mast*, 62; Briggs, *Harry Franco*, 195.

8. Charles Briggs, "A Veritable Sea Story," *Knickerbocker*, February 1844, 151. For a discussion of the antiromantic bias in certain literary circles in the 1840s, see Miller, *The Raven and the Whale*, 55–60.

9. The segmentation of readerships during this period also contributed to this change. Dana and Cooper were read largely by educated readers, while the tales of the "tars" were read by the sailors and general readers.

10. See Jeffrey Rubin-Dorsky, *Adrift in the Old World: The Psychological Pilgrimage of Washington Irving* (University of Chicago Press, 1988).

11. *Knickerbocker*, February 1839, 79–81.

12. Dana, *Two Years before the Mast*, preface, 9–10. Further references to this book will be made in the text. For analyses of Dana's method in *Two Years before the Mast*, see review, *Knickerbocker*, October 1840, 349–52; *North American Review*, January 1841, 56–75; D. H. Lawrence, "Dana's Two Years before the Mast," in *Studies in Classic American Literature* (New York: Thomas Seltzer, 1923), 163–92; Robert C. Gale, *Richard Henry Dana* (New York: Twayne Publishers, 1969); and Robert A. Ferguson, *Law and Letters in American Culture* (Cambridge, Mass.: Harvard University Press, 1984), 257–66.

13. *Graham's*, January 1844, 46. In *Ned Myers*, Cooper employs the stance of an "editor" who merely relates the story of a sailor's life. This was a technique popular during this period. Marryat, Poe, and Hawthorne all acted as "editors" in at least one of their novels, a strategy that allowed their works to appear as "authentic" narratives by common people. This rhetorical stance foreshadows the "sub-sub editor" of *Moby-Dick*.

14. For examples of nautical reminiscences from the early 1840s, see *Life in a Man-of-War, by a Fore-Top-Man* (New York: n.p., 1841), and John Sherbourne Sleeper, *Tales of the Ocean and Essays of the Forecastle, by Hawser Martingale* (Boston: S. N. Dickinson, 1841).

15. John Codman, *Sailors' Life and Sailors' Yarns, by Captain Ringbolt* (New York: C. S. Francis and Co., 1847), 251.

16. For an account of the conventions of the picaresque novel, see Gidding, *The Tradition of Smollett,* 9–36.

17. See letter to John Murray, 15 July 1846, in Melville, *The Letters of Herman Melville,* ed. Merrell R. Davis and William II. Gilman (New Haven: Yale University Press, 1960), 25.

18. Briggs, *Working a Passage.* Further references to this book will be incorporated into the text.

19. J. Ross Browne, "Journal of a Whale Cruise," *American Review: A Whig Journal,* September 1845, 234, and Dana, *Two Years before the Mast,* 43, 64.

20. See Charles R. Anderson, *Melville in the South Seas,* (New York: Columbia University Press, 1939), 283–88. John Samson argues that Melville parodies the accounts of missionaries, in "Profaning the Sacred: Melville's *Omoo* and Missionary Narratives," *American Literature* 56 (1984): 496–509.

21. See David S. Reynolds, *Beneath the American Renaissance: The Subversive Imagination in the Age of Emerson and Melville* (New York: Alfred A. Knopf, 1988), 48, and also chapter 1 of this book.

22. For an interesting discussion of the comic conventions of the time and humor as a sign of authorial confidence and strength, see Nancy Walker, "Wit, Sentimentality, and the Image of Women in the Nineteenth Century," *American Studies* 22 (1981): 5–22.

23. Letter to John Murray, 25 March 1848, in Melville, *Letters,* 70.

24. See Anderson, *Melville in the South Seas,* 200–206.

25. Roper, "Historical Note," *Omoo,* 322.

26. Newton Arvin long ago identified Doctor Long Ghost as the story's hero; see Arvin, *Herman Melville* (New York: William Sloane, 1950), 16.

27. For a brief mention of the similarity of Smollett's character with Doctor Long Ghost, see William B. Dillingham, "Long Ghost and Smollett's Count Fathom," *American Literature* 42 (1970): 233–35.

28. See Edward H. Rosenberry for a detailed analysis of Melville's use of these "comic matters," in *Melville and the Comic Spirit* (Cambridge, Mass.: Harvard University Press, 1955), 33–45.

29. Jay Leyda, ed., *The Melville Log: A Documentary Life of Herman Melville, 1819–1891* (New York: Harcourt, Brace, 1951), 263.

30. The following squib appeared in the *New York Daily Tribune* in reference to Melville's marriage: "Breach of Promise Suit Expected.—Mr. Herman Typee Omoo Melville has recently been united in lawful wedlock to a young lady of Boston. The fair forsaken Fayaway will doubtless console herself by suing him for breach of promise" (Leyda, *The Melville Log,* 1:256). For other allusions, see excerpts from the letters of Duyckinck, Fanny Longfellow, Henry Dana, Sr., Ellery Channing, and others in idem, 1:254–73.

31. See Laurie Robertson-Lorant, *Melville: A Biography* (New York: Clarkson N. Potter, 1996).

32. See N. P. Willis's account of the event in the *New York Home Journal*, 4 March 1848.

33. *New York Tribune*, 10 May 1849.

34. Duyckinck claimed Melville lacked originality and modeled "his writing evidently a great deal on Washington Irving" (Leyda, *The Melville Log*, 1:253).

35. For the first detailed study of Melville's relation with Duyckinck's elite group of critics and writers, see Luther S. Mansfield, "Herman Melville: Author and New Yorker, 1844–1851," Ph.D. dissertation, University of Chicago, 1936. Perry Miller recounts at length the creation, ideas, and dissolution of Duyckinck's coterie in *The Raven and the Whale*, 203–79. Recent analyses of Evert Duyckinck and his literary circle are found in John Stafford, *The Literary Criticism of "Young America": Study in the Relation of Politics and Literature, 1837–1850* (1952; rpt. New York: Russell and Russell, 1967), and John Paul Pritchard, *Literary Wise Men of Gotham: Criticism in New York, 1815–1860* (Baton Rouge, 1963; rpt. Westport, Conn.: Greenwood Press, 1977), 114–32, 61–78.

36. *Literary World*, 14 April 1849.

37. Letter from H. Melville to John Murray, 25 March 1848, in Melville, *Correspondence*, ed. Lynn Horth (Evanston and Chicago: Northwestern University Press and the Newberry Library, 1993), 106; Wai-chee Dimock, *Empire for Liberty: Melville and the Poetics of Individualism* (Princeton: Princeton University Press, 1989), 42–43.

38. See letters to John Murray, 15 July 1847, 29 October 1847, and 1 January 1848, in Melville, *Letters*, 41, 66, 68.

39. See Nina Baym, *Novels, Readers, and Reviewers: Responses to Fiction in Antebellum America* (Ithaca: Cornell University Press, 1984), 224–35, and Janet Giltrow, "Speaking Out: Travel and Structure in Herman Melville's Early Narratives," *American Literature* 52 (1980): 20, for discussions of fictional incidents in the conventional travel narrative. That Melville was aware of this leniency for a "taint of fiction" in the "factual" travel narrative, see his letter to John Murray, 2 September 1847, in Melville, *Letters*, 46.

40. Letter to John Murray, 25 March 1848, in Melville, *Letters*, 70–71.

41. Ibid.

42. For the classic discussion of the tripartite structure of *Mardi*, see Merrell R. Davis, *Melville's Mardi: A Chartless Voyage* (New York: Archon Books, 1967). For recent discussions which essentially adapt the argument presented by Merrell Davis, see Elizabeth S. Foster, "Historical Note," *Mardi* (Evanston and Chicago: Northwestern University Press and the Newberry Library, 1970), 657–64, and James Jubak's analysis of *Mardi* as

a "travel narrative," "romantic quest," "political charade," and "satiric travelogue," in "The Influence of the Travel Narrative on Melville's *Mardi*," *Genre* 9 (1976): 121–33. Joseph Flibbert argues that the components of the tripartite structure are criticized and rejected by the narrator, thus *Mardi* is a travelogue "turned upon itself"; see Flibbert, *Melville and the Art of Burlesque* (Amsterdam: Rodolphi Press, 1976), 73. To date, no analysis of *Mardi* exists that demonstrates how the book's structure corresponds to the conventions of veridical and fictional travel narratives.

43. Warner Berthoff, *The Example of Melville* (Princeton: Princeton University Press, 1962); Richard H. Brodhead, *Hawthorne, Melville, and the Novel* (Chicago: University of Chicago Press, 1976); Edgar A. Dryden, *Melville's Thematics of Form: The Great Art of Telling the Truth* (Baltimore: Johns Hopkins University Press, 1968); Charles A. Feidelson, *Symbolism and American Literature* (Chicago: University of Chicago Press, 1953).

44. Herman Melville, *Mardi* (Evanston and Chicago: Northwestern University Press and the Newberry Library, 1970), 3. Further references to this work will be incorporated into the text.

45. William Ellis relates a sentimental legend of a beautiful blond-haired native who reaches for a flower blossom and sinks into a whirlpool; see also his sensational account of infanticide, *Polynesian Researches* (London: Fisher, Son and Jackson, 1831), 3:87; Benjamin Morrell, *Narratives of Four Voyages* (New York: J. and J. Harper, 1831); Charles S. Stewart, *Narrative of a Voyage to the South Pacific* (London: Fisher, Son and Jackson, 1831);

46. See Richard H. Brodhead, "*Mardi*: Creating the Creative," in *New Perspectives on Melville*, ed. Faith Pullin (Edinburgh: Edinburgh University Press, 1978), 29–53.

47. See Sylvester Judd, *Margaret: A Tale of the Real and Ideal, Blight and Bloom* (Boston: Jordan and Wiley, 1845), and Leyda, *The Melville Log*, 1:250. In a letter to his brother, Duyckinck describes "a very dramatic story" related by Melville, who heard it from Judd regarding his stay at Lahina.

48. See David Harrison, *The Melancholy Narrative of the Distressfull Voyage and Miraculous Deliverance of Captain David Harrison, of the Sloop, Peggy, of New York, on his Voyage from Fyal, one of the Western Islands, to New York*, in *The Trough of the Sea: Selected Sea Deliverance Narratives, 1610–1766*, ed. Donald P. Wharton (Westport, Conn.: Greenwood Press, 1979), 261; see also the introduction (22–26), in which Wharton argues that Poe's and Melville's symbolic use of the sea stems from their reading of Puritan and colonial sea deliverance narratives. For Poe's indebted-

ness to Harrison, see Keith Huntress, "Another Source for Poe's *Narrative of Arthur Gordon Pym," American Literature* 16 (1944): 19–25.

49. See Brodhead, "*Mardi:* Creating the Creative," 34–37.

50. Friedrich Karl, the Liebhier de la Motte-Fouqué, *Undine* (New York: Wiley and Putnam, 1845). Melville read this story in the spring of 1847. For the similarity of Yillah to Undine, see Davis, *Melville's Mardi,* 137.

51. For a discussion of Melville's sources for Yillah's origin, see Davis, *Melville's Mardi,* 132–41.

52. See Meade Minnigerode, *The Fabulous Forties, 1840–1850: A Presentation of Private Life* (Garden City N.Y.: Garden City Pub. Co., 1924).

53. For the continual popularity of Irving during the 1840s, see Martin Roth, *Comedy and America: The Lost World of Washington Irving* (Port Washington, N.Y.: Kennikat Press, 1976).

54. For a discussion of the aesthetics of comedy, see Stuart Tave, *The Amiable Humorist* (Chicago: University of Chicago Press, 1960). For discussions of Melville's use of satire and burlesque in *Mardi,* see Rosenberry, *Melville and the Comic Spirit,* 52–60; Flibbert, *Melville and the Art of Burlesque;* S. Mushebac, *Melville's Humor* (New York: Archon Books, 1982); and John Bryant, "Melville's Comic Debate: Geniality and the Aesthetics of Repose," *American Literature* 55 (1983): 151–69.

55. See Davis, *Melville's Mardi,* 142–59; Flibbert, *Melville and the Art of Burlesque,* 35–86; and Rosenberry, *Melville and the Comic Spirit,* 67.

56. See Percy G. Adams, *Travel Literature and the Evolution of the Novel* (Lexington: University Press of Kentucky, 1983), 140–45, for a discussion of the *conte philosophique* as a conventional form of the travel narrative.

57. As a factual exposition of an incident devoid of subjective impression and commentary, the story of Ravanoo illustrates Mohi's method; see *Mardi,* 352.

58. For an example of Yoomy's method, see ibid., 560.

59. See Feidelson for the classic analysis of *Mardi* as a symbolic journey, in *Symbolism and American Literature,* 183–84. For thematic analyses of the meaning behind the narrator's journey or search, see Milton R. Stern, *The Fine-Hammered Steel of Herman Melville* (Urbana: University of Illinois Press, 1957), and James E. Miller, Jr., "*Mardi:* The Search for Innocence," in his *Reader's Guide to Herman Melville* (New York: Noonday Press, 1962), 36–53.

60. N. P. Willis, *New York Home Journal,* 21 April 1849.

61. *London Atlas,* 24 March 1849, and *London Examiner,* 31 March 1849.

62. Yillah was "well nigh as beautiful as Maturin's *Immalee*" (Henry Fothergill Chorley, *London Athenaeum,* 24 March 1849).

63. *Boston Hunt's Merchant Magazine,* May 1849.

64. Duyckinck, *Literary World,* 14 April 1849.

65. George Ripley, *New York Tribune*, 10 May 1849; and *New York Saroni's Musical Times*, 29 September 1849.
66. *Graham's*, May 1849.
67. Henry Good Watson, *New York Saroni's Musical Times*, 29 September 1849.
68. *Southern Literary Messenger*, May 1849.

4. *Writer and Community in* Redburn *and* White-Jacket

1. See William Charvat, "Melville and the Common Reader," in *The Profession of Authorship in America, 1800–1870: The Papers of William Charvat*, ed. Matthew J. Bruccoli (Columbus: Ohio State University Press, 1968), 262–82; Henry Nash Smith, *Democracy and the Novel: Popular Resistance to Classic American Writers* (New York: Oxford University Press, 1978), 3–55; Ann Douglas, *The Feminization of American Culture* (New York: Alfred A. Knopf, 1977), 289–326; Michael T. Gilmore, *American Romanticism and the Marketplace* (Chicago: University of Chicago Press, 1985); Sacvan Bercovitch, *The American Jeremiad* (Madison: University of Wisconsin Press, 1978), 28–30, 191–94; Emory Elliot, "Art, Religion, and the Problem of Authority in *Pierre*," in *Ideology and Classic American Literature*, ed. Sacvan Bercovitch and Myra Jehlen (Cambridge: Cambridge University Press, 1986), 337; and Myra Jehlen, "The Novel and the Middle Class in America," in *Ideology and Classic American Literature*, 35.
2. Elliot, "Art, Religion, and the Problem of Authority in *Pierre*," 350–51, and Michael Paul Rogin, *Subversive Genealogy: The Politics and Art of Herman Melville* (New York: Alfred A. Knopf, 1983).
3. Elliot, "Art, Religion, and the Problem of Authority in *Pierre*," 361.
4. William H. Gilman, *Melville's Early Life and Redburn* (New York: New York University Press, 1951), 206; Hershel Parker, "Historical Note," in Melville, *Redburn, His First Voyage, Being the Sailor-boy Confessions and Reminiscences of a Son-of-a-Gentleman in the Merchant Service* (Evanston and Chicago: Northwestern University Press and the Newberry Library, 1969), 319–23; Willard Thorp, "Historical Note," in Melville, *White-Jacket, Or the World in a Man-of-War* (Evanston and Chicago: Northwestern University Press and the Newberry Library, 1970), 408–9; further references to these works will be incorporated into the text. Howard P. Vincent, *The Tailoring of White-Jacket* (Evanston: Northwestern University Press, 1970), 1–2; Wai-chee Dimock, "*White-Jacket*: Authors and Audiences," *Nineteenth-Century Fiction* 36 (1981): 296–97; Gilmore, *American Romanticism and the Marketplace*, 61, 124.
5. Letter to Lemuel Shaw, 6 October 1849, in Melville, *Correspondence*, ed. Lynn Horth (Evanston and Chicago: Northwestern University Press and

the Newberry Library, 1993), 139; Gilman, *Melville's Early Life*. 209; Parker, "Historical Note," *Redburn*, 316–18; James H. Justus, "*Redburn* and *White-Jacket*: Society and Sexuality in the Narrators of 1849," in *Herman Melville: Reassessments*, ed. A. Robert Lee (London: Barnes and Noble, 1984), 41–42.

6. Letter to Evert Duyckinck, 5 April 1849; letter to Lemuel Shaw, 6 October 1849, in *Correspondence*, 128, 139.

7. Richard Poirier uses this phrase to describe the metaphysical worlds found in the works of the American romantic writers; see Poirier, *A World Elsewhere: The Place of Style in American Fiction* (New York: Oxford University Press, 1966).

8. See Bercovitch, *American Jeremiad*, 142–210; Michael T. Gilmore, *The Middle Way: Puritanism and Ideology in American Fiction* (New Brunswick, N.J.: Rutgers University Press, 1977); and Jehlen, "The Novel and the Middle Class in America," 31–35.

9. See Smith, *Democracy and the Novel*, 3–55; Douglas, *The Feminization of American Culture*, 289–326; Nina Baym, "Melville's Quarrel with Fiction," *PMLA* 94 (1979): 903–23; and Justus, "*Redburn* and *White-Jacket*," 56.

10. Gilmore, *The Middle Way*, 47.

11. Elliot, "Art, Religion, and the Problem of Authority in *Pierre*," 339.

12. Jehlen, "The Novel and the Middle Class in America," 57–64.

13. The following were some of the more popular nautical reminiscences from the 1840s: *Life in a Man-of-War, by a Fore-Top-Man* (New York: n.p., 1841); John Sherbourne Sleeper, *Tales of the Ocean and Essays of the Forecastle, by Hawser Martingale* (Boston: S. N. Dickinson, 1841); Jack Swifter [James Fenimore Cooper], *Afloat and Ashore* (1841); James Fenimore Cooper, *Ned Myers: Or a Life before the Mast* (Philadelphia: Lea and Blanchard, 1843); Charles Briggs, *Working a Passage; Or, Life in a Liner* (New York: John Allen, 1844); and J. Ross Browne, *Etchings of a Whaling Cruise* (1846).

14. Robert A. Ferguson, *Law and Letters in American Literature* (Cambridge, Mass.: Harvard University Press, 1984), 260.

15. Charles R. Anderson, *Melville in the South Seas* (New York: Columbia University Press, 1939); Gilman, *Melville's Early Life*, 205–7; Leon Howard, *Herman Melville: A Biography* (Berkeley: University of California Press, 1951); and Parker, "Historical Note," *Redburn*, 330–31.

16. See Robert C. Gale, *Richard Henry Dana* (New York: Twayne, 1969), 130–34, and Ferguson, *Law and Letters*, 259–61.

17. Frederick Hardman's unsigned review of *Redburn* reflects general critical opinion when he instructs the author to "take time and pains . . . and avoid certain affectations and pedantry unworthy of a man of his ability"; see Hardman, *Blackwood's Magazine*, November 1849, 567.

18. Melville borrowed several incidents from these works for *Redburn* and *White-Jacket*. See Thomas Philbrick, "Melville's Best Authorities," *Nineteenth-Century Fiction* 15 (1960): 171–79; George Perkins, "Death by Spontaneous Combustion in Marryat, Melville, Dickens, Zola, and Others," *Dickensian* 60 (winter 1964): 57–63; Kenneth Alan Hovey, "*White-Jacket* vs. *Mr. Midshipman Easy*," *Melville Society Extracts* 56 (1983): 13–15; Bernard Rosenthal, "Melville, Marryat, and the Evil-Eyed Villain," *Nineteenth-Century Fiction* 25 (1970): 221–24.

19. See Gilman, *Melville's Early Life*, 159–76. The narrative voice has been a major topic of discussion: see F. O. Matthiessen, *American Renaissance* (New York: Macmillan, 1941); Lawrence Thompson, *Melville's Quarrel with God* (Princeton: Princeton University Press, 1952); Merlin Bowen, "*Redburn* and the Angle of Vision," *Modern Philology* 52 (November 1954): 100–109; and Parker, "Historical Note," *Redburn*, 308.

20. Charles F. Briggs, *The Adventures of Harry Franco; Or, Tales of the Panic* (New York: Saunders, 1839); Briggs, *Working a Passage;* Frederick Marryat, *Mr. Midshipman Easy* (London: Saunders and Otley, 1836); Marryat, *Frank Mildmay or the Naval Officer* (London: Saunders and Otley, 1829); and Marryat, *Peter Simple* (London: Saunders and Otley, 1834).

21. Christopher W. Sten, "Melville's 'Gentlemen Forger': The Struggle for Identity in *Redburn*," *Texas Studies in Language and Literature* 21 (1979): 363.

22. Other explanations of the commonalities among these characters have focused on "homoerotic sensibilities"; see Justus, "*Redburn* and *White-Jacket*," 54.

23. Due to *Redburn's* "retrogression," Justus designates *Redburn* an "unresolved *Bildungsroman* structure"; see ibid., 42.

24. Ibid., 55.

25. Vincent, *The Tailoring of Melville's White-Jacket*, 13–14.

26. Ibid.

27. One notable exception is the narrative of John Codman, who as a captain surprisingly stresses the humanity and equality between officers and crew; see John Codman, *Sailors' Life and Sailors' Yarns, by Captain Ringbolt* (New York: C. S. Francis and Co., 1847), 250–52. See also Samuel Leech, *Thirty Years from Home, Or a Voice from the Main Deck* (Boston: Tappan and Dennet, 1843), 39, and Briggs, *Working a Passage*, 92–93.

28. With the secularization of moral issues pervading the sermons of the revivals of the 1830s and 1840s into pleas for reform, many writers from this period concerned themselves with moral themes. See Perry Miller, *Life of the Mind in America: From the Revolution to the Civil War* (New York: Harcourt, Brace, and World, 1965); Douglas, *The Feminization of American Culture;* and Nina Baym, *Novels, Readers, and Reviewers:*

Responses to Fiction in Antebellum America (Ithaca: Cornell University Press, 1984).

29. Larry J. Reynolds, "Antidemocratic Emphasis in *White-Jacket*," *American Literature* 48 (1976): 19.

30. Bercovitch, *American Jeremiad*, 133–75.

31. Duyckinck, review of *White-Jacket*, 318.

32. William Saroni pointed out in his review of *White-Jacket* that Melville "substituted rhetoric for logic," in *New York Saroni's Musical Times*, 30 March 1850, 350.

33. Denis Berthold, "Factual Errors and Fictional Aims in *White-Jacket*," *Studies in American Fiction* 11 (autumn 1983): 233–37.

34. Duyckinck, review of *White-Jacket*, 318.

35. *Southern Literary Messenger*, April 1850.

36. *John Bull*, November 1851.

5. Originality: The Case of Moby-Dick

1. See *The Journal of Sir Walter Scott*, ed. J. G. Tait, 2 vols. (Edinburgh: Oliver and Boyd, 1939), 1:100, quoted in Edwin M. Eigner, *The Metaphysical Novel in England and America: Dickens, Bulwer, Melville, and Hawthorne* (Berkeley: University of California Press, 1978), 15; Anthony Trollope, *An Autobiography*, 2 vols. (London: W. Blackwood and Sons, 1883), 1:207–8; and J. I. M. Stewart, introduction to William Makepeace Thackeray, *Vanity Fair* (Harmondsworth, Middlesex: Penguin, 1968), 8.

2. Richard Brodhead, *Hawthorne, Melville, and the Form of the Novel* (Chicago: University of Chicago Press, 1976), 130. Brodhead continued his belief that Melville wrote improvisationally; see his "Trying All Things: An Introduction to *Moby-Dick*," in *New Essays on "Moby-Dick*," ed. Richard Brodhead (Cambridge: Cambridge University Press, 1986), 1–21.

3. Harrison Hayford, "Historical Note I," in Melville, *Moby-Dick, Or, The Whale* (Evanston and Chicago: Northwestern University Press and the Newberry Library, 1988), 583.

4. Ibid.

5. Harrison Hayford, "Unnecessary Duplicates: The Key to the Writing of *Moby-Dick*," in *New Perspectives on Melville*, ed. Faith Pullin (Edinburgh: Edinburgh University Press, 1978), 128–61.

6. In *The Metaphysical Novel in England and America*, Eigner provides an informed discussion of the genre of the "metaphysical" or "mixed form" novel in England. He describes the theoretical tenets of the form as detailed by its chief proponent, Edward Bulwer-Lytton, and he spends considerable time outlining its characteristics as found in some of the more well-known examples, such as *Wuthering Heights*, and several

novels by Bulwer-Lytton and Dickens. Eigner also discusses Melville's works more generally in terms of their links to the mixed form novel.

7. Brodhead, "Trying All Things," 2.

8. See Charles Olson, *Call Me Ishmael* (New York: Reynal and Hitchcock, 1947); Larzer Ziff, "Shakespeare and Melville's America" in *New Perspectives on Melville;* David S. Reynolds, *Beneath the American Renaissance: The Subversive Imagination in the Age of Emerson and Melville* (New York: Alfred A. Knopf, 1988); and Lawrence W. Levine, *Highbrow/Lowbrow: The Emergence of Cultural Hierarchy in America* (Cambridge, Mass.: Harvard University Press, 1988), 11–82.

9. See Hershel Parker, *Flawed Texts and Verbal Icons: Literary Authority in American Fiction* (Evanston: Northwestern University Press, 1984).

10. See Hayford, "Historical Note I," *Moby-Dick,* 583; James McIntosh, "The Mariner's Multiple Quest," in *New Essays on "Moby-Dick,"* 26; George R. Stewart, "The Two *Moby-Dicks,*" *American Literature* 25 (1954): 414–48; and Ziff, "Shakespeare and Melville's America," 55.

11. Eigner, *The Metaphysical Novel.*

12. Edward Bulwer-Lytton, "On the Different Kinds of Prose Fiction with Some Apology for the Fiction of the Author," in *The Disowned* (London: Bentley, 1835), 1:i–ix; quoted in Eigner, *The Metaphysical Novel,* introduction, 1–12.

13. See David Masson, "British Novelists since Scott, Lecture IV," in his *British Novelists and Their Styles: Being a Critical Sketch of the History of British Prose* (Cambridge: Macmillan, 1859), 214–27; partially reprinted in Edwin Eigner and George J. Worth, eds., *Victorian Criticism of the Novel* (New York: Cambridge University Press, 1985), 148–58.

14. Masson, "British Novelists," 275–76. For a general discussion of the metaphysical novel, see Eigner, *The Metaphysical Novel,* 1–13.

15. See Eigner, *The Metaphysical Novel,* 15.

16. See John Butt and Kathleen Tillotson, *Dickens at Work* (London: Methuen, 1957), and Eigner, *The Metaphysical Novel,* 29–38; see also *The Pilgrim Edition of the Letters of Charles Dickens, Volume Four, 1844–1846,* ed. Kathleen Tillotson (Oxford: Clarendon, 1977), 203, 589–93.

17. Edward Bulwer-Lytton, "Dedicatory Epistle to John Aldjo," in *Deveroux: A Tale* (London: Bentley, 1852), 1:v.

18. Melville, *Correspondence,* ed. Lynn Horth (Evanston and Chicago: Northwestern University Press and the Newberry Library, 1993), 162.

19. Ibid., 212–13.

20. Hobson Quinn was the first to detect *Kaloolah's* influence on *Moby-Dick,* in *American Fiction:* (New York: D. Appleton Co., 1936). Other scholars have noted some of the similarities between the works of Mayo and Melville: Luther S. Mansfield and Howard P. Vincent, *Moby-Dick*

(New York: Hendricks House, 1962); Perry Miller, *The Raven and the Whale* (New York: Harcourt, Brace, 1951), 254–55; Cecil D. Eby, "William Starbuck Mayo and Herman Melville," *NEQ* 35 (December 1962): 515–20. In his descriptions of the three types of women in *Kaloolah*, Mayo may have offered a source for Melville's next work, *Pierre*, in the depiction of the woman of affections as Isabel.

21. See Brodhead, "Trying All Things," 4, and John Samson, *White Lies: Melville's Narrative of Facts* (Ithaca: Cornell University Press, 1989).

22. See Edward Bulwer-Lytton, preface to *Harold: The Last of the Saxon Kings* (London: Richard Bentley, 1848); Richard Burleigh Kimball, *St. Leger; Or, The Threads of Life* (London: Richard Bentley, 1850); Sylvester Judd, *Margaret: A Tale of The Real and Ideal, Blight and Bloom* (Boston: Jordan and Willey, 1845). George William Curtis, preface to *Nile Notes of an Howadji* (New York: Harper Bros., 1851).

23. See William Starback Mayo, *Kaloolah, Or Journeyings to the Ojébel Kumri: An Autobiography of Jonathan Romer* (New York: Harper Bros., 1849), 143.

24. Howard P. Vincent coined the term *cetological center* in *The Trying-Out of Moby-Dick* (New York: Harcourt, Brace, 1949), 119.

25. See ibid., 119–20. For a review of the scholarship regarding Melville's use of scientific materials, see Hershel Parker, "Historical Note II," *Moby-Dick*, 635–59. The factual center of Melville's masterpiece has recently received attention. For a discussion of the economic language in *Moby-Dick*, see Paul Royster, "Melville's Economy of Language," in *Ideology and Classic American Literature*, ed. Sacvan Bercovitch and Myra Jehlen (Cambridge: Cambridge University Press, 1986), 313–36.

26. See Ziff, "Shakespeare and Melville's America," 55.

27. Levine has recently traced these cultural divisions in *Highbrow/Lowbrow*, 11–82.

28. Ziff, "Shakespeare and Melville's America," 55; Brodhead, "Trying All Things," 3.

29. Hayford, "Historical Note I," *Moby-Dick*, 583.

30. Brodhead, "Trying All Things," 3.

31. See Hayford, "Unnecessary Duplicates," 128–61.

32. Vincent, *The Trying-Out of Moby-Dick*, 136; McIntosh, "The Mariner's Multiple Quest," 26, 29.

33. Michael T. Gilmore, *American Romanticism and the Marketplace* (Chicago: University of Chicago Press, 1985).

34. Melville, *Moby-Dick*, 109, 460. Subsequent references to this work will be made parenthetically in the text.

35. Charlene Avallone discusses this notion within the context of classical literary tradition, a tradition that precludes practices within Melville's

contemporary culture; see Avallone, " 'Vast and Varied Accessions . . . From Abroad': Herman Melville and Edward Young," *Studies in the American Renaissance* (1984): 409–24.

36. Although he does not discuss Ishmael's quest for a multiple comprehension of existential matters, James McIntosh treats the multiple quest theme in *Moby-Dick* in "The Mariner's Multiple Quest," 23–52.

37. *John Bull*, 25 October 1851.

38. Stewart, "The Two *Moby-Dicks,*" 414–18; James Barbour, "The Composition of *Moby-Dick,*" *American Literature* 17 (1975): 343–60; Robert Milder, "The Composition of *Moby-Dick:* A Review and a Prospect," *Emerson Society Quarterly* 23 (1977): 203–16; Leon Howard, *The Unfolding of Moby-Dick,* ed. James Barbour and Thomas Quirk (Glasboro, N.J.: The Melville Society, 1987).

39. Parker, "Historical Note," *Moby-Dick,* 635.

40. Hayford, "Unnecessary Duplicates," 68–121; Parker, *Flawed Texts and Verbal Icons;* Carolyn Porter, "Call Me Ishmael, or How to Make Double-Talk Speak," in *New Essays on Moby-Dick,* 79.

41. Hayford, "Historical Note," *Moby-Dick,* 584.

42. Bryan Wolf, "When Is a Painting Most Like a Whale?" in *New Essays on Moby-Dick,* 175.

43. Ibid.

6. *(Un)Popularity:* Moby-Dick *and* Pierre

1. *London Examiner,* 8 January 1848, 14 December 1850.

2. Ibid., 8 November 1851. See Hugh W. Hetherington, *Melville's Reviewers, British and American, 1846–1891* (Chapel Hill: University of North Carolina Press, 1961), 191.

3. E. P. Whipple, "Novels of the Season," *North American Review,* March 1848, 363.

4. *Literary World,* 17 August 1850.

5. Ibid., 5 January 1850.

6. See Jay Leyda, ed., *The Melville Log: A Documentary Life of Herman Melville, 1819–1891* (New York: Harcourt, Brace, 1951), 1:409.

7. *Literary World,* 22 November 1851.

8. *Harper's,* 1851.

9. *London Morning Advertiser,* 24 October 1851.

10. Brian Higgins and Hershel Parker, "The Flawed Grandeur of *Pierre,*" in *Critical Essays on Pierre,* ed. Brian Higgins and Hershel Parker (Boston: G. K. Hall, 1983), 240–65, and idem, "Reading *Pierre,*" in *A Companion to Melville Studies,* ed. John Bryant (Westport, Conn.: Greenwood Press, 1986), 211–39.

11. Higgins and Parker, "Flawed Grandeur," 241.

12. Charlene Avallone, Anne French Dalke, and David Reynolds have examined *Pierre* in light of the subgenres and American variants of the French sensational romance, forms which often do not underscore the highly ideological orientation of their French precursor or of *Pierre:* see Avallone, "Calculations for Popularity: Melville's *Pierre* and *Holden's Dollar Magazine*," *Nineteenth-Century Literature* 43 (1988): 82–110; Dalke, "The Sensational Fiction of Hawthorne and Melville," *Studies in American Fiction* 16 (1988): 195–207; and Reynolds, *Beneath the American Renaissance: The Subversive Imagination in the Age of Emerson and Melville* (New York: Alfred A. Knopf, 1988), 275–308.

13. Duyckinck, *Literary World*, 18 September 1852, 185.

14. Melville, *The Letters of Herman Melville*, ed. Merrell Davis and William H. Gilman (New Haven: Yale University Press, 1960), 127. This list represents a compilation of Anne Dalke's, David Reynolds's, and my research into the reviews and writers of the day; see Dalke, "The Sensational Fiction of Hawthorne and Melville," and Reynolds, *Beneath the American Renaissance,* 167–334. For an account of the sensational novel in England, see Winnifred Hughes, *The Maniac in the Cellar* (Princeton: Princeton University Press, 1980).

15. Herman Melville, *Israel Potter: His Fifty Years in Exile* (Evanston and Chicago: Northwestern University Press and the Newberry Library, 1982), 48.

16. Higgins and Parker, "The Flawed Grandeur of *Pierre.*" 265.

17. Nina Baym argues that no true distinction can be made about literary cultural formulations of the terms *romance* and *novel*. She bases her conclusion on her survey of some twenty magazines of the period from 1840 to 1860. Her conclusion can be explained, however: by mixing magazines aimed at the various classes of readers and considering their critical assumptions collectively as she does, Baym does not distinguish among the various formulations made by different groups for different audiences. A distinction between novel and romance does surface in my analysis of magazines that catered to the general reader. See Baym, *Novels, Readers, and Reviewers: Responses to Fiction in Antebellum America* (Ithaca: Cornell University Press, 1984), 234.

18. Avallone discusses in "Calculations for Popularity" how these conventions informed the editorial policies and practices in *Holden's Dollar Magazine* and argues that the magazine served as the source for Melville's choice of narrative form in *Pierre*. For studies of the French influence in middle-class antebellum culture, see Howard Mumford Jones, *America and French Culture, 1750–1848* (Chapel Hill: University of North Carolina Press, 1927); Grace B. Sherrer, "French Culture as Pre-

sented to Middle-Class America by *Godey's Lady's Book,*" *American Literature* 3 (1931): 277–86; and Elizabeth White, *American Opinion of France from Lafayette to Poincaré* (New York: Alfred A. Knopf, 1927).

19. Melville, *Correspondence,* ed. Lynn Horth (Evanston and Chicago: Northwestern University Press and the Newberry Library, 1993), 226.

20. For discussions of the form and the readers of the sentimental or domestic romance, see Nina Baym's *Women's Fiction: A Guide to Novels by and about Women in America, 1820–1870* (Ithaca: Cornell University Press, 1978) and *Novels, Readers, and Reviewers;* Mary Kelley, *Private Women, Public Stage: Literary Domesticity in Nineteenth-Century America* (New York: Oxford University Press, 1984); Reynolds, *Beneath the American Renaissance;* and Susan Harris, *19th-Century American Women's Novels: Interpretive Strategies* (Cambridge: Cambridge University Press, 1990).

21. For the variations of the sensational form see L. Karol Kelley, *Models for the Multitude: Social Values in the American Popular Novel, 1650–1920* (Westport, Conn.: Greenwood Press, 1987).

22. Anne-Marie Dibon and Cornelia Strieder discuss the sensational conventions in the novels of these French authors; see Dibon, "Form and Value in the French and English Nineteenth-Century Novel," *Modern Language Notes* 87 (1972): 885–914, and Strieder, *Melodramatik and Sozialkritik in Werken Eugène Sues* (Erlangen: Palm and Enke, 1986). The politically progressive *US Democratic Review* praised the French genre— its French authors, most notably Eugène Sue, and its American proponents, Nathaniel Hawthorne and George Lippard.

23. F. O. Matthiessen, *American Renaissance* (New York: Macmillan, 1941), 486; William Charvat, "Melville and the Common Reader," in *The Profession of Authorship in America, 1800–1870: The Papers of William Charvat,* ed. Matthew J. Bruccoli (Columbus: Ohio State University Press, 1968), 251–52; Higgins and Parker, "Reading *Pierre,*" 211–39; and Leon Howard and Hershel Parker, "Historical Note," *Pierre, Or, The Ambiguities* (New York: Hendricks House, 1962), 369–73.

24. Howard and Parker, "Historical Note," *Pierre,* 369; William Braswell, "The Early Love Scenes in Melville's *Pierre,*" *American Literature* 22 (1950): 283–89.

25. Reynolds, *Beneath the American Renaissance,* 160–81.

26. Nora Atkinson, *Eugene Sue et le roman-feuilleton* (Paris: A Nizet and M. Bastard, 1929); Frederick Charles Green, *French Novelists from the Revolution to Proust* (New York: Charles Ungar, 1964).

27. See, for example, Eugène Sue, *The Mysteries of Paris,* 2 vols. (New York: Harper Bros., 1842).

28. Henry Murray traces this theme throughout American and English literary history in his introduction to *Pierre,* lxvi. Reynolds relates its use in

the sensational novels of Thompson and Lippard to *Pierre*, in *Beneath the American Renaissance*, 293. Avallone discusses the allusions to abnormal sibling love in the pages of *Holden's Dollar Magazine* in relation to the Holden's relationship to his own sisters. She suggests that Melville's own relation to his sisters contributed to the depiction of sibling relations in his romance; see Avallone, "Calculations for Popularity," 95–97. Howard and Parker uphold various theories regarding Melville's intent —and failure—to write a popular domestic romance; see their "Historical Note" in *Pierre*, 365–73.

29. Reynolds, *Beneath The American Renaissance*, 305.

30. Dibon, "Form and Value," 885.

31. Larzer Ziff, "Shakespeare and Melville's America," in *New Perspectives on Melville*, ed. Faith Pullin (Edinburgh: Edinburgh University Press, 1978).

32. The following texts each discuss the effects of class and socioeconomic status on the forms and themes of French and Russian nineteenth-century novelists: George Lukács, *Die Theorie des Romans* (Neuwied and Berlin: Luchterhand, 1965); Lukács, *Studies in European Realism* (London: Hillway Publishing, 1950); René Girard, *Mensonge romantique et vérité romanesque* (Paris: Grasset, 1961); Lucien Goldmann, *Pour une sociologie du roman* (Paris: Gallimard, 1964); Goldmann, *Le Dieu caché* (Paris: Gallimard, 1955); and Frederic Jameson, "The Case for George Lukács," *Salmagundi* 13 (1970): 3–35. Dibon uses the works of these theorists to explain the lack of social analysis in English novels of the same period; see Dibon, "Form and Value."

33. William Gilmore Simms, *The Yemassee* (New York: Harpers, 1853).

34. Baym, *Novels, Readers, and Reviewers*, 231.

35. *Boston Daily Evening Transcript*, 2 August 1852; *New York Albion*, 21 August 1852; *Baltimore American and Commercial Daily Advertiser*, 6 August 1852.

36. *Morning Courier and New York Enquirer*, 21 August 1852; *Spirit of the Times*, 28 August 1852; *Graham's*, October 1852.

37. *Church's Bazaar for Fireside and Wayside*, 21 August 1852.

38. *Literary World*, 30 March 1850.

39. Henry Fothergill Chorley, *London Athenaeum*, 15 June 1850.

40. E. P. Whipple, *Graham's*, May 1850.

41. Nathaniel Hawthorne, *The Scarlet Letter* (1850; rpt. Columbus: Ohio State University Press, 1962).

42. *New York Evening Mirror*, 27 August 1852.

43. *Southern Literary Messenger*, September 1852.

44. *New York Evening Mirror*, 27 August 1852.

45. Lawrence W. Levine, *Highbrow/Lowbrow: The Emergence of Cultural Hierarchy in America* (Cambridge, Mass.: Harvard University Press, 1988), 83.

7. Marketplace Conditions

1. Michael T. Gilmore, *American Romanticism and the Marketplace* (Chicago: University of Chicago Press, 1985), and David S. Reynolds, *Beneath the American Renaissance: The Subversive Imagination in the Age of Emerson and Melville* (New York: Alfred A. Knopf, 1988). The term *classic* is borrowed from F. O. Matthiessen, *American Renaissance* (New York: Macmillan, 1941). Some of the most noted studies on the subversive practices of "classic" writers are Marvin Fisher, *Going Under: Melville's Short Fiction and the American 1850s* (Baton Rouge: Louisiana State University Press, 1977); Henry Nash Smith, *Democracy and the Novel: Popular Resistance to Classic American Writers* (New York: Oxford University Press, 1978); and Reynolds, *Beneath the American Renaissance.* The quotations are from the following works: Ann Douglas, *The Feminization of American Culture* (New York: Alfred A. Knopf, 1977), 319; Nina Baym, "Melville's Quarrel with Fiction," *PMLA* 94 (1979): 903–23; Reynolds, *Beneath the American Renaissance;* and Fisher, *Going Under.*
2. Nina Baym, *Novels, Readers, and Reviewers: Responses to Fiction in Antebellum America* (Ithaca: Cornell University Press, 1984); Lawrence Buell, *New England Literary Culture: From Revolution through Renaissance* (Cambridge: Cambridge University Press, 1986); Cathy Davidson, ed., *Reading in America: Literature and Social History* (Baltimore: Johns Hopkins University Press, 1989); Lawrence W. Levine, *Highbrow/Lowbrow: The Emergence of Cultural Hierarchy in America* (Cambridge, Mass.: Harvard University Press, 1988); Reynolds, *Beneath the American Renaissance;* Jane Tompkins, *Sensational Designs: The Cultural Work of American Fiction, 1790–1860* (New York: Oxford University Press, 1985); and Ronald Zboray, "Antebellum Reading and the Ironies of Technological Innovation," in *Reading in America,* 180–200.
3. B. Roorbach, *Bibliotheca Americana,* quoted in Hellmut Lehmann-Haupt, *The Book in America: A History of the Making and Selling of Books in the United States* (New York, 1952), 119.
4. Kate Seyton, "Fireside Talk about Magazine Tales, etc.," *Godey's,* January 1853, 44–45.
5. Parke Godwin, *George William Curtis: A Commemorative Address Delivered before the Century Association, New York, December 17, 1892* (New York: Harpers and Bros., 1892), 16.
6. *New York Daily Times,* 27 June 1856.
7. "Writing for Periodicals," *North British Review,* reprinted in *Harper's,* June 1850, 553.
8. George William Curtis, letter to Edward W. Dix, in Walter Bezanson, "Historical Note," in Melville, *The Piazza Tales and Other Prose Pieces*

(Evanston and Chicago: Northwestern University Press and the New-berry Library, 1987), 495.

9. "A Word at the Start," *Harper's*, June 1850, 1.

10. Seyton, "Fireside Talk about Magazine Tales, etc.," 45.

11. William Kirkland, "British and American Monthlies," *Godey's*, June 1845, 271.

12. *Knickerbocker*, March 1839.

13. William Charvat, *The Profession of Authorship in America, 1800–1870: The Papers of William Charvat*, ed. Matthew J. Bruccoli (Columbus: Ohio State University Press, 1968), 193–94; E. Douglas Branch, *The Sentimental Years, 1830–60* (New York: Hill and Wang, 1965), 134. For computations of the average annual wage for workers in 1850, see Sean Wilentz, *Chants Democratic: New York City and the Rise of the American Working Class, 1788–1850* (New York: Oxford University Press, 1984), 117, 405, and Stuart Blumin, *The Emergence of the Middle Class: Social Experience in the American City, 1760–1900* (Cambridge: Cambridge University Press, 1989), 108–37.

14. *New York Ledger*, 19 May 1855, quoted in Mary Kelley, *Private Women, Public Stage: Literary Domesticity in Nineteenth-Century America* (New York: Oxford University Press, 1984), 6; James C. Derby, *Fifty Years among Authors, Books, and Publishers* (New York: Putnam's Sons, 1884), 202–3; Mary Noel, *Villains Galore: The Heyday of the Popular Story Weekly* (New York: R. R. Bowkwer, 1954), 64–65, quoted in Susan Coultrap-McQuin, *Doing Literary Business: American Women Writers in the Nineteenth Century* (Chapel Hill: University of North Carolina Press, 1990), 75.

15. William Charvat, "Literary Economics and Literary History," in *The Profession of Authorship in America*, 283–97, and Gilmore, *American Romanticism and the Marketplace*.

16. See Royal Gettmann, *A Victorian Publisher: A Study of the Bentley Papers* (Cambridge: Cambridge University Press, 1960).

17. Eugene Exman, *The Brothers Harper: A Unique Publishing Partnership and Its Impact upon the Cultural Life of America from 1817 to 1853* (New York: Harpers, 1965), 285–91.

18. In a letter to Charles Eliot Norton (9 April 1851), George William Curtis described how the critic Evert Duyckinck warned him of the dangers of "experimenting" too recklessly, a term and a warning that Duyckinck repeated in his review of Melville's *Moby-Dick*; see Jay Leyda, ed., *The Melville Log: A Documentary Life of Herman Melville, 1819–1891* (New York: Harcourt, Brace, 1951), 1:409.

19. Frank Luther Mott, *A History of American Magazines* (Cambridge: Cambridge University Press, 1948).

20. Kirkland, "British and American Monthlies," 271.

21. Sedgwick, "Fanny McDermot," *Godey's*, January 1845, 13.

22. See Theodore Ledyard Cuyler, "Burial at Sea," *Godey's*, September 1849, 195–97; Epes Sargeant, "The Flower of the Family," March 1844, 125–32; Sargeant, "The Man with Two Strings Tied to His Bow," February 1844, 72–76; Margaret Coxe, "The Talisman: Wherewith Happiness Is Secured," July 1844, 77–81; and E. A. Poe, "The Cask of Amontillado," November 1846, 216–18.

23. Caroline Lee Hentz, "My Grandmother's Bracelet," *Godey's*, January 1844, 36–41; Henry William Herbert, "The Fortunes of the House of Foix: The Fatal Gift," October 1844, 155.

24. Hentz, "My Grandmother's Bracelet"; E. F. Ellet, "The Artist's Disappointment," *Godey's*, August 1844, 77–83; Poe, "The Oblong Box," *Godey's*, September 1844, 132–36.

25. Ellet, "The Artist's Disappointment," 78.

26. Robert Montgomery Bond, "The Death Cave."

27. Sargeant, "The Man with Two Strings Tied to His Bow," 72; Ellet, "The Artist's Disappointment," 79; Herbert, "The Fortunes of the House of Foix," 155; and Poe, "The Cask of Amontillado," 216–18.

28. Poe, "The Oblong Box," 132–36; Nathaniel Hawthorne, "Drowne's Wooden Image," *Godey's*, July 1844, 13–17; and Poe, "The Cask of Amontillado," 216–18.

29. Hawthorne, "Drowne's Wooden Image," 17; Poe, "The Oblong Box," 136; Poe, "The Cask of Amontillado," 218.

30. The following works discuss in detail the preference for literary realism by middle-class readers and reviewers: George Paston, *At John Murray's: Records of a Literary Circle, 1843–1892* (London: John Murray, 1932), 24–39; Kathleen Tillotson, *Novels of the 1840s* (Oxford: Clarendon Press, 1954), 13–16; Baym, *Novels, Readers, and Reviewers;* and Sheila Post-Lauria, " 'Philosophy in Whales . . . Poetry in Blubber': Mixed Form in *Moby-Dick,*" *Nineteenth-Century Literature* (December 1990): 300–316.

31. Henry Danforth, "Getting to Sea," *Graham's*, September 1844, 105–9; Catharine Sedgwick, "A Contrast," *Graham's*, January 1844, 15–18; Fanny Forrester, "Bending the Twig," *Graham's*, August 1845, 85–89.

32. Henry Danforth, "Harry Cavendish—A Pirate," *Graham's*, January–June 1842, 31, 74, 178, 237, 268, 307.

33. Wyn Kelley has also identified this theme as a mainstay in what she calls "labrynth" literature; see Kelley, *The City and Urban Form in Nineteenth-Century New York* (New York: Cambridge University Press, 1996).

34. Nathaniel Hawthorne, "Earth's Holocaust," *Graham's*, November 1844, 192–201; E. A. Poe, "The Imp of the Perverse," *Graham's*, July 1845, 1–3.

35. See, for example, Fisher, *Going Under,* and Smith, *Democracy and the Novel.*

36. Poe, "Magazine Writing: Peter Snook," *Broadway Journal*, 7 June 1845, and Hawthorne, preface to *Mosses from an Old Manse* (New York, 1851).

37. Exman, *House of Harper*, 304.

38. Fred Louis Pattee, *The Feminine Fifties* (New York, 1940), 196, quoted in Coultrap-McQuin, *Doing Literary Business*, 73. See Joyce W. Warren's discussion of Fanny Fern's contributions to the *Ledger* in Fern, *Ruth Hall and Other Writings*, ed. Joyce W. Warren (New Brunswick, N.J.: Rutgers University Press, 1986), xxii-xxvii.

39. The following publications examine the work of Fern and Southworth in Bonner's *Ledger:* Kelley, *Private Women, Public Stage;* Joanne Dobson, introduction to E.D.E.N. Southworth, *The Hidden Hand, or, Capitola the Madcap* (New Brunswick, N.J.: Rutgers University Press, 1988), xii-xlii; Dobson, "The Hidden Hand: Subversion of Cultural Ideology in Three Mid-Nineteenth-Century Women's Novels," *American Quarterly* 38, 2 (1986): 223–42; Alfred Habegger, "A Well-Hidden Hand," *Novel* 14, 3 (1981): 197–212; and Coultrap-McQuin, *Doing Literary Business*, 49–78.

40. For the most emphatic assertions of Melville's subversive practices, see Ann Douglas, "Melville's Revolt against the Reader, in her *Feminization of American Culture*, 318–64, and Fisher, *Going Under*.

41. See Johannes D. Bergmann, "Melville's Stories," in *A Companion to Melville Studies*, ed. John Bryant (Westport, Conn.: Greenwood Press, 1986), 251.

8. Creative Reliance

1. For a study of the liberal conventions of *Holden's Dollar Magazine*, see Charlene Avallone, "Calculations for Popularity: Melville's *Pierre* and *Holden's Dollar Magazine*," *Nineteenth-Century Literature* 43 (1988): 82–110.

2. Marvin Fisher, *Going Under: Melville's Short Fiction and the American 1850s* (Baton Rouge: Louisiana State University Press, 1977); Henry Nash Smith, *Democracy and the Novel: Popular Resistance to Classic American Writers* (New York: Oxford University Press, 1978), and David S. Reynolds, *Beneath the American Renaissance: The Subversive Imagination in the Age of Emerson and Melville* (New York: Alfred A. Knopf, 1988).

3. For discussions of Melville's alleged sense of failure and despair during the 1850s, see R. Bruce Bickley, *The Method in Melville's Fiction* (Durham, N.C.: Duke University Press, 1975); William B. Dillingham, *Melville's Short Fiction, 1853–1856* (Athens: University of Georgia Press, 1977); and Fisher, *Going Under*.

4. Ann Douglas argues in *The Feminization of American Culture* (New York: Alfred A. Knopf, 1977) that Melville revolted against readers who demanded specific forms, subjects, and themes that were antithetical to

the author's artistic endeavors. However, through the environments of *Harper's* and *Putnam's*, Melville found forms and audience tastes that were conducive to his personal artistic vision.

5. For discussions of the tastes of a readership Melville called "fireside people" and what Joan Hedrick has labeled "parlor" literature, see Hedrick, "Parlor Literature: Harriet Beecher Stowe and the Question of 'Great Women Artists,'" *Signs* 17, no. 2 (1992): 275–303; Ronald Zboray, *A Fictive People: Antebellum Economic Development and the American Reading Public* (New York: Oxford University Press, 1993), and chapter one herein.

6. Reynolds, *Beneath the American Renaissance,* 57–58.

7. Laura Wexler, "Tender Violence: Literary Eavesdropping, Domestic Fiction, and Educational Reform," in *The Culture of Sentiment: Gender, Race, and Sentimentality in Nineteenth-Century American Literature,* ed. Shirley Samuels (New York: Oxford University Press, 1992), 28.

8. Nina Baym, *Women's Fiction: A Guide to Novels by and about Women in America, 1820–1870* (Ithaca: Cornell University Press, 1978; Urbana: University of Illinois Press, 1993), 12. Susan Harris has recently recovered —and refashioned—this term in her perceptive study of the writing strategies of nineteenth-century women novelists in *19th-Century Women's Noveles: Interpretive Strategies* (Cambridge: Cambridge University Press, 1990).

9. Jane Tompkins, *Sensational Designs: The Cultural Work of American Fiction* (New York: Oxford University Press, 1985); Cathy Davidson, introduction to Susan Rowson, *Charlotte Temple* (New York: Oxford University Press, 1986), Harris, *19th-Century American Women's Novels,* 13.

10. Reynolds, *Beneath the American Renaissance,* 58.

11. Maria Jane McIntosh, *The Lofty and the Lowly: Or, Good in All and None All-Good,* 2 vols. (New York: Appleton and Company, 1853).

12. Illustration, *Godey's,* January 1853, ii.

13. "The Seamstress and the Lady's Boudoir," *Godey's,* January 1853, 25.

14. Donald Mitchell, "Reveries of a Bachelor," *Harper's,* December 1850, 620–27.

15. Melville, "The Paradise of Bachelors and the Tartarus of Maids," *The Piazza Tales and Other Prose Pieces* (Evanston and Chicago: Northwestern University Press and the Newberry Library, 1987), 323.

16. Ibid., 345.

17. See Carolyn Karcher's excellent analysis of this piece in *Shadow over the Promised Land: Slavery, Race, and Violence in Melville's America* (Baton Rouge: Louisiana State University Press, 1980), 160–85.

18. See Michael Paul Rogin, *Subversive Genealogy: The Politics and Art of Herman Melville* (New York: Alfred A. Knopf, 1983), 208–20, and Wai-

chee Dimock, *Empire for Liberty: Melville and the Poetics of Individualism* (Princeton: Princeton University Press, 1989), 3–41.

19. See Stuart Blumin, *The Emergence of the Middle Class: Social Experience in the American City, 1760–1900* (Cambridge: Cambridge University Press, 1989), 127–28, 182–86.

20. "Life in Hawaii," *Putnam's*, July 1853, 22.

21. "Salt Lake and the New Saratoga," *Putnam's*, September 1853, 264.

22. Thoreau did not like editorial advice about his manuscript, so he refused to publish any further installments with *Putnam's*. See Steven Fink, *Prophet in the Marketplace: Thoreau's Development as a Professional Writer* (Princeton: Princeton University Press, 1992).

23. Henry David Thoreau, "An Excursion to Canada," *Putnam's*, January 1853, 57.

24. Ibid, 58.

25. Melville, *Moby-Dick or, The Whale* (Evanston and Chicago: Northwestern University Press and The Newberry Library, 1988).

26. Karcher, *Shadow over the Promised Land*, 109–20.

27. Ibid., 109.

28. Several popular shilling novels published during this time have been offered as possible sources for "Bartleby," such as James A. Maitland's 1851 *The Lawyer's Story*, suggested by Leon Howard in *Melville: A Biography* (Berkeley and Los Angeles: University of California Press, 1951), 208, and discussed by Johannes Deitrich (Hans) Bergmann in " 'Bartleby' and *The Lawyer's Story*," *American Literature* 47 (1975): 432–36. As David Reynolds has pointed out, the author of *New York in Slices*, George Foster, portrays the rigidity of Wall Street and the individuals who suffer from business reversals. The sensational style of George Foster's novel, however, does not stylistically complement either Melville's style or his focus in "Bartleby." Sensationalist rhetoric was not popular with *Putnam's*, as evidenced in its condemnation of Melville's *Pierre*, where the author successfully (though not always popularly) employed this style.

29. Dan McCall, *The Silence of Bartleby* (Ithaca: Cornell University Press, 1989), 99.

30. See also "Our Best Society," *Putnam's*, February 1853, 170–79, and "Elegant Tom Dillar," May 1853, 525–30.

31. George William Curtis, "Andrew Cranberry, Attorney-at-Law," *Putnam's*, January 1853, 18.

32. Michael T. Gilmore, *American Romanticism and the Marketplace* (Chicago: University of Chicago Press, 1985), 142.

33. Melville Papers, Duyckinck Collection, New York Public Library. See also Walter E. Bezanson, "Historical Note," *Piazza Tales*, 575.

34. Douglas, *The Feminization of American Culture*, 298; H. Bruce Franklin, "Herman Melville: Artist of the Worker's World," in *Weapons of Criti-*

cism: Marxism in America and the Literary Tradition, ed. Norman Rud-ich (Palo Alto, Calif.: Ramparts, 1976), 287–309; Rogin, *Subversive Genealogy,* 192–201; and Gilmore, *American Romanticism and the Marketplace,* 132–45, especially 142.

35. Hershel Parker, "The 'Sequel' in 'Bartleby,' " in *Bartleby the Inscrutable,* ed. M. Thomas Inge (Hamden: Archon Books, 1979), 163.

36. Stanley Brodwin, "To the Frontiers of Eternity: Melville's Crossing in 'Bartleby, the Scrivener'," in *Bartleby, the Inscrutable,* 174–96, and McCall, *The Silence of Bartleby,* 143.

37. Allan Emery, "The Alternatives of Melville's Bartleby,' " *Nineteenth-Century Fiction* 31 (1976): 186–87, referred to in McCall, *The Silence of Bartleby,* 100.

38. Quoted in Inge, *Bartleby, the Inscrutable,* 31.

39. *Putnam's,* July 1854 to March 1855. The story was published in book form by Putnam in 1855 as *Israel Potter: His Fifty Years of Exile.* The quotation is from Walter E. Bezanson, "Historical Note," in Herman Melville, *Israel Potter: His Fifty Years of Exile* (Evanston and Chicago: Northwestern University Press and the Newberry Library, 1982), 194.

40. Melville, letter to *Harper's,* 25 May 1854, in *Correspondence,* ed. Lynn Horth (Evanston: Northwestern University Press and the Newberry Library, 1993), 263–64.

41. No letter from *Harper's* to Melville concerning this serial has been located; see *Correspondence,* 263.

42. See Bezanson, "Historical Note," *Israel Potter,* 184.

43. Melville, letter to G. P. Putnam, 7 June 1854, in Melville, *Correspondence,* 265. While other scholars have suggested 12 June as a more probable date for this letter (see Bezanson, "Historical Note," *Israel Potter,* 181–82), Lynn Horth in her splendid edition of Melville's correspondence refutes this claim decisively by providing the actual letter dated 7 June.

44. Melville, letters to George P. Putnam, 16 May 1854 and 7 June 1854, in *Correspondence,* 261, 265.

45. The 16 May letter concerns Melville's attempt to solicit continued support from the editors at *Putnam's* despite their rejection of "The Two Temples": "I have your note about the "Two Temples." . . . Ere long I will send down some other things, to which, I think, no objections will be made on the score of the tender consciences of the public" (*Correspondence,* 261).

46. Charles Briggs, letter to Herman Melville, 12 May, 1854, in ibid., 636.

47. Henry Trumbull, *Life and Remarkable Adventures of Israel Potter* (Providence: Henry Trumbull, 1824); Bezanson, "Historical Note," *Israel Potter,* 182.

48. Bezanson, "Historical Note," *Israel Potter,* 184.

49. "Editorial Notes—American Literature," *Putnam's,* February 1854, 223.

50. Fitz-James O'Brien, "Our Young American Authors," *Putnam's*, February 1853, 77.

51. For a discussion of midcentury debates on genre, see Sheila Post-Lauria, " 'Philosophy in Whales . . . Poetry in Blubber': Mixed Form in *Moby-Dick*," *Nineteenth-Century Literature* 45, no. 3 (December 1990): 300–316, and chapter 6, herein.

52. Jacob Abbot, "Benjamin Franklin," *Harper's*, January-February 1852, 145–65; 289–309; and idem, "Napoleon Bonaparte," *Harper's*, June 1853, 50–70.

53. Abbot, "Benjamin Franklin," 145.

54. A recent collection of essays addresses the essential bivalent thematics inherent in the sentimental mode; see Samuels, *The Culture of Sentiment*.

55. Bezanson, "Historical Note," *Israel Potter*, 188.

56. See Sheila Post-Lauria, "Canonical Texts and Context: The Example of Herman Melville's 'Bartleby, the Scrivener: A Story of Wall Street,' " *College Literature* 20, no. 2 (June 1993): 196–205.

57. See Sheila Post-Lauria, "Editorial Politics in 'Benito Cereno,' " *American Periodicals* (1995):1–13.

58. Bezanson, "Historical Note," *Israel Potter*, 187–91.

59. Ibid., 194.

60. Charles Gordon Greene, *Boston Post*, 15 March 1855, cited in *Melville: The Critical Heritage*, ed. Watson G. Branch (London: Routledge and Kegan Paul, 1974), 338.

61. John Bryant, "Melville's Comic Debate: Geniality and the Aesthetics of Repose," *American Literature* 55 (1983): 151–70.

62. See Lea Bertani Vozar Newman's excellent summary of the criticism on this topic in *A Reader's Guide to the Short Stories of Herman Melville* (Boston: G. K. Hall, 1986), 130–36.

63. Parke Godwin, *George William Curtis: A Commemorative Address Delivered before the Century Association, New York, December 17, 1892* (New York: Harpers and Bros., 1892): 29–30.

64. Thomas Bender, *New York Intellect: A History of Intellectual Life in New York City, from 1750 to the Beginnings of Our Own Time* (Baltimore: Johns Hopkins University Press, 1988), 167.

65. Letter from Frederick Law Olmsted to Parke Godwin, 1 July 1856, Bryant-Godwin Collection, New York Public Library.

66. Kimball, "Cuba," *Putnam's*, January 1853, 7.

67. See the review of Maturin M. Ballou's *History of Cuba* in "Editorial Notes," October 1854, 448. Only one exception exists: see "Annexation," February 1854, 183–94, in which the author ardently supports American policy on Mexico, Texas, and North American Indians. The point of the article, however, is to silence British condemnation of American policies

toward annexation and to demonstrate that the British, along with many other countries of the world, have continually held their own annexationist policies.

68. In recent years some critics have attributed a radically opposite political stance to the magazine's editorial policy. Allan Moore Emery, for example, mistakes editorial policies when he states: "For the prophets of *Putnam's,* America's mission was to 'extend' democracy throughout the Western Hemisphere, to spread the 'living seeds of freedom' among the subject peoples of the world"; see his " 'Benito Cereno' and Manifest Destiny," *Nineteenth-Century Fiction* 39 (1984): 55.

69. "Is Man One or Many?" *Putnam's,* July 1854, 1–14; "Are all Men Descended from Adam?" January 1855, 79–88; "Hayti and the Haytians," January 1854, 58.

70. "Is Man One or Many?"

71. "Are All Men Descended from Adam?"

72. "Hayti and the Haytians."

73. "African Proverbial Philosophy," *Putnam's,* October 1854, 362–71.

74. Yet despite *Putnam's* clear stand on manifest destiny, this opinion is one against which Melville reputedly argues; see Emery, " 'Benito Cereno,' " 50.

75. I am referring specifically here to the essays by Joyce Adler, *War in Melville's Imagination* (New York: New York University Press, 1981), 88–110; Karcher, *Shadow over the Promised Land;* Joshua Leslie and Sterling Stuckey, "The Death of Benito Cereno: A Reading of Herman Melville on Slavery," *Journal of Negro History* 67 (winter 1982): 297–301; Joshua Leslie and Sterling Stuckey, "Avoiding the Tragedy of Benito Cereno: The Official Response to Babo's Revolt," *Criminal Justice History* 3 (1982): 128–31; Robert Levine, *Conspiracy and Romance* (New York: Cambridge University Press, 1989); Toni Morrison, "Unspeakable Things Unspoken: The Afro-American Presence in American Literature," *Michigan Quarterly Review* 28 (winter 1989): 1–24; Charles E. Nnolim, *Melville's "Benito Cereno": A Study in Meaning of Name Symbolism* (New York: New Voices, 1974); Rogin, *Subversive Genealogy;* Sterling Stuckey, *Slave Culture: Nationalist Theory and the Foundation of Black America* (New York: Oxford University Press, 1987); Eric Sundquist, *To Wake the Nations: Race in the Making of American Literature* (Cambridge, Mass.: Harvard University Press, 1993), 135–224; Jean Fagan Yellin, *The Intricate Knot: Black Figures in American Literature, 1776–1863* (New York University Press, 1972), 215–27; and Thomas D. Zlatic, " 'Benito Cereno': Melville's 'Back-Handed-Well-Knot,' " *ArizonaQuarterly* 34 (1978): 327–43. For an excellent summary of the various interpretations of Melville's tale, see Newman, *A Reader's Guide to the Short Stories of Herman Melville,* 130–53.

76. See, among other articles already discussed, "American Despotisms," November 1854, 524–31.
77. See my " 'Philosophy in Whales . . . Poetry in Blubber.' " Rosalie Feltenstein suggested the allusion to the Dominican order in her pioneering study, "Melville's 'Benito Cereno,' " *American Literature* 19 (1947): 245–55. Two works discuss the allusion to the Santo Domingo slave revolt: H. Bruce Franklin, *The Wake of the Gods: Melville's Mythology* (Stanford: Stanford University Press, 1963), 145, and for a more recent study of this name change that ties the allusion to the monks with the slave revolt, see Charles Swann, "Two Notes on 'Benito Cereno,' " *Journal of American Studies* 19 (1985): 111–14. See also Sundquist's excellent reading of "Benito Cereno" in light of this allusion, in *To Wake the Nations*, 140–48.
78. Karcher, *Shadow over the Promised Land*, 126–45, and Rogin, *Subversive Genealogy*, 210–20.
79. Elsewhere I have pointed out the parallels between magazine practice and Melville's contributions in "Canonical Texts and Context" and in "Magazine Practices and Melville's *Israel Potter*," in *American Social Texts and Periodical Contexts*, ed. Kenneth Price and Susan Belasco Smith (Charlottesville: University of Virginia Press, 1995), 115–32.

9. Writing the American Novel

1. *United States Magazine and Democratic Review,* September 1856.
2. *New York Dispatch,* 8 June 1856, cited in Walter E. Bezanson, "Historical Note," *The Piazza Tales and Other Prose Pieces* (Evanston and Chicago: Northwestern University Press and The Newberry Library, 1987), 506.
3. *American Publishers' Circular and Literary Gazette,* 31 May 1856.
4. See Harrison Hayford, Watson Branch, and Hershel Parker, "Historical Note," in Melville, *The Confidence-Man: His Masquerade* (Evanston and Chicago: Northwestern University Press and The Newberry Library, 1984), 278–79.
5. *New York Churchman,* 30 April 1857.
6. *Putnam's,* January 1853, 102.
7. *Putnam's,* October 1854, 394.
8. Letter to George Duyckinck, 31 March 1857, in *The Melville Log: A Documentary Life of Herman Melville, 1819–1891,* ed. Jay Leyda (New York: Harcourt, Brace, 1951), 2:563.
9. Hayford et al., "Historical Note," *The Confidence-Man,* 284.
10. *Literary World,* 18 August, 1849.
11. Johannes Dietrich Bergmann, "The Original Confidence Man," *American Quarterly* 21 (1969): 560–77, and Michael S. Reynolds, "The Prototype for Melville's Confidence-Man," *PMLA* 86 (1971): 1009–13, discuss

the various news accounts in New York papers concerning the swindling activities of William Thompson in 1849.

12. Hayford et al., "Historical Note," *The Confidence-Man*, 284.

13. David S. Reynolds, *Beneath the American Renaissance: The Subversive Imagination in the Age of Emerson and Melville* (New York: Alfred A. Knopf, 1988), 176–81.

14. For a review of contemporary research on these popular allusions in *The Confidence-Man*, see John Bryant, "*The Confidence-Man*: Melville's Problem Novel," in his *A Companion to Melville Studies* (Westport, Conn.: Greenwood Press, 1986), 330–31.

15. For example, "Our Relations with England," *Putnam's*, May 1856, 544.

16. "Lewes' Life of Goethe," *Putnam's*, February 1856, 201.

17. "The Compensation Office," *Putnam's*, May 1855, 459–68.

18. Leon Howard, *Herman Melville: A Biography* (Berkeley and Los Angeles: University of California Press, 1951), 408, lists the characters that appear in both "The Compensation Office" and *The Confidence-Man*.

19. "Elegant Tom Dillar," *Putnam's*, May 1853, 525–32.

20. Ibid., 525.

21. Ibid., 526.

22. Ibid., 463.

23. Ibid., 530.

24. "Ancient Peru," *Harper's*, June 1853, 9. Melville both read and wrote for *Harper's* in 1853. Jane D. Eberwein was apparently not aware of this article in *Harper's* when she suggested Joel Barlow's *The Columbiad* as a potential source; see her "Joel Barlow and *The Confidence-Man*," *American Transcendental Quarterly* 24 (1974): 28–29.

25. In her statistical analysis of 101 studies of Melville's work published between 1922 and 1980 regarding the identity of the confidence man, Mary K. Madison reports the following: sixteen as the Devil, sixteen as unknowable, two as Christ, four as God, four as a beguiling God, six as both God and Satan, ten as a man, nineteen as miscellaneous identities ranging from an artist to a salesman, twenty-four do not offer interpretations; see Mary K. Madison, "Hypothetical Friends: The Critics and *The Confidence-Man*," *Melville Society Extracts* 46 (1981): 10–14.

26. For an analysis of the confidence man as a Christlike figure, see Elizabeth S. Foster, introduction to *The Confidence-Man* (New York: Hendricks House, 1954).

27. Letter to George Duyckinck, 31 March 1857, in Leyda, *The Melville Log*, 2:563.

28. *Boston Evening Transcript*, 10 April 1857.

29. *Albany Evening Journal*, 2 April 1857.

30. *Putnam's*, July 1853, 102.

31. "The Genius of Charles Dickens," *Putnam's*, March 1855, 264.

32. Ibid.
33. Hayford et al., "Historical Note," *The Confidence-Man*, 298.
34. "Literary Imitations," *Putnam's*, August 1856, 113–20.
35. Ibid., 114.
36. Ibid., 120.
37. Fitz-James O'Brien, "Melville and Curtis," *Putnam's*, April 1857.
38. *Berkshire County Eagle*, 19 June 1857.
39. *Worcester Palladium*, 22 April 1856.
40. *London Leader*, 11 April 1857.
41. *Westminster and Foreign Quarterly Review*, July 1857.
42. *Boston Evening Transcript*, 10 April 1857.
43. *Putnam's*, September 1854, 325–30.
44. Hans Joachim-Lang and Benjamin Lease argue conclusively that Melville based his portrait of the cosmopolitan on the representative American traveler Bayard Taylor. In this rigorous analysis Joachim-Lang and Lease point out the parallels between Bayard Taylor's descriptions in his various travel books and Melville's portrait of that "king of traveled good-fellows" (*The Confidence-Man*, 131), the cosmopolitan. Taylor, whose daguerreotype appeared in *Putnam's* (August 1854), was a popular personality with *Putnam's* audiences. See Joachim-Lang and Lease, "Melville's Cosmopolitan: Bayard Taylor in *The Confidence-Man*," *Amerikastudien* 22 (1977): 287–89.
45. *Literary Gazette*, 11 April 1856.
46. "American Travelers," *Putnam's*, June 1855, 563.
47. "The Genius of Charles Dickens," *Putnam's*, March 1855, 263–64.
48. Ibid., 264.
49. Q. D. Leavis, "Melville: The 1853–1856 Phase," in *New Perspectives on Melville*, ed. Faith Pullin (Edinburgh: Edinburgh University Press, 1978), 218.
50. Edgar A. Dryden, *Melville's Thematics of Form: The Great Art of Telling the Truth* (Baltimore: Johns Hopkins University Press, 1968), 154.
51. James E. Miller, Jr., *A Reader's Guide to Herman Melville* (New York: Noonday Press, 1962), 171.

10. The Move to Poetry

1. *Putnam's*, July 1857.
2. Q. D. Leavis, "Melville: The 1853–1856 Phase," in *New Perspectives on Melville*, ed. Faith Pullin (Edinburgh: Edinburgh University Press, 1978), 211.
3. See Melville, *Journal of a Visit to Europe and the Levant, October 11, 1856-May 6, 1857*, ed. Howard C. Horsford (Princeton: Princeton University Press, 1955), 31–32.

4. Ibid., 40.

5. Merton M. Sealts, Jr., *Melville as Lecturer* (Cambridge, Mass.: Harvard University Press, 1957), 7–10, 59–60.

6. Lemuel Shaw, Jr., to Samuel Shaw, 2 June 1857, in Jay Leyda, ed., *The Melville Log: A Documentary Life of Herman Melville, 1819–1891* (New York: Harcourt, Brace, 1951), 2:580.

7. Lewis Mumford, *Herman Melville* (New York: Literary Guild of America, 1929), 308.

8. For an account of Melville's developing interest in writing poetry, see his *Journal of a Visit to Europe and the Levant*, 36–41.

9. Sealts, "Statues in Rome," in *Melville as Lecturer*, 144–45.

10. John Allison, "The Later Melville: Tragedy and the Paradox of Form," Ph.D. dissertation, University of Chicago, 1982, 7–8.

Index

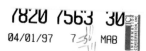